School Guidance and Counselling

T0345571

Hong Kong Teacher Education

General Series Editor: Kerry J. Kennedy, The Hong Kong Institute of Education

The volumes in the series set out to provide contextualized reflections on issues that most teachers come across. Each volume will delve into discussions that will enhance and improve teaching skills. The series covers a wide range of topics including curriculum and assessment, understanding and managing diversity, guidance and counselling, and human development.

Also in the series:

School Guidance and Counselling

Trends and Practices

Edited by

Pattie Y. Y. Luk-Fong and Yuk Ching Lee-Man

香港大學出版社

HONG KONG UNIVERSITY PRESS

Hong Kong University Press
The University of Hong Kong
Pokfulam Road
Hong Kong
www.hkupress.org

ISBN 978-988-8083-41-1

British Library Cataloguing-in-Publication Data
A catalogue record for this book is available from the British Library.

10   9   8   7   6   5   4   3   2   1

Printed and bound by Cheer Shine Enterprise Co., Ltd., Hong Kong, China

Contents

Foreword

Teachers play a fundamental role in the social and economic development of any society. Their preparation as professionals to meet the challenges of post-modern living is a key priority for both governments and universities. Many changes have taken place in teacher education since the establishment of formal institutions of teaching training in Hong Kong over one hundred years ago. Today, the Hong Kong government is committed to an "all graduate, all trained" profession and university level institutions are now responsible for all teacher education across early childhood, primary and secondary education. It is against this background that the Hong Kong Teacher Education Series has been developed.

The incentive behind the series is simple: the need for resources that reflect local values, professional contexts and cultures. The market for resources is dominated by Western materials that are either embedded in non-local contexts or that assume there is a general context that is relevant across cultural boundaries. Such resources, of course, can be useful but they do not help Hong Kong's future teachers appreciate and understand the unique contexts that characterize Hong Kong's schools. Thus the Hong Kong Teacher Education Series will provide culturally relevant resources that embed both theory and practice in local classroom contexts.

Hong Kong's aspirations to be a bilingual triliterate society will be reflected in the Hong Kong Teacher Education Series. Dual-language versions of the resource material will be produced for use in either Chinese or English teacher education contexts. This is recognition of the centrality of language in the lives of Hong Kong people. It places value on both English and Chinese in the teaching/learning process and will ensure that the resources are accessible to all teacher education students in Hong Kong.

The initial titles that have been selected for this series reflect the needs of future teachers in Hong Kong's classroom: classroom management, assessment for learning, managing and understanding diversity. Subsequent titles will deal with curriculum, human development, and school guidance and counselling. These professional areas will introduce teacher education students directly to the concepts, ideas and practices they will need as young professionals in Hong Kong's classroom. Case studies of actual school practice will bring the text to life as students engage with the realities of actual teachers and classrooms. This will help to prepare them in a realistic and practical way so that they are well prepared for their own students and classrooms.

As important as the focus on practice is in this series, it does not mean that theory has been neglected. Concepts, ideas and issues are located in broader theoretical and cultural contexts but not in an abstract way. For teachers, classrooms and students provide the ultimate context against with theories can be tested and cultures can be better understood. In these challenging and demanding times, teachers need to be fully equipped with the latest thinking and ideas based on research and advances in understanding. Yet these must always be tested in the laboratory of practice so that teachers are not only knowledgeable but they also know how to translate this knowledge into action that can benefit students.

In developing this series, I have been grateful for the dedication of my colleagues at the Hong Kong Institute of Education. They have taken up the challenge of writing and shown great commitment in providing meaningful and relevant resources for their students. I am also grateful to Senior Management at the Hong Kong Institute of Education since they supported this endeavour from the very beginning. I have also been encouraged by Hong Kong University Press which has seen the value of the series and the need to support Hong Kong's future teachers. As is so often the case in educational matters, collaboration and cooperation can produce great outcomes, and I believe such has been the case in this instance.

Hong Kong's future is in no small way linked to the quality of its teachers and their capacity to support the learning of young people throughout this new century. Hopefully, the Hong Kong Teacher Education Series will contribute to this important objective.

Kerry J. Kennedy
General Series Editor
The Hong Kong Teacher Education Series

Preface

School Guidance and Counselling is a book written for teachers to enable them to master their guidance role at school. This book draws extensively on the most up-to-date theories in the field of school guidance and counselling, with a strong emphasis on the local contextual factors that affect school guidance and counselling in Hong Kong. Chinese Confucian practices such as the emphasis on examinations, the contestation between discipline and guidance, and the role of class teachers in school guidance, are highlighted. The book adopts a systems approach to analyse and reflect on the practices of school guidance and counselling at the individual, the classroom, the whole school and the family systems levels.

Pattie Yuk Yee Luk-Fong

About the Authors

(In chapter sequence)

Pattie Yuk Yee LUK-FONG holds a Ph.D. in education from the University of Canberra, Australia. She has been an adjunct associate professor in the Department of Special Education and Counselling at the Hong Kong Institute of Education (HKIEd) since her retirement in 2011. For over three decades she has been a teacher educator. She has worked as a secondary school teacher, teaching consultant in the Faculty of Education at the University of Hong Kong, and senior lecturer and principal lecturer at the Hong Kong Institute of Education. Her primary research interests are guidance and counselling, personal identity, gender identity in teachers, and family changes. She lectures on guidance and counselling, the self and personal development module for liberal studies, and family education and support. She has published many articles in international academic journals, including 'Competing Contexts for Developing Personal and Social Education in Hong Kong' and 'Towards a Hybrid Conceptualization of Chinese Women Primary School Teachers' Changing Femininities: A Case Study of Hong Kong'. Pattie Y. Y. Luk-Fong is a founding member of the HKIEd's Gender Matters Group, and a founding and council member of the Consortium of Institutes on Family in the Asian region (CIFA). She received the Award for Outstanding Contribution to School-Based Family Counselling in 2011 and was a committee member of the Assessment Working Group of the Chief Executive's Award for Teaching Excellence (2012–2013) in the discipline and counselling area.

Tuen-yi CHIU graduated with first class honours from Hong Kong Baptist University where she read sociology. Her honours project, 'Home Sweet Home: A Family Case Study of the Poor Chinese New Immigrants in Hong Kong and Their Utilization of Space' (*An le wo: Xianggang pinqiong xinyimin jiating zhi kongjian yunyong*) was awarded third prize in the 11th National Challenge Cup Contest, and was later published as a book chapter. Chiu is pursuing her MPhil studies in the Department of Sociology at the Chinese University of Hong Kong. At the time of writing, she is a research assistant in the Department of Special Education and Counselling at the Hong Kong Institute of Education.

Yuk Ching LEE-MAN holds a doctorate in education in counselling psychology from the Chinese University of Hong Kong. She was an assistant professor in the Department of Special Education and Counselling at the Hong Kong Institute of Education (HKIEd), and programme coordinator of the Institute's part-time Bachelor of Education (Honours) (Special Needs) programme before her retirement. She took up her first teaching position in 1977 and became a teacher educator in 1986. Her current research focuses on the prevention of child abuse, the mental health of teachers, parent education, and life education. Her teaching areas include guidance in schools, career guidance, sex education and behavioural problems in adolescents. Among the titles she has edited include *Counselling Cases: Illustrations and Insight*; *Guidance and Counselling: A Multimedia Self-Learning Course*, an educational package comprising a video cassette and a resource manual; *Aerogramme Project for Children: Children's Responses;* and *The Four 'Q's: Parenting Tips.* Yuk Ching Lee-Man is an executive committee member of Against Child Abuse, council member of the Hong Kong Professional Counselling Association, committee member of the Information, Education and Communication Department of the Family Planning Association of Hong Kong, board member of the Hong Kong Institute of Family Education, and course consultant (parent programme) for the Life Education Activity Programme (LEAP).

Mabel Mei Po SHEK holds a master's degree in education and a master of social science in counselling, and is currently a senior teaching fellow in the Department of Special Education and Counselling at the Hong Kong Institute of Education (HKIEd). She received the Excellence in Teaching Award from the Faculty of Education Studies and the President's Award for Outstanding Performance in Teaching from the HKIEd in 2011 and 2012 respectively. She previously worked at a boy's home, secondary schools and the Education Bureau's Guidance Section, and has many years of experience in teaching, training and counselling. She provides parent education at schools and organizes workshops to enhance teachers' personal and professional development. She teaches courses on school counselling, sex education and life skills, and is currently an Ed.D. candidate at the University of Bristol, specializing in narrative inquiry into the professional identity of school counsellors.

Ching Leung LUNG holds a doctorate in education from the University of Durham, UK, and is an assistant professor in the Department of Special Education and Counselling at the Hong Kong Institute of Education. He used to be a guidance coordinator in a secondary school, and has extensive experience in managing school guidance services and supervising programmes on moral and civic education. He has published a series of textbooks on guidance and personal and societal education, titled *Same Class, Good Relationship*. Lung lectures on guidance in school, the self and personal development module for liberal studies, intimate interpersonal relationships such as dating and marriage, and life skills. His research focuses on personal and social education, dating relationships in adolescents, the personal growth of teachers, the guidance roles of class teachers, and the administrative aspects of school-based guidance.

Ming Tak HUE previously taught in secondary schools in Hong Kong, where he coordinated guidance and discipline programmes in the form of individual guidance, peer support and classroom behaviour support. During his career as a school teacher, he had accumulated invaluable practical experience in handling behavioural issues and mentoring students in their personal growth. He obtained his master of education from Bristol University, UK, and completed his Ph.D. at the Institute of Education, University of London. Ming Tak Hue now works in the Department of Special Education and Counselling at the Hong Kong Institute of Education. His teaching areas include guidance in school, students' personal and social development, classroom management, behaviour management and inclusive education. His research interests include school discipline, pastoral care for ethnic minority students, students' holistic development, and the development of school-based guidance and discipline programmes.

Suk Chun FUNG holds a master of education in counselling and a doctorate in education from the Chinese University of Hong Kong. She has also pursued professional development in marital counselling, play therapy and gambling counselling, and is a registered gambling counsellor. Suk Chun Fung was actively involved in school guidance and counselling work when she taught in primary and secondary schools. She has extensive experience in individual and group counselling and in organizing student personal growth activities. In 1998, she was awarded a Commendation Certificate by the Hong Kong Education Bureau and the Committee on Respect Our Teachers Campaign. Suk Chun Fung is currently a senior teaching fellow in the Department of Special Education and Counselling at the Hong Kong Institute of Education. Her teaching areas include school guidance work, counselling theory and practice, and intervention strategies for Autism Spectrum Disorders. Her current research focuses on the effectiveness of animal-assisted therapy for children with autism.

1

The Fundamentals, Definition, Philosophy, Goals and Current Trends of School Guidance in Hong Kong

Pattie Yuk Yee Luk-Fong

Guidance has been considered a pervasive force within the school curriculum or instructional process that aims at the maximum development of individual potentialities.

(Myrick 1993: 2)

Confucius says: To teach regardless of what kind of person that is.

– *The Analects*, Book 15, *Duke Ling of Wei* (Analects 15: 39)

Abstract

This chapter begins by studying the relationship between East-West cultural traditions and guidance, before coming to a definition of 'guidance' and 'counselling', and moving on to explore the philosophical values, functions, targets and stages of school guidance. The complementary role that discipline and guidance play in school education is emphasized, while the need to integrate discipline, guidance and teaching as one holistic educational process is also pinpointed. The chapter concludes with an overview of the trends of the development of guidance in Hong Kong.

Objectives

This chapter will help you:
- describe the relationship between East-West cultural traditions and guidance;
- differentiate between guidance and counselling;
- understand the philosophical values, functions, targets and stages of guidance;
- identify the similiarities and differences between discipline and guidance;
- comprehend the importance of integrating the three related educational processes of discipline, counselling and teaching; and
- recognize the current trends in the development of school guidance in Hong Kong.

Before You Start: Think and Discuss

1. How does the East-meets-West context of Hong Kong impact on school guidance?
2. What are your views on the 'three-in-one' approach to integrate discipline, guidance and teaching? What would be the difficulties in the implementation of such an approach?
3. In the school where you are studying or where you are a teacher-in-training, are you able to detect any particular trends in the development of guidance? Does the overlap of discipline and counselling create any problem?

Introduction

It has long been in the Chinese tradition to uphold the Confucian school of thought, with the Confucian concept very much ingrained in education. There is an often quoted dictum in *Book 15* of *The Analects*, 'Confucius says, "To teach regardless of what kind of person that is",' which points out that a teacher should teach his students irrespective of their wealth, birthplace, social status, and intelligence level. In these words, Confucius not only points out the importance of education, but also underlines his preaching of the egalitarian principle. His philosophy has been the guiding principle for many generations. The Western concept, on the other hand, proposes that 'guidance has been considered a pervasive force within the school curriculum or instructional process that aims at the maximum development of individual potentialities' (Myrick 1993). It is quite clear that the individual is as important in the educational tradition of the East as it is in the West.

Guidance in Hong Kong

In studying the guidance and counselling services of Hong Kong, the unique context of Hong Kong as a place where East meets West must be taken into consideration. More than 150 years as a British colony (1840–1997) has established deep roots of Western traditions in indigenous Chinese soil in education and guidance. Stevenson and Stigler (1992), Cheng (1990; 1995) and Cheng and Wong (1996) have written extensively on differences between Eastern and Western traditions in terms of education and schooling. Cheng (1990) talks about the constant conflicts and struggles between Western and Chinese cultures in education. Yet he points out that although 'in education, educators seem to accept both traditional and Western ideas without much hesitation, they are now in process of trying to combine the two into a coherent system' (1990: 171). King (1996: 274) also posits that 'in a way the entire culture of Hong Kong has been shaped by the struggle between conflicting values.'

As guidance essentially comes from the West and it has been grafted onto an essentially Chinese educational system in Hong Kong, it is expected that guidance in Hong Kong will comprise both Western and Chinese traditions.

Aspects of Chinese Traditions Associated with Guidance

The Chinese traditions attach great importance to the five aspects of whole person development for students: moral, intellectual, physical, social and aesthetic, while strong emphasis is put on discipline and moral education. Teachers in the Discipline Teams would inculcate the value of discipline and moral uprightness through the weekly assemblies devoted to moral education. Class teachers would be responsible for looking after the personal growth of students. As such, the form-class structure becomes the major framework for facilitating students' personal growth. This common practice is in line with the traditional role of the teacher as a vehicle for 'pointing the way, imparting knowledge and resolving problems'. The perceived role of Chinese teachers to resolve issues for students is quite similar to the aim of guidance in helping students find solutions to their problems. Yet it must be understood that the Chinese traditions dictate that problem resolution should be teacher-led, which contrasts the Western concept of 'helping others to help others to help themselves.' To firmly grasp the concept of guidance in Hong Kong, we must take Hong Kong's East-meets-West cultural context as the starting point.

Defining Guidance

Guidance is a process of helping people make important choices that affect their lives, such as choosing a preferred lifestyle. One distinction between guidance and counselling is that guidance focuses on helping individuals make important decision, whereas counselling focuses on helping them make changes. Most of the early occurrences of guidance take place at in schools where an adult would help a student make decisions, such as on a course of study or a vocation. The unequal relationship between teachers and students helps the less experienced person find directions in life. Similarly, children have long received 'guidance' from parents, ministers, scout leaders, and coaches. In the process they have gained an understanding of themselves and their world (Shertzer and Stone 1981). This type of guidance will never become passé; regardless of one's age or one's stage of life, a person often needs help in making choices. Yet such guidance is only one part of the overall service provided by professional counselling (Gladding 2000).

According to M. C. Shaw (1973: 7), 'Guidance is ... a third force within the educational framework'.

> Guidance will be defined as a program . . . within the school system whose primary task is the application of skills and theory derived from the behavioral sciences. These skills will be primarily toward the accomplishment of goals related to the affective domains. (1973: 10)

Milner (1980) views guidance as 'the presentation of knowledge, information and/or advice to individuals or groups in a structured way so as to provide sufficient material upon which they may base choices or decisions'. Miller, Fruehling, and Lewis (1978: 7) offer a different definition:

> Guidance is the process of helping individuals achieve the self-understanding and the self-direction necessary to make informed choices and to develop the behaviour necessary to move toward self-directed goals in intelligent or self-correcting ways.

They also elaborate on the fundamental principles of guidance:

1. Guidance is for all students.
2. Guidance is for students of all ages.
3. Guidance must be concerned with all areas of growth of the students.
4. Guidance encourages self-discovery and self-development.
5. Guidance must be a co-operative enterprise involving students, parents, teachers, administrators and counsellors.
6. Guidance must be an integral part of any education programme.
7. Guidance must be responsible both to the individual and society. (Miller, Fruehling and Lewis 1980: 8–12)

Myrick (1993: 2) further points out that:

> Guidance has been considered a pervasive force within the school curriculum or instructional process that aims at the maximum development of individual potentialities.

He goes on to discuss that there are the programme, service, activities, lessons, personnel, counsellor and resources for guidance. Stone and Bradley (1994: 24) define guidance as:

> a programme of experiences aimed at assisting individuals in better understanding themselves, others, and the world in which they live so that they might make informed choices, solve problems and become responsible members of the community in which they live.

In summary, guidance comprises the following characteristics:
1. It involves a planned programme.
2. It is part of the school curriculum.
3. It is a force for the affective domain of the curriculum.
4. Its goal is for the maximum development of individual potentialities for all.
5. It helps individuals understand oneself and others, make informed choices, resolve problems and become responsible members of society.
6. It involves behavioural science theory and skills.
7. It requires concerted effort from students, teachers, parents, support professionals and administrators.

School guidance has these special features:
1. It promotes the students' whole person development.
2. Guidance service should have a developmental nature.
3. Guidance should be preventive. (Hui 1998)

Case Study 1

On school-leaving day, Miss Fung receives a letter from an unknown sender with a thank-you card inside. The card reads, 'Miss Fung, thank you very much for your unfailing support as well as teaching. Even though I am leaving school today, it is still my sincere wish that you remain a happy teacher forever!' The card was signed, but gave no name of the sender. Miss Fung was puzzled and tried to figure out who would have sent this card to her. At last, she was amazed to learn that it was from Chi-kit, whom she had taught for more than four years. He was remembered as being aloof, reticent and mediocre at the beginning. As he seldom talked to the teachers, he did not leave any deep impression on Miss Fung when they first met. Later, when Chi-kit joined the drama club run by Miss Fung, she discovered that although he appeared to be taciturn, Chi-kit was willing to try new things, diligent in his study, and highly creative. Miss Fung was pleased as she learnt from this experience that a person is like a blank sheet, but given the opportunities and suitable stimuli for exerting oneself and developing one's potentials, it is possible to achieve a life of glorious colours.

Broadly speaking, this is a case of guidance at work. Miss Fung was able to help her student realize and eventually fully develop his potential through extra-curricular activities. It illustrates that guidance is an integral part of the total educational process. Having taught Chi-kit for four years, Miss Fung has established a good teacher-pupil relationship with him. His participation in the drama club organized by her led to his transformation from a reticent, withdrawn student to a prized student who was open to new experience, diligent in study, and highly creative. This is a good example of how extra-curricular activities as part of school life can be an important means to discover students' talents.

Defining Counselling

'Guidance' and 'counselling' are by definition fundamentally different. As yet, there is still no consensus on the definition of counselling. According to the American Counselling Association (2004), professional counselling refers to 'the application of mental health, psychological, or human development principles, through cognitive, affective, behavioural or systematic intervention strategies, that address wellness, personal growth, or career development, as well as pathology'. In 2010, the representatives of the American Counselling Association announced a new definition of counselling as 'a professional relationship that empowers diverse individuals, families, and groups to accomplish mental health, wellness, education, and career goals'.

This definition is an extension of those expounded by previous scholars. According to Lewis (1970), 'counselling is a process by which a troubled person (the client) is helped to feel and behave in a more personally satisfying manner through interaction with an uninvolved person (the counsellor) who provides information and reactions which stimulate the client to develop behaviours which enable him to deal more effectively with himself and his environment' (cited in Hui 2003: 9). This interpretation is shared by Murgatroyd (1985) who undertook to develop a definition of counselling on behalf of the Division of Psychotherapy of the American Psychological Society, viz., 'to help an individual in the process of growing up to overcome personal difficulties so as to enable him/her to realize his/her potentials to the fullest'(cited from APA website).

Counselling in education may be described as a relationship developed between a counsellor and a person in a temporary state of indecision, confusion or distress. It can help the individual to make his/her own decisions and choices, to resolve his/her issues or cope with his/her distress in a realistic and meaningful way (Milner 1980). Later, A. Jones (cited by Murgatroyd 1985) points out that guidance is an empowering process, the aim of which is to help an individual make sense of his/her life, grow and reach maturity through learning, taking responsibilities and coming to his/her own decisions. Nelson-Jones (1983) also considers that the aim of counselling is to help the client (basically one receiving consultation outside of a clinical environment) help himself/herself. The psychological skills expected of a counsellor include establishing a relationship with the client and helping him/her change his feelings, thoughts and behaviour.

Rogers (1942) also states that effective counselling consists of a structured, permissive relationship which allows the client to gain an understanding of himself to a degree which enables him to take positive steps in the light of this new orientation.

To sum up, counselling may be said to have the following essential elements:

1. Counselling is an empowering process of the client;
2. Counselling can facilitate the individual's attempts to overcome hurdles, resolve confusions and distress, and take innovative measures;
3. Counselling is a process whereby an individual attains his personal growth and cope effectively with his environment; and
4. Counselling is a relationship.

Case Study 2

Wing-man is an S. 2 student. She used to take her little sister, who was in P. 2, to school every morning before she went to school. One day, because Wing-man had to go to school earlier than usual, she asked her grandma to take her little sister to school instead. Unfortunately, the little girl was knocked down by a car and died as a result of the accident. Her sudden death caused great distress to Wing-man and her family to the point of near breakdown. Her grandma blamed herself for the accident and had to be hospitalized for emotional trauma. Feeling over-burdened, Wing-man's mother decided to call her class teacher, Miss Chow, to help comfort Wing-man. Miss Chow arranged a private meeting with Wing-man, who broke into tears as soon as she saw Miss Chow. She blamed herself for not taking her sister personally to school on that fatal day. Miss Chow held Wing-man's hand and explained that she should accept her sister's death as accident. She encouraged Wing-man to be strong for the sake of her parents. Miss Chow then prayed with her that her sister might rest in peace. After that, Wing-man pulled herself together and went to school as usual. As time passed, she learnt to live with the sad fact of her younger sister's death.

This is an example of a counselling case. Whenever a family problem comes up, it is not uncommon for the parents to request teachers' help to counsel the student concerned. It is easy to see that Miss Chow enjoyed a good relationship with Wing-man for as soon as she was alone with Miss Chow, she could no longer hold back her tears. Miss Chow cared for her student and took the initiative to talk to her about her sister's death as she knew quite well that Wing-man was very close to her little sister. Miss Chow's readiness to show concern and willingness to listen not only helped calm down Wing-man in her agitated state, but also removed any damaging misconception that her sister's death might be linked to her failure to take her to school on that day. The case shows that Miss Chow has succeeded in helping Wing-man to accept her sister's death and in bringing herself gradually back to normal life. But as to whether it is appropriate for Miss Chow to hold Wingman's hand, to pray with her, to urge her to be strong, and not to add to her parents' worries, some may think that such actions are open to debate.

Philosophy behind Guidance

From a philosophical point of view, guidance focuses on the individual, with understanding as the core. There is also the belief that, as all are born equal, everyone should be able to benefit from the educational opportunity for the fullest development of one's potentials.

Functions of Guidance

The functions of guidance encompass prevention, development and therapy. Prevention refers to the provision of guidance services before the onset of the problems. Development refers to the requirement for guidance to suit the students' developmental needs. Personal growth education (including whole person development) forms an important part of preventive and developmental guidance in Hong Kong, often disseminated through cross-curricular programmes such as civic and moral education, and extra-curricular activities such as sports and cultural activities, and academic subject societies. Therapy refers to the intervention by the guidance personnel when students encounter problems.

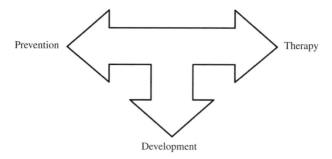

Figure 1.1 The functions of guidance

Goals of School Guidance

School guidance aims at enhancing the quality of students' learning and personal development (Johnson 2000; Campbell and Dahir 1997) and fostering their growth towards whole person development. Since prevention is an inherent nature of guidance, guidance service should be made available to students before real problems arise. In the article 'Gender, Class, Race', Lee (2001) states that differences in gender, class and race do exist and have significant impacts on students' growth and development, so they must not be overlooked.

Goals, Targets and Phases of Guidance and the Guidance Personnel

General mode of guidance at schools

According to Yau-Lai (1998), school guidance at the early stages of its development lacked coherent organization, leading to nebulous goals. Shaw (1973) later formulated a mode of organization which takes into account the goals, targets, timing and strategy of guidance. In other words, it is to consider 'why', 'who', 'when' and 'how' to guide at the same time. Table 1.1 shows that the early phase of guidance is concerned with general prevention and development, and it points to the need of providing long-term guidance service to all students. In the middle phase of guidance service, students with problems are the major targets. The goal of guidance is to ensure the timely identification and provision of guidance for the students with problems. Lastly, if the situation continues to worsen until it reaches the final phase, the goal of guidance service will shift to one of diagnosing and treating students with severe problems.

Table 1.1 illustrates the goals, targets, phases of guidance service and the suitable guidance personnel. It also points out how important it is for the guidance personnel to work together as a team within the school.

Table 1.1 The goals, targets, phases of guidance and the guidance personnel

Phases of guidance	Goals	Targets	Guidance personnel
Early phase	Developmental and preventive	All students	All teachers (class teachers in particular), career masters/mistresses (only present in secondary schools)
Middle phase	Timely identification and counselling	Students with problems	Student guidance teachers, remedial teachers, school social workers
Final phase	Diagnosing and therapeutic treatment	Students with severe problems	Clinical psychologists

The goals of guidance are to prevent problems from arising, help students grow up healthily, identifying those with problems so as to provide them with the timely assistance, and, if necessary, referring those with severe problems to external psychotherapists for diagnosis and treatment.

Because of its preventive and developmental nature, guidance service should be made available to all students, at an early stage and as a long-term service. Since the entire student body is in need of such prolonged and developmental guidance, it is imperative that all teachers in the school be involved. In general, if a student is found to be in need of professional counselling attention, he/she should be referred to the guidance teacher. Should the student's problem stem from the family, the student should be referred to the school social worker for counselling. The severe cases should be referred to external psychotherapists. With the emphasis on developmental and preventive guidance, the number of students requiring individual counselling will be largely reduced, while the number of severe cases which require referral to psychotherapists will be kept to the minimum.

Similarities and Differences between Guidance and Discipline

Within the school setting, guidance and discipline are equally important as the two are complementary (Kehas 1970; Sherzer and Stone 1980). Lam (1988) points out that discipline and guidance are inter-dependent, gearing towards the same goal. Table 1.2 illustrates the similarities and differences between guidance and discipline:

Table 1.2 Guidance and discipline (Yau-Lai 1998)

Guidance	Discipline	Area of comparison
1. Affirming the individual's worth 2. Exercising responsibly the individual's rights and freedoms 3. Facilitating the individual's overall growth 4. Accepting and respecting the individual's personal uniqueness 5. Personal and confidential	1. Affirming the importance of the community 2. Keeping discipline and order within the community 3. Helping the individuals make necessary adjustments in the community 4. Focusing on orderliness and uniformity 5. Collective and open	The whole group versus the individual
6. Being concerned with the whole person 7. Moving the focus from internal to external 8. Exploratory and emphasizing self-awareness 9. Focusing on the cultivation of self-control	6. Being concerned with outward behaviour 7. Moving the focus from external to internal 8. Suppressive and restrictive 9. Focusing on the establishment of external control	Internal versus External

(continued on page 11)

Table 1.2 *(continued)*

| 10. Focusing on love, compassion and forgiveness | 10. Abiding by the spirit of law and order | Strictness versus leniency |
| 11. Self-discipline being central to education | 11. Education with the aid of punishment and reward | Positive versus negative |

The group or the individual

In general, the discipline approach is more effective with groups as its emphasis is on keeping discipline standards prescribed for discipline and outer behaviour are easily observable. It is possible to get fast short-term results through such measures as honour, authority and legal rules and regulations. However, we should not ignore the distinct differences among individuals in the student body. Very often, the maladjusted students are punished for their inability to conform, but there is no guarantee that punishment will achieve the intended results. It is time to consider the guidance approach, so as to help them and resolve problems which might be physical, psychological, educational, environmental and family conditions. From the standpoint of the school as an organization, the guidance approach, which can only cater for individual students, should support the discipline approach, even though the latter would not be able to take care of the students' individual needs without the assistance of the former. This is also the reason why the two approaches must go together in order that all students will be offered the necessary help and assistance to grow up into healthy and happy individuals (Yau-Lai 1998).

The internal and the external

From the educational standpoint, discipline is concerned with external order and uniformity. School rules are therefore set up to control students' behaviour and restrict them from any breach or deviations. However, external control like this can only mould students into law-abiding persons, but cannot help them come to grips with their internal struggles and conflicts. On the other hand, the guidance approach would foster a good degree of self-control, thus encouraging students to establish self-control, which in turn govern their outward behaviour. In so doing, they would also develop the correct social skills. In fact, guidance and discipline are equally important in the educational process. It is imperative that we adopt these complementary approaches, so as to ensure both the internal and external well-being of the student (Yau-Lai 1998).

Strictness or leniency

As said, discipline has to do with the whole school. It requires all students to abide by a set of rules and regulations made known to all. Offenders will be punished according to the rules, while good behaviours will be suitably rewarded. The orderly and pleasant environment thus created will be to the interest of the majority of students and conducive to a good learning atmosphere, encouraging students to maximize their strengths on the one hand, and help them improve their weaknesses on the other. Nevertheless, to some students, harsh punishment can only control their external behaviour, but it fails to relieve or release their psychological and emotional stress. Under such circumstances, guidance would be a good 'complementary alternative' to discipline. A compassionate guidance teacher understands individual students' needs and helping them resolve any internal or emotional strife which would then smooth the way for the discipline approach and enhance the effectiveness of education (Yau-Lai 1998).

Positive versus negative

Lam (1988) points out that after being reprimanded and punished for his/her offence by the discipline teacher but the student's negative feelings are overlooked, the student in question may be so overcome with resentment and shame that he would turn rebellious, give up on himself, or take an escapist route. To avoid this from happening, it is better to solicit the help of the guidance teacher, who will assist the student in learning from his mistake and turning it into an experience of growing-up.

We can therefore see that discipline and guidance should go together in order to achieve the best effects. While the ways to handle the situation are different, their goals are the same. It follows that discipline teachers and guidance personnel in the school should maintain good communication and work together to achieve the ultimate goal of teaching and realize the function of school education.

Guidance and Discipline in Local Schools

In the past, guidance service and discipline work are undertaken by two separate teams of teachers. The guidance committee, also called the guidance team, is responsible for providing counselling service to the needy students as well as designing programmes to promote the whole person development of students. The Education Bureau of Hong Kong (Education Department 2001) states in its guidelines on student guidance that:

School guidance work is considered to be of paramount importance to help our adolescents maximize their own potential, acquire acceptable social skills, discriminate right from wrong, develop appropriate values, adjust to social-economic changes and in general, be better equipped for real life. In addition, school guidance work can help prevent or overcome students' problems through prompt assistance and appropriate advice. It is also a supplement to the guidance they get at home.

In its guidelines for discipline teachers (EMB 2004), the subject is taken a step further:

Discipline in the context of quality education should mean more than rules and control. We do not want our students to behave only when they are closely monitored and threatened by the punishment imposed. We want to educate them so that our students are able to think critically, to analyze the situations, to solve problems and make appropriate decisions on the action to take. Students learn more from how teachers behave and what teachers believe in than what they teach. When teaching is meaningful and personalized, students develop a high sense of achievement and belonging to the class and the school. Thus when they leave school, they will behave responsibly even in the absence of the watchful eyes of teachers. We want our students to develop self-control and self-discipline. We want them to develop into responsible and well-adjusted adults.

Case Study 3

The mode of integration between discipline and guidance is different from school to school. Compare the mode of integration between School A and School B. Then, recall the school you went to or the one in which you did your teaching training, and see if you can describe the ways in which they organize their discipline and guidance work?

School A

- Most teachers attach great importance to discipline and uphold the concept of 'class management first, teaching second'.
- During the lesson, the teacher plays the role of a commander, and the discipline approach is always preferred in dealing with the behavioural problems of students.
- At the class level, the school emphasizes obedience, subservience and collectiveness.

School B

- The principal advocates whole person education and adopts the whole school approach to discipline and guidance.

(continued on page 14)

Case Study 3 *(continued)*

- Guidance and discipline are regarded as collaborative partners so that the working relationship between the guidance team and the discipline team is a close one.
- In the lesson, the teacher often plays the role of a counsellor, but he/she will always uphold the necessity of keeping order in class.
- The school has been described as an organic entity which is 'forward looking' and 'becoming healthier and healthier'. It contributes positively to the improvement in student behaviour, increasing students' sense of belonging to the school, and enhancing the team spirit in school, and the academic performance of students.

The Integration of Discipline, Guidance and Teaching

In the course of their learning process, children and adolescents will invariably encounter all sorts of difficulties and needs. We should provide them with suitable guidance whenever necessary and help them meet their needs and cope with their difficulties. Fundamentally, guidance may be summed up as a spirit, an attitude, a style, or a medium (Ng Mo-dan 1980). It is the responsibility of all educators to give guidance to students. Besides having the whole body of teaching and administrative staff involved in guidance which goes together with teaching and discipline at school, it is also necessary to match the social resources in the community and develop accordingly, in order to realize the educational precept of 'development precedes prevention, and prevention is better than cure'. Teaching can include programmes of personal development directly or immersed in the academic subjects, but the most important thing is to be led by the spirit of guidance. School teachers, class teachers, guidance teachers, guidance personnel, and administrators must have a clear understanding of the role they play in guidance.

Trends in the Development of Guidance in Hong Kong

Developing from remedial to preventive approach

The guidance and counselling services in Hong Kong have followed the international trend in evolving from case work or remedial approach to developmental and preventive in nature (Baker 1996; Branden 1992; Canfield 1990; Hui 1997; Lam 1984, 1995; Luk-Fong and Lung 1999). Actually, the guidance and counselling services in Hong Kong have also undergone tremendous changes over the years. In the 1950s, these services took the form of career guidance in secondary schools. In the 1970s and 1980s, guidance was provided in the form of case work, supplemented with group activities (Hui 1991). Finally, in the 1990s, the mode of operation transformed into the 'whole school approach'.

The first government document on school guidance, 'Guidance Work among Secondary School Students: Guidelines for Principals and Teachers' (Education Department 1986), stresses the importance of coordination and collaboration among teachers, form teachers, guidance teachers, heads of the guidance team, social workers, school staff, parents and other professionals in the endeavour. In 1990, the Education Commission advocated the whole school approach to guidance in the Education Commission Report No. 4. In 1993 and 1995, the Education Department released the guidelines on the whole school approach to guidance for secondary schools (Education Department 1993b). Since then, the 'whole school approach' has been recognized as the blueprint for guidance in Hong Kong schools.

Discipline and guidance: From competition to integration

Guidance is a Western concept. Its introduction to Hong Kong schools at first led to strong struggles and conflicts from the traditional discipline approach. In general, secondary schools have a discipline team and a guidance team as part of the establishment. The discipline team is responsible for handling students' behavioural and discipline problems, while the guidance team looks after the students' emotional development and helps them cope with the distress brought on by the family, study and social circle. Due to the nature and orientation of their work, discipline teachers often give students the impression of being harsh, so students tend to keep their distance, while guidance teachers often convey a kind and sympathetic image to the students and enjoy popularity among them. Since discipline teachers tend to arrest the problem by means of punishment and achieve tangible results in a short time, they are often copied by other teachers. However, if the discipline team and guidance team do not work in coordination, they will each go their own way, or worse, work against each other.

In 2002, the implementation of the comprehensive guidance system in all schools in Hong Kong made it a policy to merge the discipline team and the guidance team into one single committee. Then, in 2004, the Education and Manpower Bureau decided to merge the Discipline Section and the Student Guidance Section, which reflects the added importance of integrating discipline and guidance services. At present, varying modes of combining the discipline and guidance services are being implemented at different schools, such as one in which the two teams work closely together, another in which the two teams are supervised by a higher-level committee in overall charge of students' personal development, and lastly one in which the two teams are completely merged. However, it must be noted that different schools have their own culture, values and beliefs. Their teachers, students and parents have long established a set of assumptions and expectations about what discipline and guidance services should be like. They may not be able to make adjustments and accept the new mode of service, thus reducing the effectiveness of the delivery of service (Mak 2010).

Developments of personal growth education curriculum

Personal growth education is an important component in a comprehensive system of student guidance, which shows how important it is to align discipline, guidance and teaching in practice. The Guidance Section of the Education Department took the initiative in 1993 to pilot the adapted version of the 'Grow with Guidance System' developed by Radd (1993) in four local pilot secondary schools and eight primary schools. According to the evaluation carried out by the Guidance Section of the Education Department, the pilot scheme achieved quite good results, in that the responses of students, teachers, parents and principals were all positive (Education Department 1999).

Teachers and students in Hong Kong both welcome class teacher periods and personal growth curriculum

The findings of Hui (1998) among local secondary schools reveal that students prefer to consult class teachers rather than social workers. There is a clear consensus among teachers and students that they welcome guidance service in the form of personal growth programmes or class teacher periods that are forward looking and designed with long-term objectives in mind. Yet they still have some reservations about guidance as a remedial measure.

Invitational education

A communication model developed by William Watson Purkey in America, invitational education has been widely implemented in Hong Kong since the 1990s. According to Purkey and Novak (1996: 34), 'Teachers who believe in the ability, value, and responsibility of each student are more committed to developing ethical approaches that summon students to take ownership of their learning'. Invitational education is a realization of a pedagogical, educative process that centres on five basic principles, viz.:

1. People are able, valuable, and responsible and should be treated as such.
2. Educating should be a collaborative, cooperative activity.
3. The process is the product in the making.
4. People possess untapped potential in all areas of worthwhile human endeavour.
5. This potential can best be realized by developing the five Ps: One's personal and professional potential are best manifest in the place, policy, process, programme and people that invite such potential.

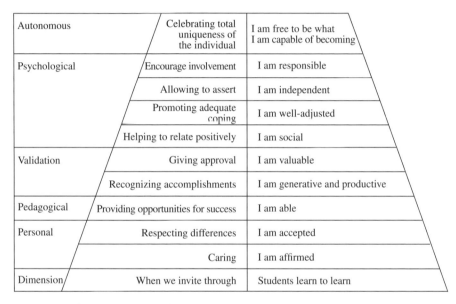

Figure 1.2 Hierarchy of invitational education (Stillion and Siegel 1985)

Raising resilience levels against adversity

Resilience refers to man's inborn ability and potential to rise to the occasion in face of adversity, i.e. the power to adjust, change, attune and recover, when one is faced with a crisis or caught in a predicament (The Boys' and Girls' Clubs Association of Hong Kong 2010). That is to say, when a person is confronted with a crisis or a difficult situation, there may emerge a capacity which will minimize the pain or contain the harm wrought by the adverse situation (Education & Manpower Bureau 2003). Resilience draws on three elements: the sense of competence, sense of belongingness and sense of optimism, or 'CBO' in short. They have the following characteristics:

Table 1.3 The three characteristics of resilience

Sense of competence	Sense of belongingness	Sense of optimism
I can • find the solution to the problem • control my emotions and impulse at critical moments • seek help whenever necessary • communicate positively with others and lay open my inner feelings • set suitable goals for myself and commit to them	I have • people whom I can trust • people who make clear rules for me to follow • people who can be my role models • people who wish that I will learn to be independent and autonomous • people who will help me when I am in need	I am • a likeable person • a person who cares for other people and is always ready to help • a person who knows how to respect myself and others • a person who is willing to take responsibility for my own actions • a person who has faith in finding a way out of every problem

Resilience is a universal capacity which enables the individual, family, or community to prevent, reduce and/or overcome the damage that adversities can bring. Resilient people are able to turn the adverse situation around and make life more endurable (Education and Manpower Bureau 2009). They can continue to push forward in face of adversity and are psychologically prepared to cope with all the difficulties coming their way. To children especially, it is important that they grow up through learning from their mistakes, and build up the capacity for shouldering the pressures of adversities in life. Therefore, in recent years, many guidance programmes set their goal on improving the capacity of the students' resilience, in the hope that they will be able to remain optimistic and positive in the face of adversities.

Since whole-day school became the norm in most primary schools, school time has been extended for primary pupils and there is an apparent trend in schools making use of this opportunity to improve their resilience in the school context. Figure 1.3 is the Resilience Wheel developed by Henderson and Milstein (1996), which can be used as the blueprint for resilience capacity building programmes at school:

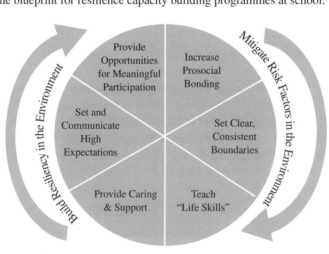

Figure 1.3 Resilience wheel (Henderson and Milstein, 1996)

As we can see, there are diverse ways of building the culture of resilience. A series of intensive group-based and theme-based activities will offer students opportunities for participation and give them the chance to understand and actually experience the real advantages of resilience. When conducting the activities, we must pay due attention to these two points: a caring culture and clear expectations.

Positive psychology

Positive psychology is a relatively new term, which is widely used in many branches of behavioural sciences (including applied psychology). Positive psychology tends to target adults as the subject of study, with the focus on the individual's strength and subjective well-being. As the core of positive psychology is related to optimism, creativity, self-efficacy, and different types of virtues. Childhood and those social units that are closely related to children in the process of growing up—family, peers and school—are bound to attract the interest of positive psychologists. As far as schools are concerned, they concentrate on how children can master the basic academic skills, and how to improve their academic performance through the development of positive intrapersonal and interpersonal skills (Gilman, Huebner and Furlong 2009).

Although the top priority of the school is to help students in academic performance, it also makes available a community in which children and youngsters are facilitated to develop a sense of civic pride and responsibility, as well as experiment with different roles and activities. Just as a community can make adults feel threatened or blessed, the school may also have similar impacts on their young students. There is an urgent need to develop the school as a strength-based community to facilitate students in the process of their learning and growing up. Since extra-curricular activities can also facilitate students in expressing their creativity and developing their sense of empowerment, their importance is indisputable. Nevertheless, since not many extra-curricular activity programmes have been scientifically proven as being effective, further research will be required in this regard.

School-based family counselling

School-based family counselling is an approach used to help children at school achieve success and overcome personal and interpersonal problems. It applies a systems approach to combine school guidance and family counselling to form an integrated whole. The school-based family counsellors use systems thinking as the theoretical basis and offer their service to children within such systems as family, school, peers and community. The efficacy of this counselling mode is based on the partnership and close collaboration between the school and the community. The school-community collaboration project consists of strategies used to render support to students, schools, school development and community development (Sanders 2001). The strategies include: (1) a high degree of involvement in learning; (2) principal's support for community involvement; (3) friendly atmosphere at school; (4) two-way communication regarding the level and type of community involvement (Epstein et al. 2009). Such collaboration will provide the school with a challenging and nurturing environment for learning, thus raising the standards in students' academic performance and general behaviour (Epstein et al. 2009).

Promoting equality education and supporting students to succeed

Equality education and supporting students to succeed are the current trends in the development of guidance (Paisley and Hayes 2003). They originate from the Transformation School Counselling Initiative (TSCI), which aims at helping students achieve academic success, tackle the problem of poverty, and break up the social and ethnic barriers that exist between young people of the ethnic minorities and others. This initiative can enable the guidance personnel to: (1) be knowledgeable about schools and schooling; (2) be equipped to assist students in meeting their educational and personal goals; (3) remove barriers that impede the academic success of poor and minority students (Paisley and Hayes 2003). To achieve these goals, the guidance personnel will be required to take part in activities comprising the following five components: educational leadership, advocacy, team building and collaboration, counselling and coordination, as well as use of assessment data (Perusse, Goodnough, Donegan and Jones 2004). The implementation of inclusive education in Hong Kong has already taken into account these elements.

Conclusion

This chapter has discussed the fundamental concepts of guidance, its international development trends, and its actual development in Hong Kong. The aim is to facilitate the examination and discussion of school issues from the perspectives of guidance.

Questions for Discussion

1.   From the perspectives of guidance, what do school, student and education each refer to?

2. To provide guidance in the 'East meets West' hybrid cultural contexts of Hong Kong, what special considerations should one bear in mind?

Related Websites

1. Hong Kong Psychological Counselling Centre
   http://www.hkpcc.hk/
2. The Boys' and Girls' Clubs Association of Hong Kong
   http://www.bgca.org.hk/bgca06/main/press.asp?lang=C&id=317
3. Hong Kong Association of Careers Masters and Guidance Masters
   http://www.hkacmgm.org/
4. Hong Kong Youth Counselling Association
   http://www.hkyca.org.hk/
5. Hong Kong Institute of Christian Counsellors
   http://www.hkicc.edu.hk/index.php
6. Student Guidance and Discipline Services
   http://www.edb.gov.hk/index.aspx?nodeID=1972&langno=1
7. Counselling and Guidance
   http://www.youth.gov.hk/tc/counselling/index.htm
8. Asian Journal of Counselling
   http://www.fed.cuhk.edu.hk/en/ajc/index.htm
9. 學校行政專題報告──教訓輔三合一制度
   http://web.ed.ntnu.edu.tw/~minfei/schooladministration/91-2share-1.pdf
10. 建立學生輔導新體制實驗方案：教學、訓導、輔導三合一整合實驗方案
    http://www.psees.tyc.edu.tw/~adm04/g10/g1011.htm

Extended Readings

Campbell, C. A., and Dahir, C. A. (1997). *Sharing the Vision: The National Standards for School Counselling Programs.* Alexandria, VA: American School Counsellor Association.

Education Commission. (1990). *Education Commission Report No. 4: The Curriculum and Behavioural Problems in School.* Hong Kong: Government Printer.

Education Department. (1993a). *Guidelines on Whole School Approach to Guidance (for Primary Schools) Part (1).* Hong Kong: Government Printer.

——— (1995a). *Guidelines on Whole School Approach to Guidance (for Primary Schools) Part (2).* Hong Kong: Government Printer.

Geldard, K., and Geldard, D. (2002). Practice Frameworks (Part 2, pp. 25–70) and Conclusion (Part 6, pp. 235–70). In *Counselling Children: A Practical Introduction (2nd ed.).* Wiltshire, London: The Cromwell Press Ltd.

Hui, E. K. P. (2003). *Teaching in Hong Kong: Guidance and Counselling.* Hong Kong, China: Longman.

Shertzer, B., and Stone, S. (1981). Guidance in the Educational Setting (Ch. 2, pp. 39–59) and Counselling with Individuals (Ch. 6, pp. 167–95). In *Fundamentals of Guidance* (4th ed.). Boston: Houghton Mifflin.

Wagner, W. G. (2003). A Multidimensional Approach to Intervention with Children (Part 1, pp. 3–16). In *Counselling, Psychology, and Children: A Multidimensional Approach to Intervention.* Upper Saddle River, NJ: Merrill.

馮觀富（1996）：《輔導原理與務》。台北：心理出版社。

林孟平（1995）：《輔導與心理治療》（增訂版）。香港：商務印書館。

區祥江（2008）：《輔導小百科》。香港：突破出版機構。

吳武典（1996）：《學校輔導工作》。台北：心理出版社。

游黎麗玲（1998）：《學生輔導》（增訂版）。香港：中文大學出版社。

References

American Counselling Association. (2004). ACA in the News: Definition of Professional Counselling. Accessed 11 November 2010. http://www.counselling.org/PressRoom/NewsReleases.aspx?AGuid=d41c4491-1df5-46a5-a06b-f104c02c8c5a

——— (2010). ACA Milestones. Accessed 11 November 2010. http://www.counselling.org/AboutUs/OurHistory/TP/Milestones/CT2.aspx

Baker, S. B. (1996). *School Counselling for the Twenty-First Century* (2nd ed.). Englewood Cliffs, NJ: Merrill.

Branden, N. (1992). What is Self-Esteem? In G. R. Walz and J. C. Bleuer (eds.), *Student Self-esteem: A Vital Element of School Success (vol. 1)* (pp. 15–26). Ann Arbor, MI: ERIC Counselling and Personnel Services.

Campbell, C. A., and Dahir, C. A. (1997). *Sharing the Vision: The National Standards for School Counselling Programs.* Alexandria, VA: American Counselling Association.

Canfield, J. (1990). Improving Students' Self-esteem. *Education Leadership*, 48: 48–50.

Cheng, K. M. (1990). The Culture of Schooling in East Asia. In N. Entwistle (ed.), *Handbook of Educational Ideas and Practices* (pp. 163–73). London: Routledge.

——— (1995). *Zhengzhi biandong zhong de Xianggang jiaoyu.* Hong Kong: Oxford University Press. (In Chinese.)

Cheng, K. M., and Wong, K. C. (1996). School Effectiveness in East Asia. *Journal of Educational Administration*, 34(5): 32–49.

Education and Manpower Bureau. (2004). *Personal Growth Education.* Accessed 6 September 2007. http://www.emb.gov.hk/index.aspx?nodeID=121&langno=1

Education Department. (1993a). *Guidelines on Whole School Approach to Guidance (for Primary Schools) Part (1).* Hong Kong: Government Printer.

——— (1993b). *Guidelines on Whole School Approach to Guidance (for Secondary Schools) Part (1).* Hong Kong: Government Printer.

——— (1995a). *Guidelines on Whole School Approach to Guidance (for Primary Schools) Part (2).* Hong Kong: Government Printer.

———— (1995b). *Guidelines on Whole School Approach to Guidance (for Secondary Schools) Part (2)*. Hong Kong: Government Printer.

Epstein, J. L. et al. (2009). *School, Family, and Community Partnerships: Your Handbook for Action*. Thousand Oaks, CA: Corwin Press.

Gilman, R., Huebner, E. S., and Furlong, M. (2009). *Handbook of Positive Psychology in Schools*. New York: Routledge.

Gladding, S. T. (2000). *Counselling: A Comprehensive Profession* (4th ed.). Upper Saddle River, NJ: Merrill.

Gysbers, N. C., and Henderson, P. (1994). *Developing and Managing Your School Guidance Program*. Alexandria, VA: American Counselling Association.

Henderson, N., and Milstein, M. M. (1996). *Resiliency in Schools: Making it Happen for Students and Educators*. Thousand Oaks, CA: Corwin Press.

Hui, E. K. P. (1991). A Whole School Approach to Guidance. In N. Crawford and E. K. P. Hui (eds.), *The Curriculum and Behavior Problems in Schools* (pp. 17–28). Hong Kong: Faculty of Education, The University of Hong Kong.

———— (1997). *Guidance and Counselling in Hong Kong Schools: Policy, Practice and Future Directions*. Paper presented at the Cross-Cultural Counselling in Chinese Communities, 16 May 1997, Hong Kong.

———— (1998). Guidance in Hong Kong Schools: Students' and Teachers' Beliefs. *British Journal of Guidance and Counselling*, 26(3): 435–47.

Johnson, S. L. (2000). Promoting Professional Identity in an Era of Educational Reform. *Professional School Counselling*, 4: 257–61.

Kehas, C. D. (1970). Towards a Redefinition of Education: A New Framework for Counselling. In B. Shertzer and S. C. Stone (eds.), *Education, in Introduction to Guidance*. Boston: Houghton Mifflin Company.

King, A. Y. C. (1996). The Transformation of Confucianism in the Post-Confucian Era: The Emergence of Rationalistic Traditionalism in Hong Kong. In W. M. Tu (ed.), *Confucian Traditions in East Asian Modernity: Moral Education and Economic Culture in Japan and the Four Mini-Dragons* (pp. 265–76). Cambridge, MA: Harvard University Press.

Lam, M. P. (1984). Teacher-Student Relations. *Educational Research Journal,* 12: 18–23. (In Chinese.)

———— (1995). Self-Esteem as the Core in Whole School Approach in Guidance. In P. K. Siu and T. K. Tam (eds.), *Quality in Education: Insights from Different Perspectives* (pp. 148–71). Hong Kong: Hong Kong Educational Research Association. (In Chinese.)

Lee, C. C. (2001). Culturally Responsive School Counsellors and Programs: Addressing the Needs of All Students. *Professional School Counselling*, 4: 289–99.

Lewis, E. C. (1970). *The Psychology of Counselling*. New York: Holt, Rinehart and Winston.

Luk-Fong, Y. Y. P. , and Lung, C. L. (1999). Guidance and Counselling Services in Hong Kong Secondary Schools: Profiles and Possibilities. In Y. C. Cheng (ed.), *Paper Series in Education, 1999* (pp. 1–23). Hong Kong: Centre for Research and International Collaboration, Hong Kong Institute of Education.

Miller, F. W., Fruehling, J. A., and Lewis, G. J. (1978). *Guidance Principles and Services*. New York: Charles E. Merrill.

Milner, P. (1980). *Counselling in Education*. London: P. Milner.

Murgatroyd, S. (1985). *Counselling and Helping*. London: Methuen.

Myrick, R. D. (1993). *Developmental Guidance and Counselling: A Practical Approach* (2nd ed.). Minneapolis, MN: Educational Media Corporation.

Nelson-Jones, R. (1983). *Practical Counselling Skills*. London: Cassell.

Paisley, P. O., and Hayes, R. L. (2003). School Counselling in the Academic Domain: Transformations in Preparation and Practice. *Professional School Counselling*, 6(3): 198–204.

Perusse, R., Goodnough, G. E., Donegan, J., and Jones, C. (2004). Perceptions of School Counsellors and School Principals about the National Standards for School Counselling Programs and the Transforming School Counselling Initiative. *Professional School Counselling*, 7(3): 152–61.

Purkey, W. W., and Novak, J. M. (1996). *Inviting School Success: A Self-Concept Approach to Teaching, Learning and Democratic Practice* (3rd ed.). Belmont, CA: Wadsworth.

Radd, T. R. (1993). *The Grow with Guidance System: Levels 1–7*. Omaha, NE: Grow with Guidance.

Rogers, C. (1942). *Counselling and Psychotherapy*. Boston: David and Charles.

Sanders, M. G. (2001). The Role of "Community" in Comprehensive School, Family, and Community Partnership Programs. *Elementary School Journal*, 102 (1): 19–34.

Schmidt, J. D. (1996). *Counselling in Schools: Essential Services and Comprehensive Programs*. Needham Heights, MA: Allyn and Bacon.

Shaw, M. C. (1973). *School Guidance System*. New York: Houghton Mifflin.

Shertzer, E. F., and Stone, S. C. (1981). *Fundamentals of Guidance* (4th ed.). Boston: Houghton Mifflin.

Stevenson, H. W., and Stigler, J. W. (1992). *The Learning Gap: Why Our Schools are Failing and What We Can Learn from Japanese and Chinese Education*. New York: Simon and Schuster.

Stillion, J., and Siegel, B. (1985). The Intentionally Inviting Hierarchy. *Journal of Humanistic Education*, 9: 33–39.

Stone, L. A., and Bradley, F. O. (1994). *Foundations of Elementary and Middle School Counselling*. White Plains, NY: Longman.

Yang, K. S. (1999). Towards an Indigenous Chinese Psychology: A Selective Review of Methodological, Theoretical, and Empirical Accomplishments. *Chinese Journal of Psychology*, 41(2): 181–211.

輔導工作手冊：《教訓輔三合一輔導人員的職責》。擷取於 2010 年 1 月 29 日，http://www.tfps.chc.edu.tw/~tfps/counsellor/page_2.htm

教育署（1986）：《中學學生輔導工作——給校長和教師參考的指引》。香港：政府印務局。

教育署（1999）：《輔導成長齊參與：實況篇》，錄影帶。

教育署（2001）：《中學生輔導工作》。香港：教育署升學及輔導服務組。

教育統籌局（2003）：《建立校園抗逆文化的理念》。擷取於 2010 年 1 月 29 日，http://www.edb.gov.hk/FileManager/TC/Content_2003/resilience%20concept.doc

教育統籌局（2009）：《成長的天空計劃（小學）輔助課程——工作員須知》。擷取於 2010 年 1 月 29 日 http://www.edb.gov.hk/index.aspx?langno=2&nodeid=1989

林孟平（1988）：《輔導與心理治療》。香港：商務印書館。

廖茂村（2003）：〈教訓輔三合一整合實驗方案建立學生輔導新體制實施問題之探討〉，《學校行政雙月刊》，第 28 期，頁 108–124。

麥德彰（2010）：〈會長的話之「訓輔合一」訓、輔的未來路向〉。《訓導通訊》，第 57 期。

吳武典（1980）：《學校輔導工作》。台北：心理出版社。

香港小童群益會：《全方位校園支援計劃》。擷取於 2010 年 1 月 29 日，http://www.bgca.org.hk/bgca06/main/press.asp?lang=C&id=323

游黎麗玲（1998）：《學生輔導》。香港：中文大學出版社。

2

Psychological Resilience and the Personal Growth of Children and Adolescents

On the Guidance and Counselling Needs of Children and Adolescents

Pattie Yuk Yee Luk-Fong and Tuen-yi Chiu

> For a theory of therapy, I think it is best not to assume that motivation comes from within the individual, but to look instead at the individual as part of the social systems.
>
> (Haley 1987)

Abstract

This chapter begins with a brief account of the guidance and counselling needs of Hong Kong students, followed by an explanatory account of the theoretical framework of 'person in context' and 'developmental contextualism'. I will then introduce the methods of evaluating students' guidance needs before concluding the chapter with psychological resilience as the conceptual framework for assisting the personal growth of youngsters.

Objectives

This chapter will help you:
* tell what the students' guidance and counselling needs are;
* explain the concepts of 'person in context' and 'developmental contextualism';
* grasp the methods to assess the students' needs in guidance; and
* use resilience as the conceptual framework to assist youngsters in their personal growth.

Before You Start: Think and Discuss

1. What is the difference between students' needs for guidance and for counselling? Are guidance and counselling complementary in the sense that they make up for each other's deficiencies, or that they give each other mutual support?
2. How does the unique East-meets-West context of Hong Kong affect a student's personal growth?

3.   As a class teacher or a subject teacher, how do you fulfil students' personal growth/guidance needs?

Introduction

Prior to providing guidance to students, it is imperative to understand students' personal growth and guidance needs. In many parts of the world, the personal growth of youngsters is not only influenced by the individual's personal characteristics and stage of personal development, but also deeply affected by his/her surroundings. The personal growth of Hong Kong's youngsters is no exception.

Person in Context

'Person in context' is built upon the theories of the ecology of human development (Bronfenbrenner 1979), which argues that personal growth (covering such aspects as personality, body, linguistic competency, cognition, social skills, emotions and moral values) is affected by the surrounding environment (such as family, school, peers, media and society values) (see Figure 2.1).

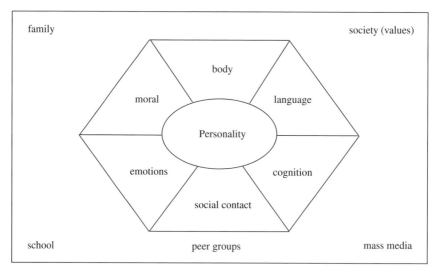

Figure 2.1 Person in context

Developmental Contextualism

'Developmental contextualism' (Lerner and Jovanovic 1990) belongs to the school of thought that stresses the interactions between development and context. It upholds the theory that no matter what developmental stages of life the students are in, their needs are both holistic and interrelated. The students' physical, emotional, cognitive and social developments affect one another in an interactive manner. For instance, students who are tired tend to be bad-tempered and have difficulty in concentrating on their study. Lerner and Jovanovic (1990) define body image as 'the functions of cognition and sensitivity of the body' within the framework of developmental contextualism. They point out that the formation of body image is not only related to person-social context relationships, but is also affected by an individual's cognitive development.

> **Case Study 1**
>
> Seven-year-old Siu-keung was noted for his attention-seeking behaviour on entering P. 1. He lived with his grandparents, an aunt with a mental illness history and a twenty-year-old uncle. His father used to be a construction worker, but unemployed for many years. His mother was a housewife. They had a lenient attitude towards Siu-keung's behaviour and did not have any explicit expectations of him as they considered that the child's happiness was most important. This laissez-faire attitude might be due to their own upbringing, which they remembered as undesirable, as their parents were very strict with them. Since his grandmother passed away six months ago, Siu-keung started using foul language at school and even pulled down his trousers in public. His teachers did not know what to do with him, and his classmates found him a nuisance. The teachers' reproach and classmates' alienation caused him to resent school so much that in the examination, he did not bother to do any questions even though he knew the answers (Luk-Fong Y. Y. P. 2005).

This case reveals the complexity of the student's behavioural problem and dramatic drop in academic performance. It is found that family factors are often involved, like family size and relationships, the parents' education level and social-economic status, incidents happening to the family (like death of a family member), influence of the extended family, and the influence of family of origin on the parents. Family issues are also induced by the external environment, for example, a father losing his job. If the school is unaware of these factors and only punish the student for not complying with the requirements of the school system, this may bring distress and chaos to the student, as well as to members in his family and school systems, while failing to render timely assistance to the student. Therefore, a close coordination between the school system and the family system is a necessary condition for student guidance.

Personal Growth and Guidance Needs of Children and Adolescents

The following is a tabulation of the personal growth and guidance needs of children and teenagers in the unique environment of Hong Kong (see Table 2.1) based on the theoretical framework of 'developmental contextualism'. While guidance emphasizes a growth orientation and the development of competence, counselling is about remedial actions, and a deficit model which would help clear the hurdles. We would like to equate guidance with the needs in personal growth, and counselling with the guidance needs.

Children's personal growth and guidance needs will be discussed from three perspectives, namely: (1) the needs in personal growth for Hong Kong children and adolescents; (2) the educational environment of Hong Kong; and (3) the social environment of Hong Kong (see Table 2.1).

Table 2.1 Children and teenagers' needs for guidance and counselling

	Guidance needs	**Counselling needs**
Nature	Developmental growth orientation	Remedial removing barrier Deficit model
Hong Kong students' needs in personal growth	(a) Children's needs at different developmental stages: holistic and interrelated (physical, cognitive, social, emotional, moral, linguistic) (b) Havighurst's developmental task checklist • Acquiring physical and academic skills • Developing morals • Achieving personal independence • Learning to develop social relationship with classmates • Recognition of gender roles	(a) What are the students' needs and worries? (b) What are the major problems encountered by students?
The educational context of Hong Kong	(a) The examination-oriented education system: students' low self-concept (b) Education reforms • Skill-oriented • Multiple intelligence (competence and attitude) • Helping students to find for themselves the meaning of education • Knowing of one's own abilities and limits • Vocational knowledge • Goal setting • Time management • Decision-making	Removing barriers for learning: • Not every student is ready for schooling • Lack of study skills • Not knowing how to do the homework • Personal or emotional problems

(continued on page 31)

Table 2.1 *(continued)*

The societal context in Hong Kong	(a) Capitalist society, consumerism, mass media, the Internet, the haves and have-nots: student's choice and value judgement (b) Changes in the family: e.g. single parent, parent re-marrying, dual career parents, weekend family (c) Political context: 'one country, two systems' (d) Cultural context: East-meets-West (e) Competence and life skills training • Communication • Problem-solving • Decision-making • Conflict resolution	Problems of Children: • Internalized problems • Externalized problems • Rule-breaking behaviours Transition needs: (a) Transitions of developmental stages : P.1, P.6, S1, S3, S6 (b) children newly-arrived from China (c) family transition: e.g. divorce, bereavement, unemployment

Personal growth needs of children and adolescents

Young people's needs for healthy personal growth comprise a sense of security, caring relationships, strength, bonding, respect, competence, problem-solving, and a sense of purpose (Morrison and Allen 2007). School children/teenagers at different stages of development, for instance during childhood or adolescence, have different needs. According to Havighurst (1972), youngsters' developmental tasks include acquiring basic physical and academic skills, developing morality, achieving personal independence, learning to get along with peers, and recognizing their gender roles.

Hong Kong is by and large a Chinese society, and Confucian influence still dominates an individual's personal development and everyday life (Cheng 1999). Table 2.2 compares and contrasts the Western and the Chinese (Confucian in particular) traditions about the individual. In order to help our students with their guidance and counselling needs, we should begin by looking at how the East-West culture impacts upon them.

Table 2.2 A comparative study of East-West views on 'self' and 'others' using a Western theoretical framework (Luk-Fong 2001)

Self and other relationships	Western traditions	Chinese traditions (especially the Confucian thinking)
Core concepts of the personal growth of adolescents		
The physical self	Body image and physical health More individualistic in form	Physical, mental and spiritual discipline Avoiding individual differences
The sexual self	Equality	Family- and male-oriented

(continued on page 32)

Table 2.2 *(continued)*

The social self	Communication	Role and harmony
The vocational self	Interest and ability	Economic ends
The moral and political self	Rights and participation	Virtues and obligations
The self as learner	Ability	Effort
The self in a collective	Participation	Conformity
Values	Self-esteem, self-respect, co-operation with others	Self-cultivation, embedded self
Skills and processes	Communication Decision-making Problem-solving Conflict resolution Reflection Transfer	Will Practice Self-examination Reflection Self-correction
Relationships	Self in relation to others Respect for differences Individual autonomy Conflict resolution	Five cardinal relationships Familism and brotherhood Authority Harmony

The embedded self

There are fundamental differences between the 'embedded self' in the Chinese tradition and the so-called 'individual self' in the West (as represented by the USA), the Confucian idea of self-cultivation, and the psychological concept of self-esteem. Take interpersonal relationships as an example, the Chinese advocate the Confucian concept of 'reconciliation for the sake of maintaining harmony' (以和為貴) and this is evident in the five cardinal relationships and the values underlying the emphasis on the family and authority. This is miles apart from the 'autonomy of the individual' as advocated in the West, where conflicts are expected to be resolved by dialogue and confrontation. Wong's (1999) study on the value system of Hong Kong youngsters clearly reveals that it is a hybrid of both worlds, viz., the youngsters in Hong Kong identify themselves with both (1) the value system of the West, which emphasizes individual achievements and freedom; and (2) the traditional Chinese value system, which respects the family and diligence.

School environment

Emphasis on obedience and observation of school regulations

Schools in Hong Kong have always attached more importance to the collective than the individual. Schools stress uniformity among students and require them to wear school uniform and take the same curriculum from primary to junior secondary levels. The weekly assembly makes an ideal occasion for students' uniformity training. The emphasis on the observance of school rules seems to be in contradiction with the recent education reforms which encourage students to undertake creative, independent and critical thinking. Such a discrepancy may bring confusion to students.

Examination-oriented education: 'Learning is not for scoring?'

The education reform emphasizes the learning process and proclaims that 'learning is not for scoring'. Despite the many efforts, it has yet to change most people's mindset. There is still a strong conviction among students that a direct correlation exists between personal success and academic excellence. Examination-oriented education can adversely affect students' self-concept. The survey on 'How Teenagers View Success and Failure' (2000) conducted by the Hong Kong Federation of Youth Groups[1] reveals that the majority admit that they have encountered more failures than successes in their experience and 10 per cent of the respondents even indicate that they regard themselves as complete failures as individuals. Among the respondents, the majority considers that the main criterion for measuring success and failure is 'academic results', with more than 40 per cent referring to 'good academic performance' and 'bad academic performance' as the pointers of success or failure. The respondents also state that in the face of failure, they would rather talk with their peers/classmates/colleagues than their parents. They do not want their parents to know for fear of being scolded or worrying them. Another opinion survey called 'How Important are Academic Scores to Students' (1998),[2] also conducted by the Federation, finds that, on average, respondents had three tests a week. When asked how they feel about academic results, the majority returned with a score of 7 or above, on a scale of 10 in ascending order, in the tension index as well as stress index. Yet over 40 per cent of the respondents agree that scores and examinations are the best ways to assess student performance. The contradiction indicates their dilemma towards scoring. Nevertheless, over half of the respondents do not agree that academic scores are the deciding factor for one's failure or success, with close to 35 per cent expressing strong disagreement. Forty-five per cent of the respondents disclose that their academic scores definitely have an impact on their self-esteem, and that they feel under pressure whenever they compare scores with classmates.

Emphasis on effort over ability

In Hong Kong, there is a general and deep-rooted concept that 'diligence can make up for stupidity' (Cheng 1990). Schools and parents share the belief that diligence and drilling can improve student performance. The following case study may throw some light on this:

Case Study 2

Mei-ling is eleven years old and a primary six student. In this academic year, within a 9-month span, she had to cope with a total of seven internal examinations, term tests and public examinations on top of regular class tests every fortnight, mock placement tests and over ten volumes of supplementary exercises. As the Education Bureau requires schools to submit the internal assessment scores before June for the Secondary School Placement Assessment, some schools organize the examinations for this purpose, and also hold end-of-term examinations so that their students will not become laxed during the summer holiday. They think that by keeping the students constantly on alert, they would obtain good grades in the pre-Secondary 1 test. Such an arrangement has put heavy examination pressure on the students and made it necessary for them to drastically reduce their extra-curricular activities. This case shows that schools which believe that more examinations and drill practices can help improve students' academic performance would often neglect their duties in cultivating students' real potentials and abilities.

Pressure on academic performance

Many students work hard in order to get into prestigious schools and through-train (一條龍) and English-medium schools, aiming to get into the science stream and enter top-ranking universities. Whether this would change after the implementation of the New Secondary Senior (NSS) curriculum and the education reforms remains to be seen. Nonetheless, the heightened stress faced by the final batch of secondary graduates who could not repeat Secondary 6 due to the implementation of the NSS curriculum has already aroused public concern.

Several surveys conducted among junior secondary and upper primary students (The Youth Centre of the Evangelical Lutheran Church Social Service 2001,[3] Caritas Tak Tin Community Youth Service 2001)[4] show that the school is the major source of pressure borne by students, in such forms as unsatisfactory academic and examination results, promotion to a higher class, and choice of school for further study. The cause of pressure is also family-related. For instance, when they do not receive any sympathetic support from the family and cannot fulfil their parents' expectations, or when they find that their homework is too much and too difficult to handle. It is because parents usually hope that their children could study in prestigious schools and have high expectations on them, which put great pressure on their children. The study by the Evangelical Lutheran Church Social Service Youth Centre even indicates that 20 per cent of the respondents consider committing suicide a solution to their problems—a mindset that should draw dire concern.

Family situations in Hong Kong

Family changes

With modernization, the family as the basic unit for providing financial support, a caring relationship (emotional support) and raising children seems to have come under fierce challenge. Modernization is a global trend and it has impacted Hong Kong families. The participation of women in the labour market has steadily increased. In 2001, 52.9 per cent of married women were in employment (Hong Kong Government Statistics Department 2009). As many women carry on working after giving birth to children, families with both parents working are common. Some of these families hire domestic helpers to look after the children and take care of housework. According to the figures released by the Hong Kong Government Statistics Department in 2009, 220,000 domestic helpers were working in Hong Kong, coming mainly from the Philippines, Thailand and Indonesia. Some families choose another option: the children are entrusted to the care of grandparents during the day, and are taken home to be with their own parents at night. Another social phenomenon called 'weekend parents' has also emerged: the children stay with their grandparents and become their charge between Monday and Friday, only returning home to spend the weekend with their parents. Lee (2000) points out that although the nuclear family is majority in Hong Kong, traditional family values and mutual aid from the extended family are still prevalent. Lee refers to this feature as 'resilient familism'. Traditional family values such 'the family should be intact' and 'family disgrace should not be disclosed to outsiders' are still common (Law et al. 1995). It is not unusual for members of the extended family such as grandparents, aunts, on both the paternal and the maternal sides, to help taking care of the children.

The number of divorce cases has steadily risen in Hong Kong, going from 9,473 in 1996 to 12,943 in 2002, representing an increase of 36.6 per cent. In 1996, with every 100 pairs of newlywed couples came 26.8 cases of divorce, and in 2002, this number had almost doubled to 40.4 (*Wen Wei Po,* 15 May 2004). While the divorce rate in Hong Kong has remained quite stable at about 0.3 per cent, far below the figures in Europe and America, it nevertheless was the third highest in Asia, which in turn leads to an increasing number of single families. In 2001, 58,460 single families (with children aged 18 or below in the household) were recorded in Hong Kong, with 45,072 being taken care of by the mother, and the other 13,388 being looked after by the father. By comparison, the single families in the care of the mother tend to be less well-off financially. As most single parents are aged between 30 and 49, the possibility for remarriage or cohabitation is relatively high. The family background will become complicated as a result of remarriage, and children growing up under these family conditions may sometimes experience difficulties in adjustment. In the meantime, the instances of household violence had increased, from 1,072 cases in 2000 to 1,665 cases in 2002; there were 179 cases of child sex abuse in 2002 while in 2003, 73 cases were reported in the first six months alone (*Oriental Daily* 15 May 2004). Research shows that children brought up in two-parent families perform better in academic study and school behaviour than those who grow up in single-parent families, or in households with the mother and a stepfather (Zill 1996).

Working parents and parent-child relationship

The long working hours of parents is a major barrier to good parenting (Social Policy Research Centre, School of Applied Social Sciences, Hong Kong Polytechnic University 2005). A survey on working parents and parent-child relationship[5] reveals that the father on average spends 3.42 hours daily with the youngest child at primary school age, and the mother on average spends about 8.37 hours. Most working mothers with higher education levels spend less than 4 hours daily with their children. On the other hand, most non-working mothers with lower education levels spend over 5 hours daily with their children. These figures show significant regional and social class divergence. The Hong Kong Confederation of Trade Unions conducted a survey[6] in Yuen Long which shows that due to the economic downturn, parents were too busy trying to make ends meet to spare time to take care of their children. Eighty-five per cent of fathers on average spent over 9 hours daily working, and 40 per cent among them spent more than 12 hours. Over 70 per cent of children considered that their fathers spent too little time with them. The children wished the most that their parents could keep them company in play and going shopping, and second, watching TV, having tea and dim-sum in the restaurants, and playing video games. However, whenever parents could find time to spend with their children, most would only concern themselves with their academic progress (Education Department and Committee on Home-School Co-operation 1999)[7] and neglect their children's subjective well-being and emotional needs.

Parents' concepts regarding children's upbringing

A survey on the concepts of parenting called 'Major Mistakes in Parenting'[8] reveals that mistaken beliefs were related to children's academic study and obedience, and parental protection. The most popular myths on bringing up children are as follows:

(1) to make themselves worthy of their parents' love, children should be obedient and obtain good grades in school;
(2) parents should take care of every little detail of their children's daily life;
(3) children should comply with each and every of their parents' wishes.

The more children the respondents had, the lower their family income or education level, and the more mistaken their parenting concepts were. Over 10%

of respondents failed to be good role models for their children. For example, many believed that 'if children are given more than the correct change in a shop, it is all right to take the money', or that 'if a child has accidentally broken something in a shop, the best solution is just slipping away before anyone notices', etc.

The three points mentioned above illustrate that although Hong Kong has long been exposed to Western culture, there are certain deep-rooted beliefs such as stress on academic achievements, focus on authority, and male-dominated family ideology like 'dutiful wife and loving mother' (賢妻良母) . The knowledge that their parents would love them only if they make good grades is burdening students with pressure, and hinders them from attaining a balance in their physical and mental well-being. Parents' over-protective attitude towards their children has not only added pressure on themselves, but also takes away the children's opportunities to learn to take care of themselves. The popular belief that 'if a child does not get good grades, he/she will not have a secure future' is putting academic before everything else. In reality, many successful people were no more than mediocre in school when they were little. This is sufficient contention for the myths for success.

What makes a healthy family?

A 'healthy family' may be defined as one which is not concerned with the external structure (form), but puts greater emphasis on the internal contents (spirit). Stinnett and DeFrain (1985) argue that a healthy family should include commitment, appreciation, communication, time together, emotional support and crisis management. Olson (2000) also points out that a resilient family should have a high degree of cohesion and flexibility, and good communication. Disharmony between parents has direct effects on children's emotional control and behavioural problems (Repetti, Tylor and Seeman 2002). Parents' conflicts before divorce have far greater adverse effects on children than absentee parents or poor financial conditions (Amato 2001). According to a half-century longitudinal study of children growing up in families with divorced parents, most of these children were able to grow up as healthy adults. Dowling and Barnes (2000) identify the following eight factors as reasonably good protections for children from divorced families:

1. Parents in residence use effective parenting methods.
2. The non-residential parent is able to participate.
3. The conflicts between parents are kept to the minimum.
4. The father or mother is easily accessible.
5. The non-residential parent makes regular (or scheduled) visits.
6. The reason for seeking a divorce is fully explained.
7. There is regular and steady support outside the family.
8. The school provides a supportive environment and is sensitive to the students' needs.

Peer groups

Peer groups are a very important contributing factor to youngsters' personal development. A survey called 'How Teenagers Look upon Their Friends?' conducted by the Hong Kong Federation of Youth Groups (2006)[9] among students in Hong Kong reveals that 91.5 per cent of the respondents yearned for peer acceptance. Over half of the respondents (55.4 per cent) were afraid of peer rejection. Youngsters regard trust as the most important thing when it comes to choosing friends, being with friends or establishing close friendship. On a scale of 0–10 (10 being the highest), the respondents gave a score of 7.76 on average for trust among friends.

The survey also reveals that the top three factors for happy times with friends are: enjoying the company of friends (52.8 per cent); being able to say whatever they want (34.8 per cent); and being cared for (14.1 per cent). What distresses them the most in their relationship with friends are: being betrayed or cheated (32.2 per cent); estrangement (19.8 per cent); and spreading gossips and damaging remarks (10.9 per cent). Selfishness (29.3 per cent) and arrogance are the most disliked traits among youths.

As to who qualify as friends, 60.1 per cent of the respondents defined them as those who can offer advice when they encounter problems and difficulties, while 34.1 per cent defined them as playmates who were willing to spend time with them. Another finding in the study is that, when they encounter problems or difficulties, most youngsters would talk to their friends about them. The most often discussed problem is related to studies.

Mass media

The Internet

The most powerful tool that holds sway over young people in the twenty-first century is probably the Internet. It is useful to students for searching for the necessary information in their studies. But there is a growing number of students who become addicted to this virtual world: some use false identities to chat online and play online games. Young people who cannot find self-fulfilment in the real world can easily be hooked to the fantastic realm of virtual reality. As a result, a group of *hikkomori*, or young people opting for social withdrawal, has emerged. Being online addicts means these young people not only give up their studies and withdraw from social contacts, but also suffer setbacks in physical health and intellectual development. They are also likely to get involved in activities such as cyber porn and online dating which may sometimes lead to Internet crimes.

Television, films and newspapers

There is a recent trend that, in the name of 'reflecting reality', television and film screens are filled with dirty language and underworld lingo. Violence as well as figures of triad societies are idealized. To boost circulation, some newspapers try to attract readers with repulsive photographs and eye-catching headlines. The trend is reflected in schools, with a rising number of school violence cases (Leung and Tsang 2009). The 'glossy gossip' magazines are filled with exposé, and often risqué stories of artists in the entertainment world. They exert an adverse influence on students' attitude towards their own body image or towards sex.

Hong Kong's societal values

In the face of globalization and capitalism, Hong Kong has tended to accept materialism and consumerism as the implicit societal values. Youngsters are obsessed with trendy gadgets, constantly trading in their mobile phones for the latest model, competing with one another on high-end branded handbags. Their mindset regarding studies becomes short-sighted. Many students no longer pursue studies in order to acquire knowledge, but to use it as the avenue to high-pay jobs.

Assessment of Students' Personal Growth and Guidance Needs

The methods used to evaluate students' personal growth and guidance needs include the following:

Hong Kong students' needs at different stages of personal development

To assess students' personal growth and guidance needs, we can make use of the concepts of 'developmental contextualism' introduced earlier as a tool for analysis. Students' personal growth and guidance needs will change as a result of the changes that take place in the social milieu, school environment and family conditions of Hong Kong. Therefore, teachers must keep a close tab on society so as to be able to make intelligent and timely responses to their needs.

The school environment

Besides the needs specific to the different stages of personal development, it must be noted that students in different schools may have different needs for personal growth and guidance. For instance, students in a Band 1 school may need assistance from others to deal with examination pressure the most, while those studying in a Band 3 school may require more people's advice and assistance in coping with their emotional and behavioural problems. As for the needs of the school, the academic performance indicators, the student behaviour indicators, and the students' backgrounds are good sources of reference for assessing the needs of students in a particular school.

Different stakeholders

In assessing the students' needs for personal growth and guidance, it is necessary for all stakeholders of the school to take part, but it is most crucial to listen to the voice of students. Luk-Fong's research (2005b) indicates mismatches between the students', parents' and teachers' perceptions of a good parent-child relationship. The children yearn for time together with their parents, a point not well-known to their parents and teachers. While parents expect their children to be compliant and diligent, like doing their homework quickly and finishing their meals promptly, teachers wish that their students would be capable of independent and critical thinking but at the same time be obedient and compliant. The diverse views held by the students, parents and teachers show how difficult it is for students to understand exactly what a good parent-child relationship is.

Different approaches

We can assess the students' needs for personal growth and guidance by means of questionnaires, interviews and surveys. For the class teacher, another viable option is to ask the whole class to fill in a questionnaire which allows them to express their needs either in writing or in the form of pictures. Figures 2.2 (a), (b) and (c) show that children of both genders at different ages may have different kinds of worries or fears.

Table 2.3 shows the findings of the survey called 'A Study of Students' Sentiment Index' conducted by the Student Guidance Association (Primary School) (2005). It enables us to have a more comprehensive understanding of the types of emotional stress faced by students. The findings reveal that academic study and examination pressure are the major sources of stress for students in primary school. After that is poor interpersonal relationship, for instance, quarrelling with classmates, being isolated by classmates, being bullied and having no friends. The

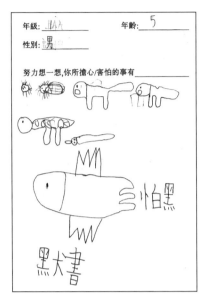

Figure 2.2(a) A 5-year-old boy is afraid of darkness and dictation

Figure 2.2(b) A 10-year-old girl is afraid of making the teacher angry

Figure 2.2 (c) A 9-year-old boy is worried about not having any friends

most shocking finding is that students feel that they do not have time for play and rest. After the education reform, which has much emphasized the importance of other learning experiences, students not only have to work hard at their studies, but also need to perform well in extra-curricular activities. In effect, this has increased the burden as well as stress for the students. The other items that concern the family include: lack of time spent with the father; family discord, being bullied by elder siblings, and financial problems.

Table 2.3 Findings of 'A Study of Students' Sentiment Index[i]

Which of the following items below are the difficulties you face and give you a bad mood?	No. of times selected	Rank
3) Poor academic results	910	1
9) Tests and examinations	880	2
7) Too much homework	792	3
1) Quarrelling with classmates	722	4
5) Being scolded by teachers	668	5
10) No time to play	646	6
17) Not enough time for rest	641	7
2) Being isolated by classmates	614	8
6) Being bullied by schoolmates	499	9
11) Lack of time spent with parents	492	10
13) Discord among family members	445	11
4) Having to attend tutorial class after school every day	398	12
12) Financial problems in family	397	13
14) Being bullied by siblings	379	14
16) Having no friends	344	15
8) Extra-curricular activities	275	16
15) Addicted to video games and Internet surfing	252	17
Others: (Please describe explicitly the behaviour) Worrying about puberty, making friends, worrying about the possibility of mother being unemployed, being given nicknames by classmates, teachers requesting to see parents, relatives migrating abroad, no time for sports, not allowed to play football, boredom, playing on the computer, gradually falling behind in class, shorter than normal for the age, falling ill too often, etc.	37	

[i]   The study conducted by the Student Guidance Association (Primary School) Company Limited has successfully interviewed 1200 P. 4–6 students in 29 primary schools using this questionnaire.

From the above discussion, the problems of children/adolescents can be summed up as related to: homework, interpersonal relationships (with parents and peers), self-esteem, sexual behaviour, psychological health (like drug abuse, and slimming) and anti-social behaviour (such as shoplifting, joining juvenile gangs).

Based on the issues of students' emotions and behaviours, the problems of children/adolescents can also be categorized as follows:

1. Internalized problems

Internalized problems arise when an individual chooses to obey the dictates of his/her internal feelings, which adversely affects his/her mental, cognitive and emotional capacities (Wong 2006). When the surrounding environment makes an impact, he/she will develop such symptoms as depression, distress, shyness, withdrawal, sensitiveness, lack of self-confidence, and somatizing.

2. Externalized problems

   Externalized problems refer to the outward behaviour that an individual chooses to perform in response to stimulus in the environment (Lerner 2002), like violence, disobedience, acting on impulse, and hyperactivity. In general, young females tend to have more internalized problems, and less externalized problems. Internalized problems and externalized problems may occur concomitantly (Wong 2006).

3. Rule-breaking behaviours

   Rule-breaking behaviours refer to those which are in breach of the law and order or regulations in society, the family, and at school (Pang 1985), such as smoking, theft, fighting, not handing in homework frequently, cheating, truanting, running away from home, and joining the triad society.

Transitional Needs

Transitions between stages of schooling

The transitions between different stages of schooling refer to the transitions from kindergarten to primary school, from primary school to secondary school, or from secondary school to university. Very often, such changes would lead to adjustment difficulties in students. The research of Lau, Leung and Wong (2008) finds that close to 10 per cent of students from well-established schools experience adjustment problems or cannot keep up with the standard when they are promoted from Chinese-medium primary schools to English-medium secondary schools. They are thus frustrated and eventually drop out of school all together. When students studying in Band 1 schools find that, after having tried their best, they are still way behind other students in academic standing and fail to get into the exclusive circle of 'elite of the elite', they would feel a sense of failure and give up on themselves. Other students are depressed on entering secondary school because they feel neglected, and eventually choose self-abandonment. Similarly, teenagers who leave school and join the work force also meet with adjustment problems. A study called 'The Transition from School to Work'[10] conducted by the Hong Kong Federation of Youth Groups (2006) shows that the major problems encountered by the respondents include: 'need to face interpersonal relations' (48.5 per cent); 'need to entertain the boss's requests' (31.5 per cent); and 'need to meet the job requirements' (21.5 per cent). The majority of respondents consider that not being sure about the direction of their career development constitutes the greatest difficulty to them. This shows that students do not have any clear understanding of their individual life goals and lack career planning. This also points to the need for career guidance for our students.

Newly-arrived children from China

In the last decade, a great influx of immigrants from mainland China (newly-arrived persons) poured into Hong Kong, only to find that the lifestyle and social customs of Hong Kong are completely different. Therefore, many newly-arrived children experience difficulties in adjusting to living in Hong Kong, especially in such areas as study, social life, and family and social integration. As a result, they come under great pressure and suffer emotional disturbance (Hong Kong YWCA 2000).[11] To sum up the findings of the 'Report on Adaptation of Newly Arrived Children from China' released by the Boys' and Girls' Clubs Association of Hong Kong (1995), and those of the study, 'The Population Poser: How do Young New Arrivals from Mainland China Adapt', conducted by the Hong Kong Federation of Youth Groups (1995), we can see that the young new arrivals from mainland China have to overcome three main hurdles:

(1) Learning adjustments

On arrival in Hong Kong, they know very little about the people and place, and they feel especially helpless when it comes to finding a suitable school. Since the teaching medium and school curriculum in Hong Kong are quite different from those in Mainland China, these young new arrivals usually take quite a long time to make the necessary adjustments to the changes. Some unfortunate ones are even made victims of discrimination or misunderstanding by their teachers and schoolmates, and so they are further disadvantaged in their drive to adapt to the new learning environment.

(2) Social adjustments

The social circle of these young new arrivals from the Mainland is restricted to their contacts at school. As many of them are only allowed to repeat the same form or start at a lower level in order to fit in with the Hong Kong school curriculum, they are usually older than their peers in class. The age gap and the language barrier make their social adjustments difficult. The lack of peer support further disadvantages their integration into Hong Kong society. Many such students seldom leave home, have to put up with loneliness and solitude, and have no effective way to release their pent-up emotions.

(3) Family relations

Due to the policy restrictions, there is a long waiting list for the family members of children to get entry permits to family reunion. They are, therefore, forced to live apart. To children growing up, long separation from family members could result in hindrance to their intellectual development and communication barriers between children and their parents, thus adversely affecting family relationships.

There is also a joint research project entitled 'A Study on Mental Health of Newly Arrival Children for Their First Two Years of Settlement in Hong Kong' (City University of Hong Kong (Division of Social Studies) and Christian Action 1999), which found that among students in P. 4–6 who had been in Hong Kong for less than two years, more than 40 per cent showed clear signs of distress and under multiple pressure, for instance, difficulties in learning English, problems in getting around in Hong Kong without assistance, having their academic performance compared unfavourably with those of friends and classmates, and being scolded or nagged by their parents.

Family transition

Family changes like parents' divorce, death of family member and unemployment of family members can cause distress to students. Homes and Rahe (1967) show that the severity of the blow dealt by divorce to adults is only second to the sudden death of the partner, while children of the family also come under great pressure. Wallerstein and Blakeslee (1989) consider that the damaging effects of divorce are greater on children than on adults. Adults may feel relieved when the marriage troubles are over, but this feeling is only shared by one in ten children in family, since children all want to live with their parents. The traumatic experience of divorce suffered by children cannot be compared with those caused by disasters because in a disaster, the adults will do their best to protect the children, whereas in a divorce the parents, who are themselves emotionally unstable, will not be able to spare energy to pay special attention to their children.

How do children involved in the divorce of their parents feel? Some may suddenly become very emotionally disturbed, unruly in behaviour, rebellious, and anti-social; they may go so far as to openly break the established rules in the group, and display such aggressive behaviours as beating others or wreaking havoc. Others may be reticent, saddened, and depressed. These children may think that they are different from other children, losing interest in the things they used to enjoy (Gestwicki 1995), or, in the words of Elkind (1988), they 'grow too fast too soon' while their classmates are too childish to understand them or share their problems. They begin to shut themselves up in voluntary self-isolation and play the role of an onlooker. They are not able to attend fully to school activities or focus on their study, giving others the impression of being bothered by worries and troubles. Since the usual order in the family has been derailed, the children may feel confused, troubled and helpless, or even develop a sense of guilt, wrongly believing that they are responsible for their parents' divorce because they did not behave well enough. They may also experience a sense of inferiority and try to hide the family misfortune from classmates. Their greatest worry and anxiety stem from this terrible feeling that 'dad and mom no longer love me'. When the parents are separated, brothers and sisters may have to live apart. The pain thus accrued can cause some children to develop symptoms of illness, a sense of powerlessness and undermine their self-concept.

It must be pointed out that divorce is not a one-off incident, but a lifelong experience for those concerned. The new life which requires necessary adjustments, including the lowering of living standards and arrangements to meet with the parents, often result in great pressures to children and adults alike. The important thing to note is that children may be easily torn between divided loyalties due to their divorced parents, making them doubt the sincerity of love between adults. If children in this dire situation do not receive proper guidance, the development of both their mind and body will be adversely affected. Teachers should understand children's experience in a parent's divorce and be aware of their own personal opinions and attitudes towards divorce. When they are certain that they have no bias towards divorce, they will be in a better position to offer suitable guidance.

Literature on 'Psychological Resilience' and Reactions from Teachers/Schools

With reference to the literature on 'psychological resilience', it is noted that when teachers and schools are faced with the students' diverse needs for personal growth and guidance, the most effectively approach that they could use to help students grow positively and overcome the troubling times would be to establish a caring relationship with the students, have positive and high expectations of them, maximize students' opportunities of participation in and making contributions to the school and society, and make optimal use of the protective factors in the environment and in the student himself/herself to ensure their growing up healthily. At the same time, teachers should pay attention to students, and the family and community should provide every assistance to the school, thus creating an environment in which they can feel safe, a sense of belonging, and being loved, respected and empowered. On the one hand, students are enabled to acquire skills and expertise, to get prepared for challenges, and to understand the meaning of life. On the other hand, they are encouraged to develop co-operation and communication skills, empathy, problem-solving skills, self-efficacy, self-understanding, and a clear goal and aspirations in life.

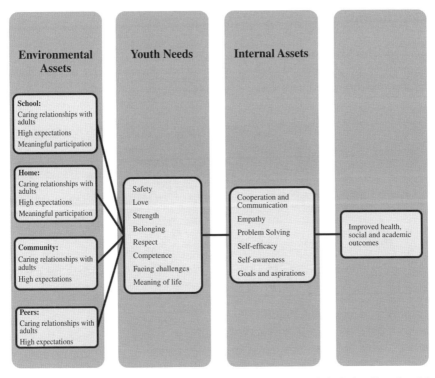

Figure 2.3 Conceptual framework for student guidance based on the 'psychological resilience' model

From the above discussion, can you propose an approach to guidance based on the conceptual framework of the 'psychological resilience' model that a teacher can apply in class or at school to ensure the healthy growth of their students?

Conceptual Framework for Student Guidance Based on the 'Psychological Resilience' Model

Youngsters' needs: _____

Internalized assets of psychological resilience: _____

Environmental assets of psychological resilience: _____

School (classroom, class teacher, other teachers): _____

Peers: _____

Family: _____ Community: _____

Conclusion

Students' growth is closely linked with the other systems such as school and family. In the Hong Kong context, the school and family are deeply affected by the unique local environment (see Figure 2.4).

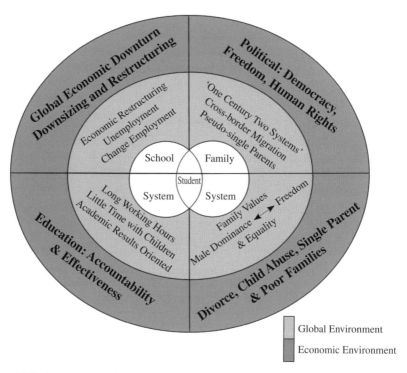

Figure 2.4 The links among student growth, the school system, the family system, and the local and global environments in Hong Kong (Luk-Fong 2005a)

Colonial rule and globalization bring with them the social systems of the West (i.e. education, law and order, finance, etc.) and value systems (i.e. democracy, freedom, human rights, etc.) of the West. These pose serious challenges to the indigenous Chinese culture and value system throughout the political, economic, social and educational arenas: the confusions thus caused are gradually undermining some of the traditions. As mentioned above, to help students grow up healthily, we must begin with 'person in context'. The person in the unique East-meets-West context will be a good starting point.

Questions for Discussion

1. Discuss how far the over-emphasis on academic performance has affected the whole person development of students in Hong Kong. What methods should schools use to redress this phenomenon?
2. What are the effects on the students' whole person development when the students, teachers and parents hold different systems of value? Discuss how the differences can be negotiated.

Notes

1. The Hong Kong Federation of Youth Groups (2000) Opinion Survey of Teenagers series, Volume 83, on 'How Teenagers View Success and Failure'. This was a telephone survey with a random sampling by telephone numbers, and 503 respondents from the 10–19 age group in Hong Kong were successfully interviewed.
2. The Hong Kong Federation of Youth Groups (1998) Opinion Survey of Teenagers series, Volume 60, on 'How Important are Academic Scores to Students'. This survey used the random sampling method to conduct telephone interviews and 537 full-time students from the 12–29 age group were successfully interviewed.
3. The Youth Centre of the Evangelical Lutheran Church Social Service conducted a survey on the pressures and stress faced by students in junior secondary school between February and April 2001. A total of 1,400 subjects were interviewed, all of them junior secondary students in the New Territories.
4. The Caritas Jockey Club Integrated Service for Young People – Tak Tin conducted a survey in March 2001 to understand the cause of students' stress and how much they were suffering from it. Questionnaires were sent out to P. 5 and P. 6 pupils in six primary schools in Kwun Tong, with a total of 1,566 subjects surveyed.
5. The Centre for Social Policy Studies of the Department of Applied Social Sciences, the Hong Kong Polytechnic University conducted 'A Survey on Parent's Working Hour and Parent-Child Relationship' in February 2005. It covered households with residential telephone lines and with children in primary school in Hong Kong. Through telephone interviews, 511 effective cases were collected.
6. The Hong Kong Confederation of Trade Unions conducted a survey in Yuen Long entitled 'The Effect of Parents' Working Hours on Their Children's Growth Development' in 2001. A total of 130 children aged between 6 and 12 were successfully interviewed on their perceptions of whether their parents had spent enough time with them.

7. The Education Department and the Committee on Home-School Co-operation jointly conducted in August 1999 a survey study called 'Research Study on the Rights and Responsibilities of Parents' Involvement in the Education of their Children'. The respondents who were successfully interviewed by telephone included 2,436 parents and 2,054 students from 18 primary and secondary schools.
8. RTHK published a survey report on parental concepts in 2001, 'Major Mistakes in Parenting', which was conducted as a street survey by the City University of Hong Kong (Division of Social Studies).
9. A survey by the Hong Kong Federation of Youth Groups, 'How Teenagers Look upon Their Friends?', was commissioned by RTHK for its programme *Salad Days* in 2006. A total of 554 students from primary to tertiary levels were successfully interviewed in this survey.
10. The research study, 'The Transition from School to Work', conducted by the Hong Kong Federation of Youth Groups in 2006 successfully interviewed 768 youths between the age of 15 and 24 by telephone. They carried out follow-up interviews on 10 cases and organized 5 focus group discussions, under the guidance of experts and scholars invited to give advice and assistance.
11. The research study 'The Condition of Emotional Adjustment of Newly-Arrived Children in Hong Kong' undertaken by the Hong Kong YWCA in 2000 targeted newly-arrived children aged 10–15 who were in Hong Kong for one year or less and studying in primary and junior secondary schools. The respondents had to answer a questionnaire by themselves and for this study 231 completed questionnaires were retrieved.

Useful Websites

1. 青少年齊抗逆
    http://www.ttmssd.org/Int/ST/Activity/2009/04/article/article.php
2. 教育局——活出精彩人生面對逆境
    http://cd1.edb.hkedcity.net/cd/mce/tc/life/main.html
3. 香港青少年服務處——青少年逆境自強篇
    http://www.cys.org.hk/education/resistence/YouthFront.asp
4. 逆境自強 11 小學生做好榜樣
    http://paper.wenweipo.com/2007/11/11/HK0711110010.htm
5. 逆境自強教案
    http://www.icac.org.hk/me/new/pri/2007/report/pdf/114_118.pdf
6. 生命鬥士
    http://www.4limb.org/view/lifefighter.0

7. ICAC 勵志故事
    http://www.icac.org.hk/icac/activities/e-reading/images/pdf/chapter5.pdf
8. 青少年及學童的憂鬱症
    http://www.healthcare2u.com/hit_youth_melancholia.html
9. 香港社會服務聯會　出版刊物　兒童及青少年
    http://www.hkcss.org.hk/cy/publication.htm
10. 青少年生涯發展服務培訓計劃教材套
    http://www.hkcss.org.hk/cy/Employment%20-%20Training.htm

Extended Readings

Luk-Fong, P. (2001). Competing Contexts for Developing Personal and Social Education in Hong Kong. *Comparative Education*, 37(1): 65–83.

Morrison, G. M., and Allen, M. R. (2007). Promoting Student Resilience in School Contexts. *Theory into Practice*, 46(2): 162–69.

蔡元雲、黃成榮、蔡志森、陳之虎（2002）：《進入 NET 新世界：揭示青少年生活面貌》。香港：突破出版社。

陳作耘主編（2003）：《青春何價（上）成長中的青年及（下）青年與社會》。香港：香港基督教服務處。

黃成榮（1999）：《青少年價值觀及違規行為探索》。香港：三聯書店（香港）有限公司。

李永年（2002）：《香港青少年問題：廿一世紀的現象、剖析與對策》。香港：香港大學出版社。

陸方鈺儀（2005）：〈從系統理念看家庭與小學輔導〉。《基礎教育學報》，第 14 卷第 1 期，頁 101–120。

曾文星（2004）：《青少年心理》。香港：中文大學出版社。

鄭漢光、盧鐵榮、黃成榮（2004）：〈少年偏差行為的自我及社會心理因素〉。《青年研究學報》，第 7 卷第 2 期。香港：香港青年協會出版。

期刊：《亞洲輔導學報》

References

Amato, P. R. (2001). Children of Divorce in the 1990s: An Update of the Amato and Keith (1991) Meta-Analysis. *Journal of Family Psychology*, 15(3): 355–70.

Bronfenbrenner, U. (1979). *The Ecology of Human Development: Experiments by Nature and Design*. Cambridge, MA: Harvard University Press.

Cheng, K. M. (1990). The Culture of Schooling in East Asia. In N. Entwistle (ed.), *Handbook of Educational Ideas and Practices* (pp. 163–73). London: Routledge.

——— (1999). Culture Matters: A Cultural Perspective of Aims of Education for Hong Kong (synopsis, draft). Paper presented at the International Conference on Teacher Education, Hong Kong.

Dowling, E., and Barnes, G. G. (2000). *Working with Children and Parents through Separation and Divorce: The Changing Lives of Children.* London: Macmillan.

Elkind, D. (1988). *The Hurried Child: Growing up Too Fast Too Soon* (rev. ed.). Reading, MA: Addison-Wesley.

Haley, J. (1987). *Problem-Solving Therapy* (2nd ed.). San Francisco: Jossey-Bass.

Havighurst, R. J. (1972). *Development Tasks and Education.* New York: Mckay.

Holmes, T. H., and Rahe, R. H. (1967). The Social Re-adjustment Rating Scale. *Journal of Psychosomatic Research*, 11: 213–18.

Law, C. K. et al. (1995). *Contemporary Hong Kong Families in Transition.* Hong Kong: Hong Kong Women Foundation (Ltd.), Department of Social Work and Social Administration, the University of Hong Kong.

Lee, M. K. (2000). *Hong Kong's Family Trends and Their Policy Implications.* Paper presented at Family Trends and Policies in OECD Countries: Issues and Lessons, Hong Kong.

Lerner, R. M., and Jovanovic, J. (1990). The Role of Body Image in Psychosocial Development across the Life Span: A Developmental Contextual Perspective. In T. T. Cash and T. Pruzinsky (eds.), *Body Image: Development, Deviance, and Change* (pp. 110–27). New York: Guilford.

Lerner, R. M. (2002). *Adolescence: Development, Diversity, Context, and Application.* Upper Saddle River, NJ: Pearson Education, Inc.

Luk-Fong, Y. Y. P. (2001). Competing Contexts for Developing Personal and Social Education in Hong Kong. *Comparative Education*, 37(1): 65–87.

——— (2005a). Pedagogical Issues in the Teaching of Classroom Guidance Curriculum: A Hybrid Hong Kong Case. *Counselling Psychology Quarterly*, 18(3): 193–206.

——— (2005b). A Search for New Ways of Describing Parent-Child Relationships: Voices from Principals, Teachers, Guidance Professionals, Parents and Pupils. *Childhood*, 12(1): 111–37.

Morrison, G. M., and Allen M. R. (2007). Promoting Student Resilience in School Contexts. *Theory into Practice*, 46(2): 162–69.

Olson, D. H. (2000). Circumplex Model of Marital and Family Systems. *Journal of Family Therapy*, 22: 144–67.

Repetti, R. L., Taylor, S. E., and Seeman, T. S. (2002). Risky Families: Family Social Environments and the Mental and Physical Health of the Offspring. *Psychological Bulletin*, 20(2): 330–36.

Stinnett, N., and DeFrain, J. (1985). *Secrets of Strong Families.* Boston: Little Brown.

Wallerstein, J. S., and Blakeslee, S. (1989). *Second Chances: Men, Women, and Children a Decade after Divorce.* New York: Ticknor and Fields.

Zill, N. (1996). Family Change and Student Achievement: What We Have Learned, What It Means for Schools. In A. Booth and J. F. Dunn (eds.), *Family-School Links: How Do They Affect Educational Outcomes?* (pp. 139–74). Mahwah, NJ: Lawrence Erlbaum Associates.

Gestwicki, C.（2008）：《親職教育：家庭、學校和社區關係探討》（陳昭伶、陳嘉珩、白秀玲、梁嘉惠、廖淑台、鄭翠娟譯）。台北：華騰文化。

城市大學社會科學部、基督教勵行會（1999）：《新來港到港適應期間精神健康研究》。香港：城市大學社會科學部；基督教勵行會。

東方日報（2004）：〈家庭團結指數倒退逾倍〉，《東方日報》，港聞 A29 版。2004
年 5 月 15 日。

黃成榮（1999）：《青少年價值觀及違規行為探索》。香港：三聯書店（香港）有限公司。

黃德祥（2006）：《青少年心理學：青少年的發展、多樣性、脈絡與應用》。台北：
心理出版社。

梁玉嬋、曾瑞霞（2009）：〈青少年成長與發展〉，輯於《青少年生涯發展服務培訓
教材套》（頁 280–290）。香港：香港社會服務聯會。

劉玉瓊、梁玉珍、王定茹（2008）：《處理學童缺課及輟學問題：家庭為本實務手冊》。
香港：香港中文大學社會工作學系新地心理健康工程。

陸方鈺儀（2005）：〈從系統理念看家庭與小學輔導〉。《基礎教育學報》，第 14 卷
第 1 期，頁 101–120。

彭駕騂（1985）：《青少年問題探究》。台灣：巨流圖書公司印行。

文匯報（2004）：〈離婚率升 暴力案增 家庭團結指數劇跌 社聯倡社會反思 加強對新
來港家庭支援〉，《文滙報》，香港新聞 A21 版。2004 年 5 月 15 日。

香港青年協會（1995）：《內地新到港青少年的適應》。香港：香港青年協會。

香港小童群益會（1995）：《新移民青少年生活適應個案調查報告書》。香港：香港
小童群益會。

香港政府統計處（2009）：《綜合住戶統計調查按季統計報告書（2009 年第四季）》。
香港：政府印務局。

3

Hong Kong School Guidance and Counselling Service
Development and Approach

Mabel Mei Po Shek

The goal of education is not only to pass on knowledge to students, but also to foster their holistic development so that they can become a new generation of people with confidence, competency and responsibility.

(Discipline and Guidance Services, Education Bureau)

Abstract

This chapter aims at giving teachers a comprehensive view of the origin of guidance, the development of school guidance in Hong Kong and the impact of social changes on the implementation of school guidance. In this chapter, two major policies concerning school guidance in Hong Kong will be introduced: (1) Whole-school Approach to Guidance, and (2) Comprehensive Student Guidance Service. The rationale, objectives, principles and strategies of the implementation of these policies will be explained with a view to reflecting on how to work with the present approach of school guidance service, help students develop the abilities required in everyday life and meet the challenges they encounter in their personal growth and development.

Objectives

This chapter will help you:
- recognize the origin of school guidance and the impact of social change on the approach of school guidance;
- understand the historical development of school guidance in Hong Kong and the rationale for school guidance policies;
- get a good grasp of the rationale, objectives, principles and strategies for the implementation of Comprehensive Student Guidance Service; and
- reflect on the teacher's role in the effective implementation of Comprehensive Student Guidance Service.

Before You Start: Think and Discuss

1. What are the social factors that will affect the implementation procedures of school guidance approaches?
2. In the past, how did schools in Hong Kong carry out school guidance?
3. What domains of work should school guidance include?
4. Who is the key personnel responsible for the implementation of school guidance?
5. How can school guidance work be effectively implemented?
6. In what specific areas can teachers render assistance in implementing school guidance?

Introduction

School guidance service emerged from the USA in the early twentieth century, in response to the changes in social environment, during a society's transformation from a predominantly agrarian economy to one with rapid industrial development. Later, with the speedy and widespread growth of information technology, school education itself evolved drastically, making it necessary for school guidance to adjust and change accordingly. School guidance first began as career guidance. Gradually, the idea of guidance was expanded to concerning students' whole person development and helping them cope with adjustment difficulties in everyday life. The demand for a developmental approach to guidance has been on the rise since the end of the twentieth century to focus further on the comprehensive and developmental nature of school guidance. There was also the conscious move of school guidance as an integral part of education, a move which departed from the responsive and remedial approach in the past and launched school guidance service in a new direction.

This chapter will trace the origin and the evolution in the approach of school guidance, followed by a discussion of the history of school guidance in Hong Kong, as well as a critical review of Western influences on its development. Next, the two major policies on school guidance in Hong Kong will be elaborated in detail, covering the rationale, objectives, principles and implementation of (1) Whole School Approach to Guidance, and (2) Comprehensive Student Guidance Service. Lastly, teachers' major responsibilities in school guidance under the current approach will be highlighted, for their participation is essential to the effective implementation of comprehensive student guidance service.

School Guidance: Its Origin and Development

Position orientation: 1900s–1930s

School guidance emerged in American schools in the early twentieth century. At first, school guidance was mainly undertaken by teachers, who were appointed as 'school counsellors', to give students advice and assistance with regard to their personal, social and career needs. Since the USA was undergoing an industrial revolution and the economic system comprising free enterprises and corporations was fast developing, career guidance was thus widely promoted in schools as a matter of necessity. In response to social demands, the focus of guidance was placed on helping students identify their personal characteristics and strengths, and the necessary skills, business ethics and concepts so as to be able to secure suitable employment after graduation and contribute to the social development (Gibson and Mitchell 1999). In order to implement career guidance systematically throughout the country, Frank Parsons, an expert in career guidance, proposed in 1908 that career guidance should be carried out by trained professionals (Gysbers and Henderson 2000). School counsellors were later renamed as 'vocation counsellors' to highlight the focus of service then. As more vocation counsellors were being trained, the school guidance service was rapidly expanded and professionalized.

As a consequence of economic development and the rise of feminism in the West, the opportunities for school education for boys and girls are becoming more equal. Since students of diverse social backgrounds had the chance to enrol in schools, the gap of learning and the diverse developmental needs were increasingly evident. At this stage, the onus of school guidance still depended on vocation counsellor with a position orientation to provide students with individual career counselling. However, many people began to question the narrow focus of school guidance on career counselling alone. Thereupon, some leaders in the profession began to promote the idea that, apart from career counselling, school guidance should also pay close attention to the students' personal development. This broad interpretation of school guidance laid the foundation for the advancement of guidance theories.

Service orientation: 1940s–1960s

From the 1940s on, various counselling theories were propounded in the West, leading to the development of counselling psychology, whose influence on the work of school guidance was most notable. Among these theories, the client-centred therapy advocated by Carl Rogers was the most important. Rogers' theory utterly broke away from the traditional counsellor-directed and counsellor-position-oriented approaches to school guidance in the past, which were mainly focused on providing clients with available information and helping them solve their problems. His growth-oriented theory opened up a new horizon to school guidance. This theory centres on the client, and the counsellor needs to cultivate a trusting relationship with the client in order to help the client reach self-actualization (Rogers 1961). Based on Rogers' theory, a new trend in school guidance targeting the personal growth of students came to the fore.

School guidance was then provided mainly in the form of counselling service for individual students, helping them cope with different types of adjustment problems and develop their potentials. The counsellor's role, function and job specification also took concrete shape slowly, as school counsellors started to set goals for guidance and evaluate the needs of students. They formulated plans for counselling activities, connected with school curriculum, and coordinated different types of student services so as to cater for the students' diverse developmental needs.

Programme orientation: Since 1970s

During the 1960s, the rapid development of information technology in the USA and around the world transformed the industrial countries into knowledge-based economies. To maintain their competitiveness, the governments recognized the urgent need to invest in human capital by increasing the resources for lifelong learning. In response to such changing social contexts, there started a movement in education reform all over the world. Aligned with the education reforms, school guidance had taken a role in facilitating students to acquire competencies in the domains of personal and social, academic and career development (Gysbers and Henderson 2000; Myrick 1993; Schmidt 1993).

From the 1970s on, an array of theories on education and career development emerged, which instigated changes in the school guidance service. Concepts of comprehensive and developmental guidance soon came to the forefront. Norman Gysbers proposed the conceptual framework of comprehensive guidance programme, which incorporated the systems theory, and highlighted the connection between school guidance and the goals of education. The importance of measurable outcomes was also emphasized. The overall aim of school guidance is to develop the competence of every student and facilitating their smooth and successful transition to further studies or employment. In effect, Gysbers thus changed the fundamental concept of school guidance from position orientation to programme orientation, and brought a significant paradigm shift in school guidance.

Since the 1980s, the comprehensive guidance programme began to spread across the USA. According to the survey conducted by Sink and MacDonald (1998), about half of the schools in the USA had implemented comprehensive guidance programme. The findings of surveys carried out in various states in the USA show that the implementation of comprehensive guidance programme had a positive effect on student learning: students considered that the learning environment was supportive and safe, and there was better teacher-student relationship (Lapan, Gysbers and Petroski 2003; Lapan, Gysbers and Sun 1997). Traditionally, the approach to school guidance emphasized service or process, and counsellors specialized in the skills of individual counselling. The contemporary mode of school guidance, however, is focused on competency or results. Yet it is found quite difficult for the school counsellor to evaluate the effectiveness of school guidance (Sprinthall 1971), especially in view of the rising demand for social accountability. This presents a direction in which school guidance requires further research and development. Henderson and Gysbers (2002) point out that the key factor in the successful implementation of comprehensive guidance programme is effective leadership. The leadership role of the school counsellor is not only apparent in the management of the guidance service, but also realized through the collaboration with the teaching and administrative staff to respond positively to the students' developmental needs, setting up effective procedures for referrals and launching various guidance activities to enhance the academic, career, personal and social development of students (Miller 1968; Shertzer and Stone 1981).

❐ **Activity 1**

Group Discussion

1. In your opinion, what kind of factors, other than economic development, could affect the development of school guidance?
2. How would the influence of Western culture affect the implementation of guidance?
3. Do you think that the Western approach to guidance is applicable to regions in Asia?

Developments of School Guidance in Hong Kong

The remedial approach: 1970s–1980s

Prior to the 1970s, guidance work used to be undertaken by social workers, who reached out to teenagers in the community. Later, as more children had the opportunity to enrol at school, adjustment and emotional problems emerged in the school context. This called for the initiation of guidance work in school. In the early stage, school guidance was normally undertaken by the class teacher, who tended to put the emphasis on career guidance as well as provided individual counselling to the students with behavioural and emotional problems (Yau Lai 1998). Since 1971, voluntary social welfare agencies set up guidance services in schools. Later on, the government provided more resources to support the development of the school social work service. Due to the shortage of professionally trained social workers and the greater demand on teenagers' adjustment support, guidance service was limited to individual counselling for students in secondary schools. This situation lasted until 1978, when the Education Department established the Student Guidance Section, which made the service available to primary schools. In the initial stage, experienced primary school teachers were recruited as Student Guidance Officers (SGO), who specialized in guidance service in primary schools. The SGO-student ratios then were as follows: 1:3000 (urban areas) and 1:2000 (rural areas) (Education Commission 1990). Meanwhile, the guidance service in secondary schools continued to be rendered by social workers and the manning ratio (social worker: students) was set at 1:4000 (Hong Kong Government 1979). The ratio of guidance personnel to students was so low that it was very common for a school social worker or SGO to serve several schools.

Owing to the shortage of trained guidance personnel, they mainly handled critical cases and lacked the time to engage other students in preventive programmes. These were the crucial drawbacks that hindered the development of school guidance. In 1986, the Education Department issued the *Guidance Work in Secondary Schools: A Suggested Guide for Principals and Teachers* (Hong Kong Education Department 1986), which emphasized the importance and aims of school guidance and then made plans for additional resources to advance guidance service in secondary schools. Although these measures showed a clear commitment of the Education Department to further develop the school guidance service, the focus of guidance work was still inclined towards the remedial approach. Teachers were merely responsible for identifying the students with problems and referring them to the school social worker (in secondary schools) or student guidance officer (in primary schools) for individual counselling. Because of the lack of a concrete direction and policy for the guidance service, the general public perceived school guidance as merely a service for the students with deviant behaviours, and school guidance was in effect labelled as a kind of auxiliary or marginal service, which discouraged students and parents from actively seeking such service.

The preventive and developmental approach: The 1990s

Since the introduction of the nine-year compulsory education, the learning gaps among students had broadened, thus giving rise to more emotional and behavioural problems (Education Commission Sub-committee on School Education 1997). With a view to the increasing demand for guidance service, and the recommendation of the *Education Commission Report No. 4*, the Education Department formally adopted the 'Whole-School Approach to Guidance' in 1992 , the first government policy on school guidance. This policy confirmed the guidance role of all teachers in the school, as well as the need for preventing behavioural problem of students and developing their individual potentials. It also stressed the need for fostering a positive and caring school ethos, to enable all students to learn and grow up in a harmonious environment (Education Department Guidance Section 1993). In line with the policy implementation, the government took steps to increase school resources for guidance. A student guidance teacher was added to the staff of the primary schools to help coordinate guidance work. The provisions for teacher training and support services for guidance were also enhanced (Education Commission 1990). The ratio of student guidance teacher/officer to students was set at 1:2500 and in 1997, the ratio was raised to 1:1680.

The 'Whole-School Approach to Guidance' marks a breakthrough in the school guidance service in Hong Kong. Through the participation of all teachers in guidance work, the orientation of school guidance gradually extended from the remedial approach focused on individual counselling to the preventive and developmental approach. Nevertheless, some scholars argue that this approach to guidance is strong on ideas but short on the specific details for organization and implementation (Yuen, Lau & Chan 2000). The policy documents also placed great emphasis on positive reinforcement and systematic award schemes, which aimed at encouraging students to form positive and good habits (Education Commission 1990; Education Department Guidance Section 1993). As the goal was mainly to prevent behavioural problems among students, there were not yet any specific indications on the developmental aspects of guidance. It was also shown by research that the remedial and preventive approach to guidance remained the dominant mode in the majority of schools (Hui 1998; 2000a). It was probably because many teachers did not have a good grasp of the whole-school approach to guidance (Hui 2002) and therefore the developmental approach to guidance was not widely practised.

In order to further the whole-school approach to guidance, the Education Department Guidance Section made reference to the guidance programmes in the USA and decided in 1995 to launch a pilot scheme, with the production and distribution of the 'Teaching Kit in Whole School Approach to Guidance', in primary and secondary schools (Radd 1996). Teachers were encouraged to incorporate the 'guidance curriculum' or 'personal growth education' into the formal curriculum and use an activity approach to inculcate in students the kind of knowledge, skills and attitudes essential to daily life (Lee and Wong 2008). This development of guidance curriculum has laid a good foundation for later developments of the comprehensive and developmental approach to guidance.

Comprehensive and developmental approach: Twenty-first century

When the rapid development of information technology gave momentum to the emergence of a knowledge-based economy, international organizations began to advocate the adoption of similar policies by all nations in order to create a new economic order. Under the impact of globalization, countries continued to improve the competitiveness of their people, the effectiveness of their education and whether the education system could produce a generation of people who are capable of creativity, communicative competency and critical thinking in order to meet the challenges of a rapidly changing world. As a cosmopolitan society, Hong Kong is not immune to the constant impact of the international trends in the education reform movement. As such, the Education Department borrowed the successful experience of the USA and adopted the conceptual framework of comprehensive student guidance in the Hong Kong context. In 2002, a system of comprehensive student guidance service (CSGS) was thus set up in primary schools, with the aim of helping students develop the necessary life skills.

The Comprehensive Student Guidance Service lays emphasis on its developmental nature and considers itself as an integral part of the total educational process. It sets out to form useful links with the other sub-systems in school to render comprehensive assistance to students and help develop the life skills that they need to meet the challenges of a fast-moving and rapidly changing society (Education and Manpower Bureau 2003). Gysbers (2000) points out that one particular feature of comprehensive student guidance service is that the organization of activities is characterized by their systematization and connectivity so that the relevant parts in other sub-systems are suitably integrated to reinforce the concept of whole-school approach to guidance (Hui 2000b). The comprehensive student guidance service has ushered in an important paradigm shift for school guidance. The change from a position orientation service to a systematic and well-organized programme (Gysbers and Henderson 2006) has provided a clear conceptual framework for guidance service and helped establish the direction of guidance towards a comprehensive and developmental model.

Following the implementation of the new policy, the government allocated additional resources for the optimization of the guidance service. Since September 2000, the policy of 'one social worker for one school' has been implemented in secondary schools. As for primary schools, the government began in 2002 to improve by stages the manning ratio on the basis of the current number of student guidance teachers/officers by introducing a new option, i.e. an allowance to schools for student guidance service. In this scheme, a primary school with 24 classes or above would be allocated a student guidance teacher or a financial allowance for guidance service. In 2006, the scheme was further improved so that a primary school with 18 classes or above would be entitled to employing a student guidance teacher or given the equivalent in CSGS allowance, thus achieving the goal of one student guidance personnel to one primary school. In 2004, the Student Guidance Section and the Student Discipline Section under the Education Bureau were merged to form the Student Guidance and Discipline Services. It was hoped that the reorganization would facilitate the integration of discipline and guidance service and encourage closer coordination and collaboration among the various sub-systems at a school, with a shared commitment to 'discipline and guidance as one service'. The team spirit thus created in the school would be a good guarantee for the comprehensive development of students.

'Personal growth education' forms the core of the comprehensive guidance service. In the same year, the Curriculum Development Committee (2002) decided to include moral education and civic education as one of the key learning areas. As these two curricula deal with personal and social topics in such similar ways that they even seem to overlap with each other in content (Luk 2004), the schools had difficulties launching the personal growth education and had to make corresponding adjustments. In addition, the leadership of school guidance personnel is commonly regarded as the key factor contributing to the successful implementation of comprehensive guidance service (Henderson and Gysbers 2002; Scgwallie-Giddis, ter Maat and Pak 2003; Trevisan and Hubert 2001). It is also stated in the policy documents that the school guidance personnel should play the roles of manager, educator, consultant as well as counsellor. However, the training provided for guidance personnel all along has been emphasizing counselling techniques rather than management skills or methods to evaluate the effectiveness of guidance service (Gysbers and Henderson 2000). Therefore, positive measures must be taken to enhance the leadership capacity of guidance personnel through continuous professional development to ensure the effective implementation of a comprehensive and developmental guidance service.

❐ **Activity 2**

Group Discussion

1. Please share your experience of the guidance activities while you were at primary and secondary schools. As far as you can tell, which programmes could be described as remedial, preventive and developmental respectively? Who were the leaders and organizers? In what ways were they delivered?
2. Who, among the principal, guidance personnel and teachers, had the most say on how to run the school guidance service?
3. Do you share the ideal of 'discipline and guidance as one service'? What would be the difficulties in putting this ideal into practice at the school level?

School Guidance Policies in Hong Kong

Whole-school approach to guidance (1992–2002)

The 'whole-school approach to guidance' required the participation of all teaching and non-teaching staff in the school, with a clear division of labour. Led by the principal, and upon consultation with teachers, the school guidance officer or teacher took responsibility for planning, coordinating efforts and rendering support, for promoting professional discourse on students' problems, achieving a common consensus on the action plan and developing a set of school-based code of ethics. A systematic award scheme would be put in place to reinforce the students' good behaviour and enhance their self-concept, creating a caring and harmonious culture in which students were able to learn and develop into whole persons (Education Department Guidance Services Division 1993). In order to ensure that the policy could be implemented smoothly, the Education Department compiled the *Guidelines on Whole-School Approach to Student Guidance I* for primary as well as secondary schools, to steer schools in the approach and the implementation procedures of school guidance (Education Department Guidance Services Division 1993). In 1995, the *Guidelines on Whole-School Approach to Guidance II* were compiled to reiterate the key points in the guidance approach and give practical examples of school-based guidance programmes for reference (Education Department Guidance Services Division 1995).

Because of the shortage of professional guidance personnel, Hong Kong had to adopt an approach to guidance characterized by a 'general orientation'. The whole-school approach was made possible by collective collaboration and participation of all teaching and non-teaching staff in guidance work. At the forefront were the class teachers, subject teachers and career master/mistress who had regular and close contact with students. Having a good understanding of their students, they were able to spot problem students or students at risk easily and offer them timely help. It was also part of their work to deliver developmental and preventive guidance programmes. Next in line were the remedial teachers, student guidance teachers and school social workers. The former two were to provide teaching assistance or individual counselling to students who had learning difficulties, behavioural or emotional problems while the school social workers would provide individual counselling and family service to students and their families. Moreover, the latter would also provide consultation to teachers in relation to student guidance and community resources available. Last in line were the external psychotherapists and educational psychologists, who worked with the school guidance personnel to provide treatment for students with severe emotional problems. To mobilize the whole body of teaching and non-teaching staff and coordinate their efforts effectively, the school should establish a student guidance team comprising some of the class teachers, all guidance teachers and the school social worker. The discipline master should also attend the guidance team meetings. During their regular meetings, the school guidance team would collaborate to plan, organize, execute and evaluate the school guidance programmes, discuss student cases and formulate the guidance approach.

The rationale of 'whole-school approach to guidance' is based on the recognition that student guidance work should serve the goal of education, and contribute to the building of a positive, collaborative and caring school ethos. This is accompanied by a gradual transition from case work of a remedial nature towards a guidance service with a preventive and developmental orientation, in order to better meet the developmental needs of most students. The aim of whole-school approach to guidance is to ensure the participation of all school staff in a concerted effort to foster good conduct in students, enhance their capacity for learning and cultivate positive teacher-student relationship.

Comprehensive student guidance service (since 2002)

Goals of student guidance service

Student guidance service is an integral part of the total educational process and as such it needs to be integrated with the other sub-systems at school (e.g. management and organization, and learning and teaching) so that student guidance personnel are able to collaborate with the whole staff body, parents and the community to provide students with a comprehensive and broad guidance service. Guidance service should suit the students' developmental needs and complement the education and curriculum reforms. The aim is to help students attain balanced development in the domains of ethics, intellect, physique, social skills and aesthetics, and be capable of lifelong learning, critical and exploratory thinking, innovating and adapting to changes, thus preparing them to meet the challenges towards adulthood (Education Bureau Circular 19/2003, Appendix 1).

Principles of student guidance service

The principles of student guidance service can be described as people-oriented, with the development of students' potential as its core mission. Through integration with the other sub-systems in school, the guidance service takes care of the developmental needs of the whole student body from childhood to adolescence, with their special characteristics.

Five prerequisites of comprehensive student guidance service (Gysbers and Henderson 2006)

- Guidance is a programme, with the aim of enhancing the students' various competencies, including self-understanding, interpersonal relationship, decision-making and planning, awareness of roles and incidents in real life. Students are taken through various activities and processes so that they can acquire the relevant life skills. Guidance programmes should have continuity and connectivity, and their effectiveness need to be constantly assessed.
- A guidance programme should be comprehensive and developmental in character. When guidance activities are planned, due consideration should be given to the developmental needs of students at different stages of their life, so that students may have the opportunity to develop their potentials in the academic, career, personal and social domains. The developmental guidance programmes should be focused on enabling students, through different personal experiences, to recognize their own competencies, and to sustain the development of their potentials.
- Guidance programmes rely on the team approach. School guidance personnel do not only run the guidance service directly for students, but they also need to consult and collaborate with the guidance team, the other teaching and non-teaching staff, parents, and the community.
- A guidance programme is a systematic process, which should include planning, design, implementation, evaluation and modification. These well-planned programmes should also reflect the priorities set for school guidance as a whole.
- Guidance programmes should have a clear leadership. School guidance personnel are the core persons to execute all the programmes, so they should take responsibility for the whole service, by monitoring the quality of work of other colleagues involved in the execution of the programmes, and make sure that the service is effective.

Components of comprehensive student guidance service

The conceptual framework of comprehensive school guidance service has originated from the USA. The cornerstone of the service is the enhancement of personal development. It is through various activities and services for the students that they are enabled to acquire the knowledge, skills and attitudes they need in daily life. When they eventually assume their roles in different social contexts, they will thus be able to cope with the challenges in lives. The components of comprehensive student guidance service in Hong Kong comprise the following four domains: policy and organization, support service, personal growth education, and responsive service.

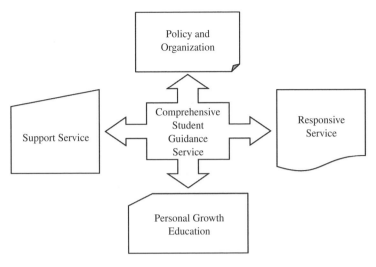

Figure 3.1 The components of comprehensive student guidance service in Hong Kong

1. Policy and Organization

   By policy and organization, it is meant that a school should try to cultivate a positive and caring culture with reference to the school's own characteristics and particular needs. The aim is to enhance the personal growth of all students. A guidance team should be set up in the school to formulate guidance policy, plan and coordinate guidance service, establish the procedure for both internal and external referrals so as to render pertinent assistance to the students in need. A mechanism for the school's self-evaluation should be established to monitor the effectiveness of the guidance service.

2. Support Service

   Support service is needed to provide teachers with the professional training and latest information related to school guidance, so that teachers are enabled to identify the students' emotional and developmental needs, acquire appropriate communication skills for working with parents and students, and implement personal growth education effectively. Support service may also contribute to the convergence of team spirit, facilitate all school staff to arrive at a common consensus, enhance mutual support, and maintain good communication in the execution of guidance service. Its other priorities may include the setting up of a consultation system, giving teachers the necessary support in handling problem students, promoting home-school collaboration, and developing parent education. Building a good relationship and partnership with the related organizations in the community is also essential for the further development of student guidance service.

3. Personal growth education

    Personal growth education takes many forms, for instance, lessons, short courses, group activities, morning assemblies and cross-curricular activities. The implementation of school-based personal growth education is catering for the developmental needs of all students. Through carefully designed learning areas, students can acquire knowledge, skills and attitudes relating to academic, career, personal and social development and realize their potentials. Furthermore, personal growth education should also suit the developmental needs of primary pupils in the different age brackets, through activities designed to achieve gradual and cumulative impacts. The activities should as far as possible be made collaborative and interactive so as to enhance students' motivation for learning. Personal growth education emphasizes experiential learning and the practice of self-exploration and self-reflection. Through the connection to the life events, students can apply what they have learnt to their daily life.

4. Responsive Service

    Responsive service refers to the individual counselling or group counselling that are made available to the students in need. It is the job of the school guidance personnel to identify and counsel students in need as well as refer students with special educational needs to the professionals for help. They also have to handle crises and provide prompt intervention and follow-up service.

Case Study 1

School background: The majority of students in this secondary/primary school live in the nearby public housing estates, and come from grassroots families. Many of them are newly arrived children from the Mainland.

Table 3.1 ABC School's annual plan on student guidance service

Area	Activities/Content	Target Group	Persons-in-charge
Policy and organization	• invite one teacher from each form to join the Guidance Team as a representative of the form so as to enhance collaboration • formulate the policy on making referrals • revise the procedures in crisis management: in dealing with bullying, suicide cases, etc.	• all teachers and students	• guidance team leader • guidance team leader • guidance team leader and crisis management team

(continued on page 69)

Table 3.1 *(continued)*

Personal growth education	*Personal growth education (one period per week)*		
	• integrated with moral and civic education, with contents such as: personal and social development, academic and career development, civic education	• all classes	• teacher-in-charge of moral and civic education and guidance team leader
	Guidance activities		
	• talk on prevention of drug abuse	• senior primary/ junior secondary	• related external organizations
	• big brothers and big sisters scheme	• P. 1 and P. 6/ S. 1 and S. 6	• guidance team
	• peer group guidance scheme	• P. 3 and P. 4/ S. 2 and S. 3	• guidance team
	• course on resilience building	• P. 4/ S. 2	• social worker of the community centre
	• love angel scheme	• all students	• guidance team
	• talk on sex education	• senior primary/ junior secondary	• Family Planning Association
Supportive service	*Support for parents*		
	• parents' meeting on P. 1/ S. 1 adjustment	• P. 1/ S. 1 parents	• guidance team leader/ class teachers
	• career talks for P. 6/ S.6 students	• P. 6/ S. 6 parents	• guidance team leader/ career master
	• talk on learning efficiency and effectiveness	• parents of junior primary/ junior secondary classes	• guidance team leader/ social worker
	• the 'walking with you' social support group	• parents of recent immigrant children	• guidance team leader/ social worker
	Support for teachers		
	• teacher development: effective strategies for classroom management	• all teachers	• invite college lecturers
	• monthly meeting: support for teachers in dealing with problem cases	• teachers with related needs	• guidance team leader/ social worker
Responsive service	• dealing with problematic cases	• students with emotional or behavioural problems	• guidance team leader/ social worker
	• group on study skills	• students with learning disabilities in the junior forms	• guidance team leader/ social worker
	• self-esteem enhancement group	• students who are newly arrived children	• guidance team leader/ social worker
	• social skills group	• P. 3/ S. 3 and S. 4 students	• guidance team leader/ social worker

❐ **Activity 3**

Class Discussion

1. With reference to the current approach of comprehensive school guidance service in Hong Kong, please comment on the suitability of the above annual plan on guidance, and make any necessary suggestions for improvement.
2. Is it possible for this annual plan on guidance to realize the concepts of the Whole-School Approach to Guidance?

Teachers' Responsibilities in Implementing Comprehensive Student Guidance Service

Concerning policy and organization, teachers can report the needs of teachers, students and parents through the guidance team, and give feedback on the guidance activities organized. Teachers can also make recommendations on policy and organization, so as to improve the quality of the guidance activities to respond positively to the needs of different stakeholders.

Regarding supportive service, teachers can take an active part in guidance-related teaching development activities so as to enhance their understanding and skills of guidance. Thus, they can be more ready to provide students with initial counselling and help them overcome the difficulties in learning and social adjustment. Teachers may also make use of the frequent contact with parents to encourage them to join the various parent education activities and talks, which are organized to offer them a better understanding of child and adolescence development as well as effective parenting. They can work together for better home-school collaboration to jointly promote the personal growth of students.

With regard to the implementation of personal growth education, teachers can collaborate with the school guidance personnel to organize and deliver courses in personal growth education. Teachers may also work with other colleagues to prepare the lessons, and, if necessary, modify the strategy and activities of the lessons to fit in with the diverse needs of students in different stages of development. Students are therefore enabled to develop the various skills that they may need in order to meet all the challenges towards adulthood. Teachers can help conduct various preventive and developmental guidance activities, and actively cooperate in the team effort of implementation strategies, work priorities, and performance indicators. In the classroom, teachers can create an atmosphere of harmony, openness and acceptance, show genuine concern about students' progress in personal growth and social development, and enhance students' interest and competencies in learning. The teachers' effort will prepare students more adequately for their eventual career development, and realize the goal of 'holistic education'.

Relating to responsive service, teachers would need to identify the students with special educational needs or adjustment problems and those who are at risk, and make referrals to the school guidance personnel for further counselling. They should collaborate with the guidance personnel and show support for the guidance strategies in a concerted effort to help students successfully overcome the many hurdles in growing up.

❐ **Activity 4**

Self-reflection

1. In the various domains of comprehensive student guidance service, namely policy and organization, responsive service, supportive service and personal growth education, what roles do teachers play? Which role do you consider to be the most important of all?
2. As a teacher, what do you think would be the difficulties in implementing the school guidance service? How to resolve these difficulties?
3. As a teacher, how can you make greater contributions to school guidance?

Conclusion

The concept of school guidance originated at the start of the twentieth century, when the countries in the West went through a transitional period marked by the decline of the agricultural sector and the rapid rise of industrial development. In order to help students make suitable adjustments to the societal transition and meet the new challenges, school guidance was then mainly oriented towards career guidance. Towards the end of the twentieth century, with the rapid development in information technology, reforms took place in the social, economic and education sectors, which pointed to a new direction for school guidance. The position orientation mode was eventually taken over by the programme orientation mode in the practice and development of school guidance. The goal was to enable students to acquire the life skills that they would need to meet the various challenges in the twenty-first century.

In Hong Kong, the school guidance service first appeared in the 1970s, when social workers began to provide individual counselling to secondary school students. By the end of the decade, the Student Guidance Section was established to formally initiate primary school guidance service, and the post of student guidance officer was filled by senior and experienced teachers. It was not until the early 1990s that the government first put forward the new direction for guidance as preventive and developmental and implemented the 'Whole-School Approach to Guidance' in secondary and primary schools. The new policy stressed the need for the whole school staff to work jointly to give students the necessary guidance in personal development, improved the manning ratio in the guidance service, and strengthened the professional training of the guidance personnel. On the advent of the twenty-first century, there were successive reforms in the social, economic and educational domains. Hong Kong decided to follow the example of the USA in adopting the comprehensive and developmental approach to guidance. With the introduction of school guidance service allowance, the manning ratio in guidance service was further improved so that it was possible to implement the 'Comprehensive Student Guidance Service' in the primary schools. The goal was to introduce a systematic guidance programme, which would help students develop their competencies in the academic, career, personal and social aspects, so as to meet the challenges of the rapidly changing society.

Since the start of the twenty-first century, Hong Kong school guidance has moved along the developmental direction. The leadership of the guidance personnel and the participation of all teachers in guidance service are the key for the successful implementation of the 'Comprehensive School Guidance Service'. Provided that teachers have a good understanding of the guidance approach, they will be able to cooperate effectively with the sub-systems in school, actively promote various guidance activities, and help students attain 'holistic development'.

Questions for Discussion

1. In your opinion, who is the most suitable person to coordinate the school guidance service, the teachers or the school social worker?
2. Under the current conditions in Hong Kong, what kind of difficulties do you think would arise in the course of implementing 'Comprehensive Student Guidance Service'? What would be the solutions?
3. When implementing the 'Comprehensive Student Guidance Service', how would the role of the guidance personnel change?
4. Try to evaluate the 'Comprehensive Student Guidance Service' currently championed by the Education Bureau and suggest any modifications that would make it better adapted to the current situation at school and responsive to students' needs.

Related Websites

1. A Model Comprehensive Guidance Program
   http://www.utm.edu/staff/aduncan/Comprehensive%20Guidance%20(786).pdf
2. Position Statements of the American School Counsellor Association
   http://www.mtschoolcounsellor.org/MT_School_Counselling_Program_Model/files/ASCA_Position_Statements.pdf

3.   Student Guidance and Discipline Service, by the Education Bureau, Hong Kong: http://www.edb.gov.hk/index.aspx?nodeID=1972&langno=1

Extended Readings

Chan, K. N. (2000). A Reflection on 'Implementing a Whole School Approach to Guidance through a Comprehensive Guidance Program' by Norman C. Gysbers. *Asian Journal of Counselling*, 7(2): 53.

Hui, K. P. (2000). Furthering a Whole School Approach to Guidance: Contributions from the Comprehensive Guidance Program. *Asian Journal of Counselling*, 7(2): 43.

Sink, C. A. (2005). *Contemporary School Counselling: Theory, Research, and Practice.* Boston, MA: Houghton Mifflin.

Yuen, M., Chan, R. M. C., Lau, P. S. Y., Gybers, N. C., and Shea, P. M. K. (2007). Comprehensive Guidance and Counselling Programmes in the Primary Schools of Hong Kong: Teachers' Perceptions and Involvement. *Pastoral Care in Education*, 25(4): 17–24.

林清文（2007）：《學校輔導》。台北：雙葉書廊有限公司。

香港社會服務聯會（2006）：《小學全方位學生輔導服務分享彙編》。香港：香港社會服務聯會。

袁文得、劉兆瑛（2003）：《生活技能發展及全方位輔導計劃：理論與實踐》。香港：香港大學教育學院生活技能發展計劃。

References

Gibson, R. L., and Mitchell, M. H. (1999). *Introduction to Counselling and Guidance* (4th ed.). Upper Saddle River, NJ: Prentice Hall.

Gysbers, N. C., and Henderson, P. (2000). *Developing and Managing Your School Guidance Program* (3rd ed.). Alexandria, VA: American Counselling Association.

——— (2006). *Developing and Managing Your School Guidance Program* (4th ed.). Alexandria, VA: American Counselling Association.

Gysbers, N. C. (2000). Implementing a Whole School Approach to Guidance through a Comprehensive Guidance Program. *Asia Journal of Counselling*, 7(2), 5–17.

Henderson, P., and Gysbers, N. C. (2002). *Implementing Comprehensive School Guidance Programs: Critical Leadership Issues and Successful Responses.* Greensboro, NC: CAPS.

Hui, E. K. P. (1998). School Guidance Focus: A Hong Kong Study. *Research in Education*, 59: 69–79.

——— (2000a). Guidance as a Whole School Approach in Hong Kong: From Remediation to Student Development. *International Journal for the Advancement of Counselling*, 22: 69–82.

——— (2000b). Furthering a Whole School Approach to Guidance: Contributions from the Comprehensive Guidance Program. *Asian Journal of Counselling*, 7(2): 43–51.

—— (2002). A Whole-school Approach to Guidance: Hong Kong Teachers' Perceptions. *British Journal of Guidance and Counselling*, 30(1): 63–80.

Lapan, R. L., Gysbers, N. C., and Petroski, G. F. (2003). Helping Seventh Graders Be Safe and Successful: A Statewide Study of the Impact of Comprehensive Guidance and Counselling Programs. *Professional School Counselling*, 6(3): 186–98.

Lapan, R. L., Gysbers, N. C., and Sun, Y. (1997). The Impact of More Fully Implemented Guidance Programs on the School Experiences of High School Students: A Statewide Evaluation Study. *Journal of Counselling and Development*, 75(4), 292–302.

Lee, B. S. F., and Wong, C. K. F. (2008). Transition to Comprehensive Student Guidance Service in Hong Kong. *Counselling, Psychotherapy, and Health*, 4(1), Counselling in the Asia Pacific Rim: A Coming Together of Neighbours Special Issue, 17–23.

Luk, F. Y. Y. P. (2004). Integration of the Personal Growth Curriculum and Education Reform. *Asian Journal of Counselling*, 11 (1 & 2): 127–42.

Miller, F. W. (1968). *Guidance: Principles and Services*. Columbus, OH: Merrill.

Myrick, D. R. (1993). *Developmental Guidance and Counselling: A Practical Approach* (2nd ed.). Minneapolis, MN: Educational Media Corporation.

Radd, T. R. (1996). *The Growth with Guidance System Manual*. Canton, OH: Grow with Guidance.

Rogers, C. R. (1961). *On Becoming a Person: A Therapist's View of Psychotherapy*. Boston: Houghton Mifflin.

Schmidt, J. J. (1993). *Counselling in Schools: Essential Services and Comprehensive Programs*. Boston: Alyn and Bacon.

Schwallie-Giddis, P., ter Maat, M., and Pak, M. (2003). Initiating Leadership by Introducing and Implementing the ASCA National Model. *Professional School Counselling*, 6(3): 170–73.

Shertzer, B., and Stone, S. C. (1981). *Fundamentals of Guidance* (4th ed.). Boston: Houghton Mifflin.

Sink, C. A., and MacDonald, G. (1998). The Status of Comprehensive Guidance and Counselling in the United States. *Professional School Counselling*, 2: 88–94.

Sprinthall, N. A. (1971). *Guidance for Human Growth*. New York: Van Nostrand Reinhold.

Trevisan, M. S., and Hubert, M. (2001). Implementing Comprehensive Guidance Program Evaluation Support: Lessons Learned. *Professional School Counselling*, 4(3): 225–28.

Yuen, M. T., Lau, P. S. Y., and Chan, R. M. C. (2000). Improving School Guidance Programs: A Conversation with Norman C. Gysbers. Asian Journal of Counselling, 7(2): 19–41.

教育署（2003）：《教育局通告第 19/2003 號》，擷取於 2010 年 2 月 25 日，http://www.edb.gov.hk/index.aspx?nodeID=73&langno=2

教育署輔導服務科（1993）：《學校本位輔導方式工作指引（一）》。香港：政府印務局。

—— (1995) ：《學校本位輔導方式工作指引（二）》。香港：政府印務局。

教育局網頁（2010）：《全方位學生輔導》，擷取於 2010 年 2 月 25 日，http://www.edb.gov.hk/index.aspx?nodeID=1974&langno=2

教育統籌委員會（1990）：《教育統籌委員會第四號報告書：課程與學生校內行為問題》。香港：香港政府印務局。

教育委員會學校教育檢討小組（1997）：《九年強迫教育檢討報告》。香港：政府印務局。

課程發展議會（2002）：《基礎教育課程指引：各盡所能．發揮所長（小一至中三）》。香港：政府印務局。

香港教育署（1986）：《中學學生輔導工作：給校長和教師參考的指引》。香港：政府印務局。

香港政府（1979）：《進入八十年代的個人社會服務》。香港：政府印務局。

游黎麗玲（1998）：《學生輔導》。香港：中文大學出版社。

4

Personal Growth Education

Pattie Yuk Yee Luk-Fong

Every person should promote his/her own beautiful attributes and, at the same time, appreciate the beauty of other people. If all are ready to share this common spirit, there will be world harmony.

(Fei Xiaotong)

Know yourself as you wish to know others. This understanding requires mutual communication. Harmony in diversity paves the way for common progress.

(P. Y. Y. Luk-Fong)

Abstract

This chapter begins with a discussion of the difference between guidance curriculum and moral education curriculum and thereupon proposes a conceptual framework for the integration of the two curricula. It then takes the idea a step further by recommending an integrated curriculum most suited to the Hong Kong context. Finally, it explores the strategies and difficulties in delivering the personal growth guidance curriculum, and concludes with some possible solutions.

Objectives

This chapter will help you:
- explore the current personal growth education/ moral education curricula in the Hong Kong context;
- acquire the methods and strategies for delivering the personal growth education/ moral education curricula; and
- resolve the difficulties encountered in the delivery of the personal growth education curriculum.

Before You Start: Think and Discuss

1. What do you think, based on the schools you have had close contact with, a personal growth education curriculum is? Does it have any specific content? On which skills and attitudes is it mainly focused?
2. What are the differences between the personal growth education curriculum and other academic subjects (e.g. general studies and English language)? Would there be any overlapping in terms of their content?
3. Do you think, speaking from your own experience, teachers would encounter any difficulties in teaching the personal growth education curriculum?
4. Can you evaluate and adapt the current teaching materials in personal growth education to cater for your students' needs?

Introduction

As pointed out in Chapter 1, guidance in Hong Kong has incorporated characteristics from the West as well as local Chinese traditions, and this unique combination has given rise to the conflicting and complementary relationships that have existed between the discipline and guidance services in Hong Kong for many years. This chapter will explore in depth the difficulties for the co-existence of the personal growth education curriculum and the moral education curriculum in Hong Kong, and make proposals for the conceptual framework as well as a way to integrate the two before identifying the areas that may need special attention in the course of teaching.

Personal Growth Education: A Definition and Conceptual Framework

International literature

Personal growth education may be defined as a process to promote the learning, growth and healthy development of children and youngsters. Borders and Drury (1992) consider that the objectives of guidance programmes are three-fold: to help students raise their academic standard; to help them form their value system; and to help them enhance their self-esteem. In America, the learning areas in developmental programmes generally include personal and social development, academic development and career development (Gysbers and Henderson 2000; Myers 1992); in Taiwan, they are referred to as 'daily life guidance', 'academic guidance', and 'career guidance'. The personal growth curriculum, as an integral part of the comprehensive student guidance service, has become a world trend. In 2000, over

34 states in America were known to have implemented such programmes. According to Gysbers and Henderson (1994), the key concept of the developmental programme lies in 'developmental contextualism', in the sense that the developmental/guidance needs arise from the person in context. The curriculum aims to provide students with suitable training in aptitude and life skills so that they can attain good academic results as well as interpersonal relations. Thus, a good foundation is laid for the later stages in the life cycle, including career, marriage and parenting.

Situation in Hong Kong

In 2002, the Student Guidance Service of the Hong Kong Education Bureau initiated the 'Comprehensive Student Guidance Service', with the personal growth education curriculum as one of its priorities (which is similar to the guidance curriculum referred to above in international literature). The guidance curriculum should, in the same way as curriculum reform, follow the school-based approach in implementation, take into consideration students' developmental needs, and focus on development and prevention. The importance attached to the guidance curriculum in Hong Kong is in line with the global trend in the development of school guidance/counselling (such as Gysbers and Henderson 2000), with no rigid preset curricular content, but rather giving emphasis on the learning process— students' active learning, self-experience, self-exploration and self-reflection. There should be an integration of learning content with students' life events (Curriculum Development Council 2002). The four key learning areas of the curriculum are 'personal development', 'social development', 'academic development' and 'career development'. 'Personal development' includes self-concept, problem-solving, and self-management; 'social development' includes respect for and acceptance of others, interpersonal communication and relationship, and management of conflicts; 'academic development' includes study skills and attitude towards learning, sense of achievement, enjoyment of school life; 'career development' include life planning, the code of conduct, and career information.

Since the launch of guidance curriculum, schools have adopted different implementation approaches. Some have formally introduced personal growth curriculum, some have combined the personal growth curriculum with moral education, while others have immersed the personal growth curriculum into general studies. As for the teaching arrangements, some schools have assigned them to the guidance team leader/ guidance teachers, others to the class teachers (sometimes with the collaboration of the guidance team leader/guidance teachers) while some have had the general studies teacher taking charge. No matter which mode of implementation is adopted, a clear conceptual framework of the guidance curriculum as well as an effective division of labour and collaboration among teachers are essential.

Similarities and Differences between Personal Growth Education and Moral Education

As a result of the education reforms, the Student Guidance and Discipline Services of the Education Bureau established the Comprehensive Student Guidance System in primary schools across Hong Kong in 2002. One of its major tasks was the implementation of personal growth education. In the same year, the Curriculum Development Council (2002) released the *Curriculum Guidelines on Basic Education*, in which moral education and civic education were formally incorporated into one of the four key learning areas. If one looks at the contents of the two curricula in detail, one will find that there are many overlapping areas.

The two curricula are both concerned with the development of the whole person, and centre on such issues as students' 'self-concept' and 'relationship between self and others'. Teaching relevance is made possible by relating teaching activities to incidents in students' life experience, so that the curriculum for school years will make use of incidents that commonly occur to students at the respective stages of life as teaching points (see Table 4.1). Table 4.2 provides a list of the important incidents in life that secondary school students commonly encounter. Apart from the fact that the moral education curriculum has the additional topic of 'communal life', the two curricula tend to select similar incidents in students' life experience.

Table 4.1 Similarities and differences between developmental and moral education programmes

Similarities	Differences
1. Focus on 'self'	1. The 'self' in the moral education curriculum is interpreted as the 'embedded self' with the obligation of the individual to the family, school, community, country and the world and it also focuses on 'self-cultivation' 2. The 'self' in the guidance curriculum focus on an 'individualistic self' and 'self-esteem'
2. Using students' events in daily life as the focus for teaching	1. The moral education curriculum focuses on values such as perseverance, respect for others, responsibility, national identity, and commitment 2. The guidance curriculum focuses on skills including problem-solving, communication, coping with changes and adversity, adaptability, conflict resolution, and study and vocational skills

However, there are differences between these two curricula. Moral/civic education aims at the inculcation of attitudes, putting an emphasis on the five core values, namely, perseverance, respect for others, responsibility, national identity and commitment. Perseverance is regarded as the ability to meet the challenges as well as to withstand the adversities in life. By 'respect for others', it means one should appreciate and tolerate the different viewpoints and beliefs of others. There is a strong social expectation that students take responsibility for their individual place in the family, society, country and the world, as it is believed that the well-being of the individual is closely tied with the well-being and prosperity of the social collective. As for national identity, the moral/civic education curriculum requires students develop a high level of understanding of Chinese history and culture, so as to raise their awareness of, and concern for, the current developments of Mainland China. Lastly, students' commitment to themselves and others (i.e. the family, society, country and the world) is also emphasized. It cultivates youngsters' respect for diversities and equips them with the positive attitudes to handle disputes and conflicts in the values of the society (Curriculum Development Council 2002, 3A: 1).

On the other hand, the objectives of the personal growth education curriculum are: to develop the individual's potentials and foster a healthy self-concept so as to enhance students' social development and enable them to establish good interpersonal relationships; to inculcate a positive outlook on life so as to meet the challenges and resolve the problems in life; to enable students to master various learning skills and nurture a diligent attitude towards learning so as to become practitioners of lifelong learning; to provide career information and prepare students for their future careers. The curriculum covers four key learning areas: self, others, academic, and career development. The 'self' focuses on enabling students to develop a healthy self-concept as well as enhance their potentials. Hence, the curriculum has to deal with their current needs, such as study skills for the academic study and interpersonal skills to build good human relationships, and their future needs, such as the work skills and life skills that they may eventually require when they start working. It may be seen from the foregoing that the moral/civic education curriculum attaches great importance to the 'embedded self' because it is where the impacts of family, school, community, Hong Kong, China and the world meet in the individual. This is rather similar to the Confucian approach in that students are to begin with self-cultivation, and then widen their scope to include family, school, the whole country and eventually the world.

The personal growth education curriculum, on the other hand, tends to promote a more 'Westernized' and more individualistic 'self'. As a matter of fact, the moral/civic education curriculum aims to promote the 'five cardinal relationships',[1] namely the relationships between oneself and the others. In the language of today, they refer to the relationships that exist between parents and children, brothers and sisters, husband and wife, teacher and pupils, as well as among friends. The moral/civic education curriculum, moreover, also emphasizes such Chinese values as perseverance, responsibility and commitment. While this comes close to the traditions of discipline in Hong Kong, the personal growth education is closer to the Western traditions of guidance. Against the background of co-existence of East-West traditions in Hong Kong, these two curricula emphasize personal values and skills respectively, and they provide an interesting example of a 'hybrid': a mixture which embraces the impacts when East meets West and when globalization clashes with localization. On the face of it, these two curricula seem to be independent of each other, but, in fact, the multifarious characteristics of the guidance curriculum showcase the reality that although we are caught up in the glocalization process, there exists a strong desire for our unique individual identity. This phenomenon may be just a representation of glocalization. However, from what we have seen in the overlapping contents of the two curricula, we may conclude that the integration of the two curricula have already taken root here. The situation may be described most concretely in terms of the *yin-yang* concept. As shown in Figure 4.1, *yin* and *yang* are two independent/dependent territories within the all-round entity formed as a result of the forces of tension and equilibrium. Within the *yin* territory, there is a round dot representing *yang*, and similarly within the *yang* territory, there is a round dot representing *yin*. In the same vein, the traditional Chinese concepts, diligence for instance, occupy a place in the comparatively Westernized personal growth education curriculum, whereas Western concepts such as tolerance of diversity also appear in the characteristically 'Chinese' moral/civic education curriculum.

Figure 4.1 The yin-yang chart

Table 4.2 A suggested list of important life events for secondary school students

(1) Personal Development and Healthy Living	
• entering puberty • making good use of pocket money • selecting reading materials • managing emotions • facing the media • worshipping idols • surfing the Internet • dressing up oneself	• managing personal finance (e.g. expenditure and savings) • handling sexual harassment • self-destruction/suicide • facing serious illness/death

(continued on page 83)

Table 4.2 *(continued)*

(2) Family life	
• showing love and concern to family members • getting along with grandparents or other adult members • negotiating for autonomy from parents • doing housework	• moving house • helping younger siblings with homework • handling family disputes • family member(s) being unemployed • parents getting divorced • illness/death of family member(s) • family violence

(3) School life	
• adapting to new life at secondary school • coping with problems in learning • choosing school activities • taking part in election of class society • having lunch at school	• taking tutorial classes • assuming important positions (e.g. head prefect or chairperson of student union) • crises faced by classmates

(4) Social life	
• meeting new friends • respecting different opinions and cultures • dating • taking care of classmates/friends (e.g. who are sick or have poor academic results) • handling negative peer pressure (e.g. drug abuse, smoking, and illegal activities) • coping with problems with friends (e.g. quarrels and financial disputes)	• wild camp/camping • falling in/out of love • taking part in religious activities • joining banquets/funerals • participating in voluntary work • helping neighbours/those in need in the community • facing undesirable temptations and social trends

(5) Life at work	
• striking a balance between part-time job and study • taking up a summer job • meeting job requirements and facing work pressure • handling interpersonal relationship at work	• being praised/reproached by supervisor • wearing uniform/ choosing clothes for work • receiving salary • being injured at work

(6) Life in the community	
• using public facilities (e.g. libraries, museums, parks, swimming pools and beaches) • riding on public transport • blood donation • joining recycle campaign • helping neighbours/the needy in society • participating in fund-raising • participating in voluntary work • participating in community activities • participating in public affairs discussion	• participating in election activities • facing temptations and undesirable societal influences • expressing opinions on issues of social injustice • participating in national flag hoisting ceremony • understanding and showing concern on major events in the Mainland • visiting the Mainland • supporting improvement projects on education and life in the Mainland • discussing current issues of local/ national/ international community

Note: Adapted from *Learning to Learn: Life-Long Learning, Whole-Person Development* (Hong Kong Curriculum Development Council 2001).

A Conceptual Framework of Personal Growth Education: Integrating Moral/Guidance Curricula

Underlying concepts

The implementation of education reforms, the guidance curriculum and the moral/ civic curriculum has blurred the boundaries between the school subjects, with overlapping and confusion in subject contents. The following discussion will take this situation into consideration and provide a conceptual framework for a personal growth curriculum so that when principals, teachers and guidance personnel undertake curriculum reforms, they are able to grasp the core of the student guidance curriculum. Taking account of the characteristics of the school and the needs of their students, schools can have a free hand to reorganize school curricula and activities, with a view to integrating learning and life, as well as connecting life events and work experience. This approach is highlighted in the Curriculum Guides as *Enhancing Life-Long Learning and Encouraging Whole-Person Development* (Education Commission 2000).

The author would use Freud's two important dimensions in life, 'work' and 'love', as the backbone of this conceptual framework of a personal growth education curriculum suitable for the development of Hong Kong students (see Figure 4.2). It is interesting to note that Freud's high regard for 'work' and 'love' coincides with the four learning areas of personal growth education. To put it simply, we can say that 'academic development' and 'career development' can be summed up by 'work', and that 'social development' can revolve around 'love', with 'individual' and 'self' as the central components. The framework has also made reference to the theory of career development put forward by Gysbers and Henderson (1994). They have identified three learning areas for the guidance curriculum: self-understanding and interpersonal skills; roles, situations and events; and career planning. Furthermore, their theory is fundamentally based on the concept of 'person in context', while due regard is paid to development of skills and techniques in different developmental stages as well as preventive measures to forestall problems. The East-West cultural conflicts and integration in Hong Kong make it necessary to understand the unique local context before we know what 'person in context' is.

Conceptual Framework

At the core of this framework is 'self-understanding', or in other words, the triangle labelled as 'self-concept'. Understanding 'self' includes knowing the outward characteristics of oneself (physical self-concept), aptitudes, preferences and abilities

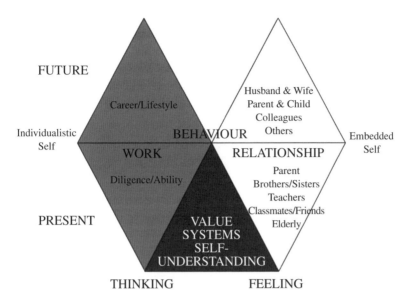

Figure 4.2 Self, work and relationship (Luk-Fong 2002)

(academic self-concept). The idea is to look at a person holistically, taking into account the interactive nature of the individual's physical, intellectual, emotional and social aspects. At the three apexes of the triangle are thinking, feeling and behaviour, which represent a psychological perspective of a person. The author has chosen to add the value system at the centre of the triangle because an individual's thinking, feeling and behaviour all spring from one's values. Here, it is also necessary to consider as additional inputs the individual's existing values as well as the fundamental values and attitudes which moral and civic education attempts to foster, including perseverance, respect, sense of responsibility, identity recognition and the spirit of commitment (Curriculum Development Council 2002, 3A). This arrangement is in agreement with what the Chinese favour as a good amalgamation of the four important human faculties of knowing, feeling, intention and action.

The diamond-shaped box on the left of the triangle represents 'work'; that on the right represents 'love' or 'relationship'. The lower halves of the two diamond-shaped boxes represent the 'present' development, while the upper halves represent the 'future' development. With regard to 'work' (the diamond-shaped box on the left), it is through learning experiences acquired from multiple channels—including intellectual development, life experiences, work-related experiences, community service, sports and aesthetic development—that students are able to understand their own aptitudes, interests and abilities. Besides balanced development in the moral, intellectual, physical, social and aesthetic domains, students can thus further develop their areas of strengths and gain greater self-confidence through their sense of competence. Hence, students' learning (studies now) can develop along a unique and personal path. From the learning process, they would not only acquire the skills of communication, self-learning, adaptation, co-operation and creativity, but also cultivate a passion for study, appreciate the effort and value of diligent work and unswerving perseverance, as well as elevate their characters including moral standards, open-mindedness, sentiments and vision. Nowadays, when implementing education reforms, many schools have applied Gardner's (1993) concept of multiple intelligence so as to enable students to develop their individual potentials. The above points have been echoed by Gardner, Csikszentmihalyi and Damon (2001) in their book, *Good Work: When Excellence and Ethics Meet*—when developing the individual's multiple intelligence. However, we must not neglect the moral code of behaviour, which is the backbone for all kinds of achievement of excellence. Fei Xiaotong (2005) has put the idea nicely in these words: 'Every person should promote his/her own beautiful attributes and, at the same time, appreciate the beauty of other people. If all are ready to share this common spirit, there will be world harmony.' If everyone can build a wholesome, healthy image of the 'individualistic self',[2] then how wonderful things will be for all of us!

The diamond-shaped box labelled as 'relationship' represents the establishment of the 'embedded or relational self'.[3] The development of the 'embedded or relational self' ought to start from the Chinese Confucian cardinal relationships. It is important for today's students to realize that they do well to establish good relationships with their parents, siblings, teachers, schoolmates, friends, senior family members and other people, based on respect, a sense of responsibility, identity recognition and the spirit of commitment. They also need to equip themselves with skills such as communication, problem-solving and empathy. In this learning area, we expect students to learn to understand this: 'Know yourself as you wish to know others. This understanding requires mutual communication. Harmony in diversity paves the way for common progress.' However, the difficulty is that the needs and expectations of teachers, parents, siblings, senior relatives and students themselves are far from the same, especially in the rapidly changing society. For instance, the interaction between the East and West as well as the traditional and modern value systems result in entanglement, and the "appropriate" cardinal relationships of parents and child, husband and wife, friends and mates, teachers and pupils, supervisor and subordinates, etc., have become blurred and hard to grasp. Daniel Shek et al. (1999) explore the differing viewpoints and blind spots of the two generations in the publication, *Two Generations of People in Conflict and in Harmony*. For instance, each of them has a different interpretation of authority, personal privacy, freedom to make friends, and parents' behaviours. Besides this, the incongruence in the family value systems is another good example. As Giddens (2001) observes: 'The family is a site for the struggles between tradition and modernity, but also a metaphor for them.' If everyone can have a good understanding of the needs and expectations of themselves and others, and are able to interpret others' ideas as well as learn to communicate in ways acceptable to both sides, then all will be able to make progress despite their differences (Luk-Fong 2005a). If today we can achieve harmony in all human relationships, then we can look forward to a future where happy and fulfilling relationships exist between husband and wife, parents and child, colleagues, friends, and other people.

Proposed Curriculum for Personal Growth Education in Hong Kong

On the basis of the above conceptual framework, the present author proposes an outline for a personal growth education curriculum which is a combination of the moral education curriculum and guidance curriculum (see Table 4.3), for the consideration of teachers and students in Hong Kong.

Strategies for Teaching the Personal Growth Education Curriculum: The Questioning Method

The teaching strategies of the personal growth education curriculum are student-centred. In the West, guidance curricula are usually taught through experiential learning so that the teaching process is regarded as more significant than its content. Williams (2001) considers that the teaching process ought to enhance the students' ability to think as well as their emotional literacy. This is in line with Brandes and Ginnis (1986) and Roger's (1983) ideas that students should learn about the self-convergence of their feelings and thoughts. Park (2001: 36) suggests that the best way to teach is to provide a context for an open and appreciative dialogue 'in which students can speak freely about their own experiences; can hear others speak equally freely about their own; can come to appreciate the thoughts and feelings of others and can learn to deal with issues that provoke strong feelings in themselves'. Best and Lang (1994: 26) point out in particular that teachers need to be skilful 'in defusing highly charged situations, and in negotiating the resolution of confrontations in ways which are face saving for all parties'.

In general, experiential learning can be divided into four stages: (1) experiencing; (2) publishing; (3) processing and generalizing; and (4) applying (Jones and Pfeiffer 1973; Vernon 1989). Teaching activities may include books, games, simulations, activities, personalized discussion, role-playing, stories, creative and artistic activities, as well as brain-storming. These learning activities are better conducted in groups

Table 4.3 A suggested curriculum framework for an integrated guidance/moral education curriculum (Luk-Fong 2005a)

Domains	Dimensions	Themes	Chinese traditions	Globalized contexts	Issues for elaboration
Self	• academic self • physical self • emotional self	• understanding own strengths and weaknesses • understanding and managing emotions and stress • body image/healthy life-style	• integrated self • know oneself (*zhiji*) • self-cultivation	• individualistic self • body image in the media • diversity of lifestyles displayed in the media and the consumer society	• individual uniqueness and value • self-reflection • self-embedded in the media and the consumer society • personal choice and core values
Self and others	• social self	*Home* • parent-child relationship • relationship with siblings • relationship with grand-parents or extended families • relationship with domestic helpers *School* • teacher-pupil relationship • relationship with classmates • relationship with senior and junior schoolmates *Community* • relationship with peers • relationship with the elderly • relationship with strangers	• know others (*zhibi*) • filial piety • male domination/seniority • respect for seniors • age hierarchy • respect for the elderly • respect for teachers • mutual care • respect for others	• social equality in education and law • changes in family structure and forms: single-parent family, dual worker family, only child family, etc.	• self-embedded in culture and contexts • changing hybrid cardinal relationships • extended kin support • domestic helpers in family • reconfiguration of gender relationship • communication (listening and expression) • problem-solving • harmony/conflict resolution • change management
Self in school	Studies • developing academic & non-academic abilities • acquiring study skills	• ability and hard work • positive attitude towards learning • master a variety of study skills	• morality & scholarship • high regards for education • diligence & perseverance	• lifelong learning • competitive, knowledge-based society	• sense of competence • realistic goals • academic pressure • time management

(continued on page 89)

Table 4.3 *(continued)*

Career planning	• knowing one's own interests and abilities • career information	• employing own abilities and interests at work • positive attitude towards work • developing personal potentials • preparation for future work	• perseverance • commitment • responsibility • upward mobility	• lifelong employment unlikely • practice and adaptability in terms of intellectual skills • moral commitment to work • teamwork • work-leisure dualism	• career choices • decision-making • stereotypes in career identity • collaboration • coping with changes
Self in community	• citizen • consumer	• civil rights and responsibilities • tolerating different views • consumer's rights and responsibilities • making wise use of money	• commitment to society	• civic society • consumerist society • democratic policies • market economy • computer technology and information flow	• make informed and responsible choices about material goods • conflict resolution • saying 'No' to bad influences (smoking, drugs, pornography, etc.)
Self in nation	• national identity	• identifying with Chinese history and culture • concern for the development of China	• commitment and concern for motherland	• one country, two systems • Hong Kong as an international city	• Hongkongese or Chinese? dual identity?
Self in world	• global citizen • global and local cultures	• helping the needy	• harmony	• global inequality	• addressing differences and value conflicts • adopting a global outlook • learning from other cultures and people
Self in nature	• nature's stewards	• wise use of resources • sustainability of ecosystem	• harmony with nature	• use of resources and environmental sustainability	• harmony with the environment • protecting the environment
Self in spirituality	• belief systems • values system • appreciation of aesthetic and cultural values	• religious beliefs • positive life views • moral courage • sincerity and integrity in actions • appreciation for literature and culture	• mutuality between human mind and spirituality	• cultural pluralism	• mutuality between human mind and heart and heaven • hybrid cultures

because it is the natural environment in which students express their thoughts and feelings, listen to others, learn to respect and empathize with others. Group learning will also encourage students to self-reflect and learn from the example of others (Morganett 1994; Schrumph, Freiburg, and Skadden 1993). Therefore, the facilitation of the group is of great importance. The effectiveness of group learning depends on the mutual trust and cohesion between the members, and the code of confidentiality observed by members is an important guarantee for their peace of mind.

Techniques in Teaching the Personal Growth Education Curriculum

Stone and Bradley (1990) point out the important items and techniques that need to be borne in mind when teaching guidance curriculum, in that we need to make good preparations, like having ready teaching notes and worksheets, and suitable arrangement for audio-visual equipment in order to facilitate students in their discussion of the important points in the lessons. The teacher should also make clear the aims of the teaching activities so that students can appreciate the importance of the personal growth education. It is imperative that in no way should we allow learning activities to turn into aimless game play.

Techniques in Leading Group Activities

When leading group activities, special attention should be paid to the teacher-student communication skills.

1.   Listening

     Because the personal growth education curriculum is student-centred, it is important that the teacher would listen actively to students in the course of the teaching and allow students to freely express their feelings and opinions.

2.   Eye contact

     Non-verbal communication such as having eye contact with students is very important as this would give students the feeling of comfort and acceptance. In such a state of mind, students are more willing to share their real personal thoughts and feelings.

3.   Teacher's self-disclosure

     The teacher's self-disclosure would not only provide a useful demonstration to students, but also help students grasp the general ideas as well as the task requirements.

4. Response

    When responding to students, please note the following:
    a. Avoid using judgemental language such as words of praise like 'Very good', 'That's correct'. Without the fear of being judged, students would be more relaxed and willing to tell the teacher and fellow students what they really think.
    b. Encourage students to make honest replies and avoid forcing students to respond to such questions as 'Are you a good boy/girl?' It is more suitable to encourage students to engage in personal self-reflection.
    c. Encourage students to actively participate by means of simple replies such as 'Thank you', 'Mei-fung said . . .'
    d. The usual class management techniques such as good voice projection, clear instructions, systematic and orderly presentation of teaching points, and smooth flow of the teaching process are very important.

5. Conclusion

    Provide a meaningful conclusion so that students are able to grasp the outcome of learning/discussion.

Characteristics of Guidance Teaching/Learning in Hong Kong

Luk-Fong (2005b)[4] discovers, during the implementation of Radd's pilot scheme of the guidance curriculum in Hong Kong, her own interpretations of the special characteristics of the guidance curriculum, as well as those of the teachers/students/parents (see Table 4.4), and the difficulties encountered in the teaching of it (see Table 4.5).

Table 4.4 Characteristics of guidance teaching and the Hong Kong experience

	Researcher (outsider who understands the difficulties and possibilities in teaching guidance in primary school)	Teachers/ principals/ parents/ students (insiders who know the teaching contexts in primary school)
Characteristics of guidance pedagogies	• need to explain the goals of guidance lessons to students • students enjoy the lesson but not sure what has been learnt • reflections, generalizations and applications need to be stressed	• different from other academic subjects • students express feelings and thoughts • emphasizing the process rather than content • enjoy the lesson

(continued on page 92)

Table 4.4 *(continued)*

Exploring how to teach	• trying to find out what is workable in the actual classroom	• exploring ways with professionals to teach guidance • some Western ideas like 'I-message' and empathy and many worksheets of Radd deemed are not suitable
Role of teacher	• the researcher, as an expert and outsider has not experienced any role conflict	• attitudes are more important than skills • teachers are kind and not too stern • facilitator's role conflicts with teacher's role • class teacher's role is compared with that of parents or elder brothers and sisters
Class teacher-student relationship	• researcher's lack of relationship with students impedes the teaching of guidance • open and relaxed, but is there any learning or growth?	• equal and intimate • communication and expression • harmonious, joyful and enjoyable

Luk-Fong (2005b) has found in her case study that the early implementation of the guidance programme is marked by the following four features:

1. Characteristics of guidance teaching pedagogies

    Teachers, students and parents all agreed that the pedagogies for teaching guidance lessons were different from those of other academic subjects. During a guidance lesson, as more emphasis was put on the process than the content, students were able to express opinions and feelings, and generally derived pleasure from the experience. However, the researcher has discovered that although students enjoyed themselves during the lesson, they were not always sure about what they were supposed to learn from it. Therefore, the researcher suggests that, when teaching the guidance lessons, teachers should put more emphasis on the students' self-reflection, generalization and application.

2. Exploring how to teach

    Many programmes developed in other countries may not suit the needs of Hong Kong students with such a strong Chinese cultural background. For instance, the method of communication used in the 'I-message' is very different from the accustomed method of the Chinese. The method of expression preferred by the Chinese tends to be subtler as they are not accustomed to talking about themselves.

3. The role of teachers

   Teachers discovered that in teaching the guidance lessons, attitudes count more than techniques. Students found that teachers seemed to be more friendly and approachable during guidance lessons than when they were teaching other subjects. They saw in their class teachers the roles of parents or elder brothers and sisters. On the other hand, teachers considered that the role of facilitator during guidance lessons might clash with that of the teacher.

4. The relationship between the class teacher and the pupils

   Teachers and students both found that in the guidance lessons, their relationship tended to be closer and on equal terms. Students enjoyed the chance to express and communicate their ideas. There was a harmonious atmosphere during the lessons, and it might be because the teacher had, in the process of teaching the guidance lessons, improved his/her relationship with the students.

Table 4.5 Pedagogical issues in the teaching of guidance

	The researcher	Teachers/ guidance professionals
Specific skills for teaching guidance in Hong Kong	1. games and activities—learning and having fun? 2. students' readiness and teachers' self-disclosure 3. teaching should be structured and concrete 4. worksheets as helpful ways of understanding individual students	1. students enjoy games, drawing, talks and chats 2. students' difficulties in talking about themselves: teachers' self-disclosure, students' personal journals and prior examples of other students help encourage the sharing among students 3. use of puppets helpful for students to talk about their own feelings 4. use of worksheets for drawing students' focus
The difficulties encountered in teaching the programme and suggestions thereupon	1. handling emotions and conflicts of students 2. clear awareness of the objectives of guidance lessons 3. emphasis on knowledge or practice? 4. giving clear instructions and exercising classroom management	1. insufficient time 2. classroom management 3. large class size—insufficient opportunity for student participation 4. establishing good relationships between students and class teacher—talking with students after class

Games, pictures, drawings and chats: Having fun and learning?

During the guidance lessons, teachers discovered that students enjoyed the chatting sessions as much as drawing and playing games. The researcher was able to verify their impressions with her own personal experience. Students were interested in group discussions and the way the group made use of discussions to solve problems. Activities involving body movements and games helped students relax and ease their embarrassment in talking about themselves (Geldard and Geldard 1997).

The key issue in teaching guidance lessons is whether students can learn through play. However, discipline is also an issue for the teacher. A relaxed atmosphere is necessary for guidance lessons, but it may not be acceptable to many Hong Kong teachers who generally expect very good discipline in their class. When students get overly involved, they may lose self-control. To maintain better class control, the researcher has attempted to ask students to stand in front of the class to read out the problem. This way the teacher would be able to look into the students' individual response while maintaining the classroom order. The researcher also discovered the importance of the dividing up into groups for the discussion and the need to set up rules. For instance, students must learn to take turns to speak, be willing to listen to others and give suitable response, and refrain from fighting. The teacher can use hand signals to give instructions to students. For instance, when the teacher makes a 'T' or 'V' sign with her hands, students must stop the activity at once. Suitable class management and grouping techniques should be able to enhance students' concentration and restore classroom discipline.

Overcoming students' unwillingness to disclose: Structured and concrete teaching

Many teachers have found from experience that it was quite difficult to ask students to talk about themselves. Some teachers realize that students need time to warm up. The researcher and teachers alike found that if some students in class could open up and take the lead to talk, others would be induced to follow. The teacher can therefore invite some of the more outgoing students to do the sharing first, so that their quieter peers are encouraged to follow suit. However, the researcher has also found that even for a group of outgoing students, it was still not easy to talk freely about matters of private concerns. A probable reason for this is that, in the Chinese culture, people who like to talk about themselves are often regarded as being boastful, and it is a completely strange concept for the children to open up and talk. The majority of the students in the research case were not accustomed to speaking their minds.

Some teachers would bring the same glove puppet with them to the lesson in the hope of encouraging students to express their feelings and thoughts. Other teachers made use of journal-writing to enable students who had difficulties in expressing themselves to write down how they felt. The researcher tried to ask children to draw self-portraits for peer sharing, starting off with her own self-portrait for a sharing session to show students how the process was like. Then she picked the volunteers randomly by means of the class numbers so as to increase the fun in class and reduce any possible embarrassment among students. Most importantly, the teacher was advised against forcing students to reveal private matters, but instead make allowance for students who were unwilling to answer personal questions.

One of the possible reasons why students were not willing to talk about issues close to home was that they did not feel comfortable about the guidance lessons, as they knew little about the objectives. The teacher should make adaptations to suit the students' emotional state and comfort zone, for instance, by starting off at the beginning of the term with discussion topics that are less personal. The researcher has discovered in the course of teaching the life skills programme at the Hong Kong Institute of Education that informing students about the programme objectives and the possible occurrence of uncomfortable feelings right at the beginning may provide students with a mental framework and the necessary psychological preparation. This will facilitate the teacher in establishing a suitable relationship with the students and encourage greater participation in class.

The effectiveness of the developmental programme

As illustrated above, implementing the school guidance curriculum is not going to be easy. However, according to the American experience in delivering personal growth education, the following results could be achieved, provided that the guidance lessons are effectively organized:
1. Improving academic performance
2. Enhancing social and emotional developments
3. Enhancing future prospects (career awareness)
4. Creating a positive school ethos on the whole

As to the effectiveness of personal growth education in Hong Kong, the conclusion remains to be seen from the future findings of relevant longitudinal studies.

The evaluation of guidance curriculum

What constitutes a good guidance curriculum? To make such an evaluation, we can start from two perspectives: the lesson content, and the teaching methods and approaches.
1. The evaluation criteria of the content of a guidance lesson should cover the following:
    (a) Is the content able to satisfy the students' needs in terms of 'developmental contextualism'?
    (b) Is it related to the 'self'—i.e. personal, social , academic and career development?

    (c) Is it able to enhance students' self-esteem, personal values and academic achievement?

    (d) Does it encompass both attitudes and skills at the same time?

    (e) Does it focus on life experience orientation and life application?

2.   The evaluation criteria of the teaching pedagogies of personal growth education programmes should include the following:

    (a) Are the teaching methods student-centred?

    (b) Do they focus more on the process than the content of teaching?

    (c) Is self-reflection stressed during the teaching process?

    (d) Can the process of teaching enhance students' self-esteem, co-operation, empathy and critical thinking?

Conclusion

This chapter discusses the implementation of the guidance curriculum in the 'East meets West' context of Hong Kong, in relation to its difficulties, special characteristics and areas of concern, so that readers are able to choose the teaching materials and methods that are most suitable for their students.

Questions for Discussion

1.   Do you agree with issues that exist in the 'East meets West' context on the teaching of guidance curriculum, which is the topic of discussion in this chapter? Why?

2.   What do you think are the differences in the teaching of guidance lessons from that of other subjects? Why?

3.   What kind of effects do you consider guidance curriculum will have on students? Why?

Notes

1.   The five cardinal relationships, originated from Confucius, comprise monarch and subjects, father and son, siblings, friends, husband and wife.

2.   The individualistic self—an individual is separated from another individual, while also being independent from the social and cultural environment.

3.   The embedded or relational self—there exists a close relationship between people, while they are at the same time immersed in the social and cultural environment surrounding them.

4. Conclusion arrived at by Luk-Fong after a two-week visit to a primary school in Hong Kong in 2009, during which she taught, observed and interviewed teachers/students/parents on the special characteristics of the guidance curriculum as well as the problems encountered in teaching guidance lessons.

Related Websites

1. Centre for Social and Emotional Education
    http://www.schoolclimate.org/educators/index.php
2. 'Classroom Curricula' programmes
    http://www2.dsgonline.com/mpg/program_types_description.aspx?program_type=Classroom%20Curricula&continuum=prevention
3. Free social and emotional literacy lessons
    http://pd.ilt.columbia.edu/projects/exsel/teachers/teacherslessons.htm
4. Key learning areas and focuses of personal growth education
    http://www.edb.gov.hk/index.aspx?nodeID=1988&langno=1
5. Life skills training
    http://www.lifeskillstraining.com/index.php
6. Personal growth education
    http://www.edb.gov.hk/index.aspx?nodeID=1976&langno=1
7. Personal growth education student checklists
    http://www.edb.gov.hk/index.aspx?nodeID=5712&langno=1
8. Sample social and emotional learning activities
    http://www.casel.org/programs/activities.php
9. Teen sex and pregnancy
    http://www.childtrends.org/_portalcat.cfm?LID=3086935F-008B-44B6-93E9C42C443B92D7
10. 'Use of Drama Elements in Conducting Personal Growth Education/ Life Education Lessons/Activities': a collection of lesson plans
    http://www.edb.gov.hk/index.aspx?nodeID=5981&langno=1

Extended Readings

Luk-Fong, P. Y. Y. (2005a). Globalisation and Localisation Enmeshed: Towards a Framework for the Development of Guidance Curriculum in Hong Kong. *Globalisation, Societies and Education*, 3(1), 83–100.

———— (2005b). Pedagogical Issues in the Teaching of Classroom Guidance Curriculum: A Hybrid Hong Kong Case. *Counselling Psychology Quarterly*, 18(3): 193–206.

陳維鄂（2001）：〈從多元智能的取向看學生輔導：結合才能發展與個人成長〉。《亞洲輔導學報》，第 8 卷第 1 期，頁 69。

郭志丕（2004）：《成長列車：小學生命成長課程》。香港：文林出版有限公司。

陸方鈺儀（2004）：〈成長課與教育改革的整合〉。《亞洲輔導學報》，第 11 卷第 1 及第 2 期，頁 127–142。

香港公開大學（2001）：《兒童成長與課堂學習》。香港：香港公開大學。

香港聖公會小學輔導服務處（2004）：《全方位學生輔導服務：成長課教材套》。香港：香港聖公會小學輔導服務處。

香港遊樂場協會（2003）：《開心教室：個人成長教育課程教材套》。香港：香港遊樂場協會。

翟錦嬋、黃秉堅、蕭穎珊（2006）：《家庭成長教育計劃：童心同心成長之旅：個人成長教育課程教材套》。香港：香港扶幼會。

References

Best, R., and Lang, P. (1994). Care and Education: The Comparative Perspective. In P. Lang, R. Best, and A. Lichtenberg (eds.), *Caring for Children: International Perspectives on Pastoral Care and PSE* (pp. 3–12). London: Cassell.

Borders, L. D., and Drury, S. M. (1992). Comprehensive School Counselling Programmes: A Review for Policy Makers and Practitioners. *Journal of Counselling and Development*, 70: 487–98.

Brandes, D., and Ginnis, P. (1986). *A Guide to Student-Centred Learning*. Oxford: Blackwell.

Curriculum Development Council. (2002). *Basic Education Curriculum Guide: Building on Strengths (Primary 1–Secondary 3)*. Hong Kong: Curriculum Development Council.

Gardner, H. (1993). *Multiple Intelligences: The Theory in Practice*. New York: Basic Books.

Gardner, H., Csikszentmihalyi, M., and Damon, W. (2001). *Good Work: When Excellence and Ethics Meet*. New York: Basic Books.

Geldard, K., and Geldard, D. (1997). *Counselling Children: A Practical Introduction*. London: Sage.

Giddens, A. (2001). The global revolution in family and personal life. In A. S. Skolnick and J. H. Skolnick (Eds.), *Family in transition* (11th ed.) (pp. 17–23). Boston: Allyn and Bacon.

Gysbers, N. C., and Henderson, P. (1994). *Developing and managing your school guidance program*. Alexandria, VA: American Counselling Association.

——— (2000). *Developing and Managing Your School Guidance Program* (3rd ed.). Alexandria, VA: American Counselling Association.

Jones, J. E., and Pfeiffer, J. W. (eds.). (1973). *The 1973 Annual Handbook for Group Facilitators*. San Diego: University Associates.

Luk-Fong, Y. Y. P. (2002). *A Study of Guidance Curriculum in Hong Kong Primary Schools*. Unpublished doctoral dissertation, University of Canberra.

——— (2005a). Globalisation and Localisation Enmeshed: Towards a Framework for the Development of Guidance Curriculum in Hong Kong. *Globalisation, Societies and Education*, 3(1): 83–100.

——— (2005b). Pedagogical Issues in the Teaching of Classroom Guidance Curriculum: A Hybrid Hong Kong Case. *Counselling Psychology Quarterly*, 18(3): 193–206.

Morganett, R. S. (1994). *Skills for Living: Group Counselling Activities for Elementary Students*. Champaign, IL: Research Press.

Myers, J. E. (1992). *Wellness, Prevention, Development: The Cornerstone of the Profession*. Alexandria, VA: ACA.

Park, J. (2001). *Think with Our Emotions*. Focus on: PSHE, http://www.teachthinking

Rogers, C. (1983). *Freedom to Learn for the Eighties*. Columbus, OH: Merrill.

Schrumph, F., Freiburg, S., and Skadden, D. (1993). *Life Lessons for Young Adolescents: An Advisory Guide for Teachers*. Champaign, IL: Research Press.

Stone, L. A., and Bradley, F. O. (1990). Foundations of Elementary and Middle School Counselling (pp. 142–43). New York: Longman.

Vernon, A. (1989). *Thinking, Feeling, Behaving: An Emotional Education Curriculum for Children Grades 1–6*. Champaign, IL: Research Press.

Williams, S. (2001). *The Philosophy in PSHE*. Focus on: PSHE, http://www.teachthinking.

費孝通：〈「美美與共」和人類文明〉。擷取於 2005 年 5 月 27 日，http://star.news. sohu.com/20050527/n225728386.shtml.

教育統籌委員會（2000）：《終身學習全人發展：香港教育制度改革建議》。香港： 教育統籌局。

課程發展議會（2002）：《基礎教育課程指引（小一至中三）3A 德育及公民教育》。 香港：課程發展議會。

石丹理、傅淑賢、趙振雄（1999）：《兩代相衝與相融：家庭價值觀異同的啟示研究 報告》。香港：香港小童群益會。

5

Person-centred Therapy
Foundations of Humanistic Approach to Counselling

Yuk Ching Lee-Man

Experience tells me that basically all human beings have a positive orientation
. . . When I can understand with great sensitivity the feelings they express,
accept them from their points of point, and admit their right to be different, I
would find that they are all willing to change towards certain directions.

(Rogers 1961: 26–27)

Abstract

This chapter describes the key stages of development of Carl Rogers's (1902–87)
person-centred therapy, including the core conditions and goals of guidance, the
role of the counsellor, commonly-used techniques, and the application of this
theory in schools. It also encourages (prospective) teachers to reflect on their views
on human nature and to involve themselves actively in school counselling work, so
as to attain a level of whole person care that embodies 'pointing the way, imparting
knowledge, and resolving problems'.

Objectives

This chapter will help you to:
- gain a clear idea of the four stages of development and the key ideas of person-centred therapy;
- come to grips with Carl Rogers's view of human nature;
- understand in concrete terms the meaning of the three basic conditions, genuineness, positive regard and empathy;
- familiarize yourself with the content and techniques of the theory through activities; and
- try to apply what has been learnt to everyday teaching/counselling work.

Before You Start: Think and Discuss

1. What is your idea of human nature? Is it benevolent, malevolent, or neutral?
2. How are students' behaviour and attitudes formed? Can they be changed? Why?
3. How can students be made to change and develop?
4   As a (prospective) teacher, what role can you play in bringing about students' change/development?

Introduction

The person-centred therapy was founded by the prominent American psychologist, Carl Rogers. His theory has been widely used in both individual and group counselling. Representative of the humanistic models, and the third force after psychoanalysis and behaviour therapy, the impact of this theory reached its peak in the 1960s and 1970s, and has continued to the present. It is hoped that through the study of this school of therapy in this chapter, we would get to know better Carl Rogers's positive regard for human nature and his pursuit of the ideal.

Person-centred Therapy: Four Stages of Development

Stage 1: Non-directive orientation

This stage took place mainly in the 1940s. In 1942, Rogers published *Counselling and Psychotherapy*, in which he advocated a non-directive mode of therapy to counter the psychoanalytic orientation in traditional individual counselling. He emphasized in the book the significance of human dignity and values, and the role of the counsellor (therapist) being only to create a free and non-directive environment and ambience to allow the client to reflect on himself/herself. Rogers disagreed with the commonly accepted therapeutic techniques such as advice, persuasion, and directive guidance and advocated the use of reflection and clarification to deliver insights to the client and facilitate changes.

Stage 2: Client-centred orientation

The second stage was during the 1950s. In 1951, Rogers's classic work *Client-centred Therapy* was published, elevating his system of therapy to a higher level.

He stressed that the counsellor should act as a 'mirror' to reflect the client's inner world and facilitate the latter's growth through empathy. Rogers pointed out that each individual has the striving force for growth and the tendency for self-actualization. As long as the client feels the acceptance, positive regard and empathy of the counsellor, the necessary conditions for positive change will be satisfied, and positive counselling results will ensue.

Stage 3: Person-centred orientation

This stage covered the 1960s. In 1962, Rogers published another of his influential work, *On Becoming a Person*, upon which his 'client-centred therapy' was renamed 'person-centred therapy'. The focus was now on 'becoming a person true to the self', i.e. living the true self. He stressed 'falling back on experience', which meant trusting one's own experience, assessing oneself from within, and accepting oneself. In 1968, he and his colleagues founded the Centre for Studies of the Person (CSP), to further hone and perfect his theory. He emphasized the relationship between the counsellor and the client in the counselling process as person-to-person rather than helper-to-helpee and least of all therapist-to-patient. From 'patient' to 'client' to 'person', it signifies the ascendance of positive regard for the person, a much lauded tenet of the humanistic approach to psychology.

Stage 4: Global relations orientation

This stage lasted from the 1970s till Rogers's passing. During this stage, Rogers was committed to extending his theory of psychotherapy to other domains. *Freedom to Learn*, published in 1969, saw his theory applied to education, in which he proposed that schools, teachers and adults should be pupil-oriented. This had a great impact on the wave of education reform of the times. His other work *Carl Rogers on Personal Power* (1977) showcased his interest and insights in the acquisition, ownership, sharing and transfer of 'power' and 'control'. During this time, he was devoted to the pursuit of peace among mankind, applying his person-centred theory to international and political issues, and hoping to resolve human problems, such as racial problems and war, with his theory. Although his influence in this area has not been as significant as in psychotherapy, it shows nonetheless his distinguished achievement.

❐ Activity 1

Summarizing the Main Points

Using the grid below, summarize the key points of the development stages of the person-centred therapy.

Stage	Name	Representative publication	Key points	Impact
1				
2				
3				
4				

Key Ideas

Humanistic view

Rogers refuted right from the beginning the pessimistic and negative determinism of the psychoanalytic school regarding human nature. Like China's Confucius, he held positive regard for human nature and had full confidence in Man himself, believing strongly in every individual's dignity and worth. He holds that every person can make decisions for himself/herself and is deeply convinced of everyone's right to express his/her beliefs and shape his/her own destiny. In his view, Man is benevolent, enterprising, trustworthy, goal-oriented, and also capable of collaborating and cultivating a harmonious relationship with others. His theory is person-based and humanistic, insistent upon the view that Man possesses the constructive will of making progress and doing good. He believes Man has two main tendencies—the formative tendency and the actualizing tendency.

Formative tendency

Formative tendency refers to the tendency of individuals or organism in the universe to go from simple to complex. This tendency is especially evident in the human consciousness—the primitive amorphous sub-consciousness gradually developing into a highly organized and self-aware consciousness. Therefore, with our awareness, we can break free from the control of the sub-consciousness and become autonomous individuals.

Actualizing tendency

Actualizing tendency refers to the positive tendency of Man to actualize his potential, create the self, change the self-concept and enhance self-direction. Rogers firmly believes that every one of us has this tendency, which is the basic motivation behind our behaviour. Through continued efforts, Man will pursue and cherish the experience that helps him realize his functions, thus growing into a more mature individual. Rogers further maintains that Man has the ability to discern his/her own psychological maladjustment and to change himself to seek psychological well-being. Negative emotions such as anger, jealousy, hostility, disappointment and sorrow will surface during the therapeutic process, but these are not instincts or impulses that have to be controlled. On the contrary, they are only reactions that spring from basic needs, such as love, a sense of belonging and a sense of security, being thwarted. The counsellor needs only to 'release the ability long existing in a person with abundant potential' (Rogers 1959) for him to self-adjust and balance out conflicting needs. This tendency to harmonize is a concrete expression of the self-actualizing tendency.

Self-concept

Self-concept is a very important concept in person-centred therapy. Some scholars even believe that Rogers's personality theory can be more aptly named the self-theory of personality (Chen and Zhang 1986). Self-concept refers mainly to how the client sees himself; in other words, the individual's overall view of 'What kind of person am I?' The self-concept does not come out of the blue, nor is it inborn; it is a product that integrates personal experience, values, meaning and beliefs. Its formation is via continuing interaction with the surrounding environment, of which the influence of significant others, i.e. adults around the individual such as parents, is the greatest. Through other people's attitudes and reactions, the individual accumulates experience continually and based on such experience he/she builds a self-concept for himself/herself—whether he/she is well-accepted or rejected.

Rogers thinks that a person's self-concept determines his approach and attitude towards accepting and dealing with experience. It can take the following three scenarios:
(I) If the experience is congruent with his existing self-concept, the individual's perception of the experience will be closer to reality. This is the most desirable scenario.
(II) The experience does not tally with his existing self-concept or is even in conflict with it. In order to obtain others' attention or approval, the individual may incorporate others' values and sacrifice his real inner needs or even twist his own cognition to try to achieve internal equilibrium.

(III) Experience that totally contradicts the self-concept may be entirely negated or neglected by the person.

Factors for emotional disturbance

As mentioned above, the self-concept determines an individual's reactions. When a person encounters experience that contradicts his self-concept, for fear of breaching of the long-held self-concept, anxiety and disturbance emerge. This is the origin of emotional disturbance for people in general. In order to alleviate the threat, the person's defence mechanism will be triggered to protect the original self-concept in order to avoid emotional torment due to change. When a person is subjected to prolonged psychological tension or when the defence mechanism becomes ineffective, the self-concept would break down, followed by self-doubt and maladjustment (alienation from others and inconsistent behaviour, etc.) In the most serious cases, the person may succumb to mental illness after prolonged emotional disturbance.

A fully functioning individual

The following are features that Rogers thinks belong to fully functioning individuals:
1. Rational and able to understand correctly their surroundings.
2. Possess a sense of security, with no need for the defence mechanism; flexible in cognition, and capable of accepting new experience and facing challenges.
3. Happy with themselves and appreciative of others; cherish and enjoy life, and live the here and now.
4. True to themselves and have positive self-regard, make decisions according to their inner needs, and have the courage to bear the consequences of their decisions.
5. Feel free psychologically and feel that they have access to many options; more confident and more self-directed.
6. Possess more positive personality attributes, and are able to make positive changes to their personality attributes.

Rogers believes that Man is a highly rational animal; he is wiser than his intellect. When he is fully functioning, he will not have to pretend, project or fear; he will not be anti-social or self-destructive; he will be relaxed and free. A fully functioning individual will be ever-changing and growing and work towards self-actualization without stop.

❑ **Activity 2**

Questions for Personal Reflection

1. Rogers maintains that Man has both a 'formative tendency' and an 'actualizing tendency'. But since individuals differ, in what way would the differences in these tendencies manifest themselves among pupils? How do we handle them?

2. Based on Rogers's theory, discuss how the 'significant others' (the principal or teachers) in the school have impact on the formation of the individual's (pupil) self-concept? How should one avoid negative impacts?

3. Are there similarities and differences between Rogers's approach and the Confucian 'benevolent' approach to human nature? How does it inspire you as a (prospective) teacher?

The Goal of Counselling and the Role of the Counsellor

The biggest concern of Rogers's person-centred therapy is the 'person', and its emphasis, the 'relationship'. It stresses the importance of helping the client to actualize his/her potential to become a fully functioning person. He believes the client has the motivation for growth to become better and benevolent; as long as the environment is suitable, every person can develop a set of appropriate and socially-acceptable behaviour. Therefore, the role of the counsellor also shifts from omniscient and omnipotent diagnosis, therapy and guidance to assistance in catalysis and companion in growth.

Since the counsellor is neither omniscient nor omnipotent, and the client is capable of change and growth, the counselling goal is hence determined by none other than the client himself/herself. The one who knows the 'problem' and the 'disturbance' best is the client himself/herself; if the counselling goal is determined by the counsellor on the client's behalf, it would constitute a kind of interference. Most significantly it would virtually imply that 'I (counsellor) am more capable, more competent and more valuable than you (client)'. Not only would it fail to yield the expected results, but it would be at odds with Rogers's theory. Hence, a counsellor who conducts person-centred therapy can only do the following: establish a good and therapeutically effective relationship with the client and provide some appropriate contexts which are conducive to the client's realization of his/her potential. If examined in detail, the counselling goal can be divided into the following:

1. Create a secure, warm and accepting environment to allow the client to explore and recognize experience and obstacles that hinder personal growth.

2. Help the client dispose of the incorrect or erroneous self-concepts accumulated, lower his/her self-defence mechanism, and realize how the defence mechanism is harmful to self-actualization.
3. Unlock the client's potential so that he/she can deal with internal conflicts naturally and explore complex emotions to facilitate his/her unique personal growth.

It can be said that helping the client become a fully functioning individual is the best goal of psychotherapy which is also the ultimate goal of person-centred therapy.

Basic Conditions for Counselling

To attain the above counselling goals, the crucial factor is 'relationship'. Rogers calls it the 'therapeutic relationship'. It encompasses three basic elements: genuineness or congruence, unconditional positive regard, and accurate empathy.

Genuineness

In person-centred therapy, genuineness or congruence is what Rogers considers the most important of the three qualities of the counsellor. He stresses that during the counselling process, the client must be able to feel the counsellor's genuineness, which is to say, in the counselling relationship the counsellor is a true person who shows congruence between his/her inner emotions and his/her behaviour and attitudes. He/she has no need of a mask or pretence, nor has he/she need of defence to protect himself/herself. He/she exists naturally, is not playing a professional role and he/she is willing to open up any time and reveal his/her inner world—including his/her thoughts and feelings. He/she likes sharing, whether the feelings are positive or negative. During the counselling process, the counsellor maintains a meaningful and warm relationship with the client to promote mutual communication. His/her manifestation of genuineness—at least his/her efforts at truth and genuineness—would become a model for the client so that the latter would imitate or emulate him/her and learn to be true to his/her own feelings to become a congruent and integrated person.

Positive regard

Unconditional positive concern, acceptance and regard are messages that the counsellor should continually convey to the client. He/she should treat the client as a person and not a 'patient', a totally independent individual who has his/her own feelings and experience. These feelings and experiences have their worth just as the client has his/hers as a person. During the counselling process, the counsellor will not make criticisms or pass judgements on the client. Neither will he/she 'interrogate' the client nor attempt to explain the client's behaviour. No matter what kind of person the client is, the counsellor will unconditionally respect and accept him/her. He/she accepts the client because the latter is his/her own self and has the freedom to express his/her feelings without being rejected. This acceptance refers to acknowledging the rights of the client but does not mean accepting all of his/her behaviour. Only with unconditional acceptance will the client be able to cast off his/her fears about the impressions that he/she might make on the counsellor, show his/her feelings and experience without reserve, and unleash his/her own inner strength to attain personal growth.

Empathy

Empathy means that the counsellor is able to understand correctly the client's mind and feelings, and to appreciate profoundly his psychological state. This empathy is built upon genuineness and positive regard. During the counselling process, the counsellor has to place himself/herself in the position of his/her client, play the role of the client with sensitivity, look at the world with the client's subjective frame of reference and feel his/her feelings. It is as if the counsellor had become the client and understood his/her inner disturbance and worries, and this is what makes psychotherapy effective. Without empathy, the counsellor will stop short of acceptance. It is only when the counsellor accepts the client's thoughts and feelings that the latter can explore freely the hidden experience in his/her subconscious and have the chance to correct erroneous self-concepts, raise self-awareness, and make changes. The client would be able to face his/her own experience—'It's not something shameful; what's more, I'm like this, but I'll still be growing!'

However, if the existence of genuineness, positive regard and empathy are not felt or realized by the client, they would be rendered worthless and ineffective. Hence, it is even more important to convey these three qualities to the client. In fact, an effective counsellor, or one who possesses the above three qualities, would express them naturally through verbal or non-verbal means. These means, if narrowly defined, are skills and techniques which are not artificial or coached but are rather the genuine expression and an integral part of a counsellor's character and refinement. If the counsellor can convey genuineness, positive regard and empathy to the client, the latter would experience a counselling relationship that is secure, unthreatened and anxiety-free. Such a relationship would enable the client to grow in a constructive individual manner. This is why the top concern of Rogers's theory is the 'person' and not the 'problem' and its emphasis is 'relationship' and not 'skills/techniques'.

❐ **Activity 3**

Whole Group/Small Group Discussion

Divide into three groups and discuss what aspects of the person-centred therapy school teachers can use as reference in their everyday work.
(a) Relationship between counsellor and client vs relationship between teacher and pupil
(b) Role of counsellor vs role of teacher
(c) Basic conditions for counselling vs conditions for teaching/student guidance

Faced with a harsh environment, a newly arrived pupil is determined to do well. He believes that only good grades in the exam will change his destiny. In his limited life experience, his parents have not been able to help, and teachers and classmates do not seem to really care; the only guarantee is his perseverance. Nevertheless, he has overlooked the fact that being too focused on grades has isolated him and put him under great pressure. If the exam performance turns out not to be as good as expected, there is a high chance of a crisis. Hence, teachers and social workers can use the three basic conditions in person-centred therapy to build a good relationship with the client and lead Xiangyang (client) to a better understanding of his experience and a re-adjustment of himself to facilitate self-reflection and change. The following response can serve as a reference:

❐ **Activity 4**

Case Study 1

Xiangyang is a 17-year-old S. 4 pupil who came to settle in Hong Kong from the Mainland when he was in S. 1. In order to do well, he works very hard. He does nothing but study, doing everything he can to get good grades, sacrificing social activities and good health. He loves saying, 'My goals are clear: in the past, I have been discriminated against for being a newly arrived student. But my grades are very good and I will always be good. I want to outperform the others even if it means giving up other things. I want to prove I'm absolutely outstanding; I don't want to be looked down upon!' Try to use Rogers's genuineness, positive regard and empathy to respond to Xiangyang.

'Xiangyang, I admire your efforts through the years and can feel your determination. Most of all, I have no doubt about your capabilities, though at the same time I understand that you have gone through a lot of hardship and made many sacrifices, and feel especially the pressure that you have brought to yourself. While I respect your choice, I hope you understand the importance of good health, interpersonal relationships and relationship with your parents. Don't ever let those who are concerned about you worry just because you have to achieve your goals . . .'

Case Study 2

Chung-mei, a playful and rather rough S. 2 student, does not do well academically and shows low concentration in her studies. On the verge of repeating S. 1, she was marginally promoted to S. 2, only to become a trouble-maker in class. She gives Miss Chan, the new class teacher, a headache whenever she sees her. Chungmei often appears in the offices of the discipline co-ordinator and the social worker for her offences. While she does not appear to be rebellious against others teachers, she only complains about Miss Chan, the new teacher. Recently, she told her teacher how she disliked Miss Chan (see below). If you were her interlocutor, how would you interact with her?

'I can assure you that Miss Chan wants me dead! If kicking me out of school doesn't involve reporting to parents and the Education Bureau, I'm sure she'll have asked the principal to expel me! I feel she's always picking on me. She blames me for every problem in class; if she gets something wrong in her teaching, she'd say it's because I'm making too much noise. She is not up to standard and she has no guts, only bluffs! Once she even asked me in front of the whole class that if I'm so unhappy at school, why don't I switch school? Huh! Actually I'd always been like this before she came and there was nothing wrong. She's just trying to pick on me. Just wait and see, what I will do to her.'

Chung-mei's behavioural problem is nothing new, only that the newcomer Miss Chan has become the 'wimp' and the 'punch bag'. Since she initiated the outpourings with other teachers, she is not anti-authority; only that she has not established a relationship with Miss Chan and is not used to her way of guidance and discipline. As the object of her outpourings and a significant other, you could try to use genuineness, positive regard and empathy to lead her to a clear perception of her circumstances and problem:

'First of all, I'd like to thank you for opening up to me and I'm also happy you've been honest and sincere. I really appreciate your trust in me. You feel that Miss Chan is picking on you; I can understand your feeling of indignation and injustice. When she asked you in public why you didn't switch school, you thought she wanted to kick you out. So it seems you do care about being expelled after all! But is switching school the same as being expelled? Can we interpret Miss Chan's remark in other ways? Perhaps you might want to think about it more carefully. Besides, your grades and your behaviour are such that other teachers (including myself) have often expressed their concern about you. And you nearly had to repeat S. 1 when Miss Chan was not here yet. I suppose it's got nothing to do with her then . . .'

Commonly-used Techniques

As the person-centred therapy is based on a humanistic approach, a main concern is the counsellor's philosophy and his attitudes towards the client. The key point is not technique; rather, the emphasis is on the counselling relationship and not the counsellor's words and behaviour. As mentioned before, person-centred therapy stresses the creation of a good rapport so that the client will feel secure, accepted and understood, and the establishment of such a rapport is reliant upon certain techniques which will be described briefly below.

Attentive listening

Listening is different from hearing. Attentive listening is a technique and attitude with which the counsellor listens with undivided attention, paying full attention to the client's expression and reaction in order to create a rapport. The techniques consist of eye contact, observation of facial expressions, posture, and arrangement of the physical environment. (Interestingly, the structure of the Chinese character for 'listen' (聽) embodies such elements as ear, eye and heart.) Attentive listening involves the counsellor sitting and facing the client squarely, assuming a natural and open posture and slightly leaning forward, maintaining eye contact, keeping a relaxed manner, but all the while listening with full attention to the client's narration. The counsellor conveys his/her concern and empathy to the client to facilitate further exploration.

Silence

The counsellor makes frequent use of silence in person-centred therapy. Silence may seem simple if merely taken as being mute but it can be a powerful tool. If used appropriately it can enhance the effectiveness of counselling. For a beginner counsellor, silence is not easy to manage, as dead air will bring in tension and uneasiness. But this tension and uneasiness are exactly the purpose of the use of silence: it urges the client (or sometimes even the counsellor) to reflect on and feel the emotions and meaning behind the client's words and descriptions of the event. Silence can be viewed as a profound empathy. It is also the counsellor's expression of trust in the client: 'I (counsellor) am confident that you (client) are capable of dealing with your personal problems. What you need is the time to learn to face it. I'm right here and always ready to offer support and encouragement.' Another function of silence is that it allows more room for the client to sort out his emotions and disclose himself/herself more elaborately. Silence allows the client to be more open, to further experience himself/herself, to be more responsible for the counselling process, and is hence a very important technique.

Clarification

Rogers stresses that during the counselling process, one of the most important responsibilities of the counsellor is to serve as a 'mirror' for the client to reflect on his/her thoughts, emotions and views, through which process the latter would discern the incongruity of his/her experiences, as well as his/her distorted or contradictory self-concept. Clarification includes making clear the key points of the client's problems and helping the client reveal the relevant aspects. Effective wordings include: 'Do you mean . . .', 'Are you telling me that . . .', 'I'd like to first make clear . . .', etc. Another function of clarification is to assist the client to make choices through a clearer discernment of the consequences of his subjective inner world and emotions. Clarification involves mainly repeating the client's thoughts and emotions to highlight his/her words and related issues.

Reflection

Reflection is considered the most powerful technique in person-centred therapy. It can capture the client's subjective experience and enables the client to receive more clearly the counsellor's signals of acceptance and understanding. Reflection consists of two main aspects:

(1) Reflection of feelings means the counsellor reflects the client's emotions (but not thoughts, notions, behaviour or disposition) with appropriate language without making criticisms or passing judgements. The counsellor conveys clearly and in concrete terms his/her understanding of the client's feelings to enable the latter to come to grips with his/her own emotions to avoid confusion.

(2) Reflection of meaning involves the counsellor reflecting what the meaning of the problem or the issue is for the client in a professional manner to enable him/her to know its impact and to further understand himself/herself. Carkhuff proposed a rather useful sentence format to reflect meaning: 'You feel ( ) because ( ).' The

first pair of brackets can be filled with items of feelings or events and the second with the meaning of the event or problem. One example would be 'You are very upset with your mother's reaction this time (feeling) because it wasn't your fault; obviously you've been made the scapegoat (meaning).'

☐ **Activity 5**

Application Exercise (Please respond to these exercises as instructed)

(a) Techniques of clarification and reflection
     Client: I don't think talking to you has had any effects at all. All along, what I hear and feel is: it was all my fault.
     Counsellor: What you mean is: _____ .

(b) Techniques of reflection of feeling and meaning
     Counsellor: You only got 59 marks for the mid-term maths exam; you _____
     _____
     _____ (feeling) because _____,
     which is why you're feeling _____
     (meaning of the event).

(c) Effective response
     Pupil: Sir, it's got nothing to do with me. Don't 'wrong' me; it was Siu-ming who asked me to steal Keung's phone; I'm innocent!
     Teacher: _____
     _____ .

     Pupil: Doing homework is boring. I know nothing and there's no one who can help me. I'd tried hard but still didn't pass. I got a beating from my mom no matter what.
     Teacher: _____
     _____ .

Conclusion

Since its founding in the 1940s, person-centred therapy has developed for over half a century. Its impact has been widespread and profound and the application of its theory has seen continual expansion. Apart from being applied in individual and group counselling, this method has also proved effective in helping clients of different categories including children and youth, with the main targets being the maladjusted and those with relatively low self-concepts. This method is also being used widely in schools.

Since person-centred therapy highlights the person rather than the problem, the mode of therapy has also switched from a 'disease' model to a 'growth' model, which proves much safer than the directive modes of psychotherapy. Its basic concepts of therapy, namely genuineness, positive regard and empathy, are straightforward and easy to comprehend. For para-helpers who lack professional training in psychology, personality dynamics and psychopathology, this mode of therapy guarantees that the client will not suffer unnecessary psychological damage. Hence, more and more organizations are training professional or para-helpers (such as teachers, social workers or medical workers) with this therapy.

As a theory, person-centred therapy also has its shortcomings and limitations.

This theory's basic assumptions that every person has the potential to grow and the tendency to self-actualize have been queried for a long time. Furthermore, even if these tendencies exist, not every client can trust his/her own inner directions to resolve the matter at hand. What is more, when the client seeks help, he/she is very likely beleaguered with a problem. He/she may have a more urgent need to find the right method or strategy to resolve his/her pressing problem than to contemplate personal growth. Also, for certain help-seekers, the non-directive and non-authoritative role of the counsellor in person-centred therapy may not appear appealing and hence may not be conducive to confidence building. This theory has made self-actualization the common goal of all help-seekers which has been challenged for overlooking the unique needs of the individual. Rogers stresses that the therapeutic relationship itself can enhance the client's growth and development but the nature of this kind of relationship is difficult to grasp and assess. Besides, person-centred therapy has been criticized for over-emphasizing emotions and feelings as determinants of behaviour while overlooking the effect of intellect, cognition and rationality on the behaviour of the individual. Some counsellors, due to their misinterpretations of the basic concepts of the theory, may limit their response and counselling mode to only reflection, empathy and listening without challenging the client's problems, hence only achieving the prerequisite of building a therapeutic relationship but stopping short of the true therapy.

Questions for Discussion

1. What do you think is the most important contribution of Rogers's person-centred therapy?
2. Do you agree with Rogers's philosophy on human nature? Why?
3. Many studies have shown that young people nowadays are lacking self-confidence and suffering from a low self-concept. In what ways can person-centred therapy help these young people?

4. How do the three basic counselling conditions of genuineness, positive regard and empathy affect the building of interpersonal (teacher-pupil) relationships? Please provide examples.
5. Person-centred therapy stresses the client's self-understanding, experience restructuring and insight. Are these suitable for counselling primary school pupils? Why?
6. As a (prospective) teacher, how would you apply Rogers's theory of psychotherapy to everyday teaching? Please elaborate.

Related Websites

1. 'Teacher-Pupil Relationship: The Foundation for Student Crisis Intervention' by Patrick S. Y. Lau
   http://www.fed.cuhk.edu.hk/ceric/ajc/0201/0201053.htm
2. 從人本心理學到超個人心理學的思索──中西方心理治療之融合　陳玉芳
   http://www.ncu.edu.tw/~phi/NRAE/newsletter/no7/08.html
3. 從人本心理學到超個人心理學的思索中西方心理治療之融合
   http://www.dabuluo.com/bllp/ShowArticle.asp?ArticleID=2378
4. 個人中心治療法（講義）
   http://blog.donews.com/drugstore/archive/2006/09/20/1042723.aspx
5. 個人中心治療法──緒論
   http://www.xinli110.com/liaofa/qzz/200906/143849.html
6. 羅傑斯的「無條件自我敬重」
   http://www.chinesechristiandiscernment.net/psychologists/Rogers_Carl.htm
7. 人本治療法
   http://www.rnd.ncnu.edu.tw/hdcheng/swtheory/clientcenter.htm
8. 學生輔導是一門科學亦是一門藝術　傅立圻
   http://home.netvigator.com/~foolapki/Essay/guide01.htm

Extended Readings

Chan, A. (1980). *Person-Centered Therapy in Hong Kong: My Local Experience*. S.l.: s.n.
Levant, R. F., and Shlien, J. M. (1984). *Client-Centered Therapy and the Person-Centered Approach: New Directions in Theory, Research, and Practice*. New York: Praeger.
Rogers, C. R. (2003). *Client-Centered Therapy: Its Current Practice, Implications and Theory*. London: Constable.
Shlien, J. M. (2003). *To Lead an Honorable Life: Invitations to Think about Client-Centered Therapy and the Person-Centered Approach. A Collection of the Work of John M. Shlien*. Ross-on-Wye: PCCS.

Tudor, K. (2008). *Brief Person-Centred Therapies*. Los Angeles: Sage.

Rogers, C. R. 著，宋文里譯（1990）：《成為一個人：一個治療者對心理治療的觀點》。臺北：桂冠圖書公司。

Thorne, B. 著，陳逸群譯（2007）：《人本心理學派代言人：羅傑斯》。上海：學林出版社。

References

Corey, G. (1991). *Theory and Practice of Counselling and Psychotherapy* (4th ed.). New York: Pacific Grove, Book/Cole.

Corsini, R. K., and Wedding, D. (eds.) (1995). *Current Psychotherapies* (5th ed.). Itasca, IL: F. E. Peacock Publishers, Inc.

Farber, B. A., Brink, D. C., and Rosin, P. M. (eds.) (1996). *The Psychotherapy of Carl Rogers: Cases and Commentary.* New York: The Guilford Press.

Gibson, R. L., and Mitchell, M. H. (1999). *Introduction and Counselling and Guidance* (5th ed.). Upper Saddle River, NJ: Prentice Hall.

Ivey, A. E., Ivey, M. B., and Sımek, Mogan. (1993). *Counselling and Psychotherapy: An Multicultural Perspective* (3rd ed.). London: Allyn and Bacon.

McLeod, J. (1997). *An Introduction to Counselling* (2nd ed.). Hong Kong: Open University Press.

Rogers, C. R. (1961). *On Becoming a Person.* Boston: Houghton Mifflin.

郭正、李文玉清、陳譚美顏（2001）：《輔導與諮商：多媒體自學教材學習指南》。香港：香港教育學院。

郭正、李文玉清（主編）（2006）：《輔導個案：示例與啟迪》。星加坡：McGraw Hill Education (Asia)。

江光榮（2000）：《輔導與心理治療》（第 11 版）。香港：商務印書館。

李茂興（譯）（1997）：《諮商與心理治療的理論與實務：學習手冊》。台北：揚智文化。

魏麗敏、黃德祥（2000）：《諮商理論與忌諱》。台北：五南圖書公司。

6

Cognitive Counselling Theory
The Light of Reason

Yuk Ching Lee-Man

I 'must' have the love and recognition of the significant others in my life.
I 'absolutely' want perfect execution of important assignments.
I strongly wish others would treat me with care and fairness; therefore they 'must' act like this!'

(Dryden & Ellis 1988; Ellis 1987b, 1988; translated by M. X. Li 1995)

Abstract

This chapter is a discussion of the background and core concepts from which Albert Ellis's (1913–2007) Rational Emotive Therapy was derived, including rational and irrational beliefs, the ABC theory, counselling objectives and commonly-used counselling techniques and strategies. It also attempts to analyse aspects that need special attention when educators apply this theory to helping pupils.

Objectives

This chapter will help you:
- grasp the relationship between rationality, emotion and behaviour;
- understand the nature of irrational beliefs;
- interpret correctly the factors behind irrational beliefs and their influence;
- familiarize yourselves with the relevant counselling strategies and techniques through activities; and
- feel confident in trying out what you have learnt to help pupils that need counselling.

Before You Start: Think and Discuss

1. Apart from environmental factors, what other major factors govern human behaviour?

2.   Do you agree with the statement, 'What is affecting your emotion is not the issue per se, but your views towards the issue'?
3.   How do you understand 'rational' and 'irrational' beliefs and behaviour? Can you cite some examples of rational beliefs and irrational beliefs?
4.   Are you good at dialectics and disputations? Do you think these processes are consistent with your counselling beliefs? Please elaborate.

Introduction

With changing times and the advance in thinking also came the change of our interpretation towards behaviour. Behaviourism began with classical and operant conditioning as the foundation of behaviour modification. In the 1960s, social learning and cognitive behaviour therapy emerged, which enriched techniques in behaviour modification and reformed the therapeutic methods. In the 1980s, the cognitive behaviour therapy became the mainstream, showing us the rationality behind human behaviour.

Rational Emotive Behaviour Therapy, the representative theory of the cognitive counselling school, was founded by the Jewish American psychologist, Albert Ellis.

Background to the Development of the Theory

During the 1940s, psychoanalysis was the mainstay in psychiatric and psychological therapy. After receiving his doctorate in clinical psychology in 1947, Ellis began to practise as a psychoanalyst. Nevertheless, he considered psychoanalysis too reliant on the ability of the therapist and too passive as it waits for the patient's 'enlightenment'. Moreover, he believed that the intricate method of psychoanalysis was too abstract and difficult to manage, and the effects were hard to verify. According to his clinical experience, most people's problems (mainly marital and familial) came from emotional disturbances originated from their personal beliefs. Starting from 1954, Ellis gradually developed his own unique method of psychotherapy, which was devoted to changing the clients' irrational beliefs. He built a set of coherent theories and techniques for helping the client resolve problems. Ellis began to publish the relevant papers in 1955, calling his therapy 'rational psychotherapy'. In 1962, he recapitulated his method in his book, *Reason and Emotion in Psychotherapy*. This method was later renamed 'Rational Emotive Therapy'—or RET.

Core Concepts

Refuting determinism, but not totally agreeing with existential humanism

Ellis holds that the Freudian school is wrong in treating human nature as deterministic; he believes an individual is more than a creature driven by pure instincts. Yet, neither does he agree totally with the existential humanistic view that Man is unique, able to understand limits and capable of changing beliefs and values as well as self-defeating views. He challenges the existential view of self-actualization: since Man's behaviour is greatly affected by instincts, even if he wants to self-actualize, he may not be able to do so. Besides, Man's mind and emotions will be conditioned to take certain forms, and even if he realizes the behaviour is self-defeating, he would still make certain mistakes! Therefore, Ellis does not believe that the emergence of an accepting, forgiving and trustworthy therapist would resolve the hidden self-defeating behaviour in the depths of a person's nature.

Opposing absolute environmental determinism

Ellis is also against environmental determinism. He believes that a person's emotions and behaviour are not purely determined by the environment but rather his adaptation to it. If a person often adopts a distorted view of his circumstances, he would easily experience frustration, become anxious about details, and further develop anxiety and hostility towards the whole world and himself. In the same way, self-acceptance and self-adjustment are interconnected; if a person recognizes his/her own worth, he/she would have higher self-regard, cherish himself/herself, and would not easily misbehave.

Man is endowed with both rational and irrational attributes

Ellis holds that Man has rational and upright thoughts and behaviour as well as irrational and crooked ones. People possess both the dispositions to self-defence, happiness, thinking, language, love, communication, growth and self-actualization, and the tendencies towards self-destruction, avoiding thinking, following conventional practice, repeating mistakes, superstition, impatience, perfectionism, self-blame, and avoidance of growth simultaneously.

Emotional disturbance originates from the self

Ellis believes that emotion is the single most essential force for an individual's survival and happiness in life. Nevertheless, Man has three obstacles in his thinking and emotion: a lack of intellect; a lack of knowledge for sensible thinking; and neurotic behaviour which prevents him from utilizing his intellect and knowledge. Ellis further maintains that only by thinking rationally can a person be happy and minimize emotional disturbance. Since thinking is subjective, whether one can lead a happy life is totally under the control of oneself and one's thinking.

Co-existence of thinking, emotion and behaviour and their interrelations

Ellis further points out that a person usually experiences emotional disturbance first, which is only intensified when exposed to the environment. A person's functioning depends on an integral operation of his cognition, action, emotions and thinking. To understand a person's behaviour, we have to adopt a holistic consideration of all the four factors. Ellis believes that irrational thinking can be traced back to the illogical learning in early life, mainly from parents and the cultural environment. A person's self-talk (inner language) also determines one's manifestation of emotions and behaviour. Cognitive attitude determines an incident is described in one's mind. This kind of sustained stimulus can result in disturbance which then affects behaviour. To change this situation, the person needs to restructure his cognition and to adopt rational thinking in order to overcome negative thinking and emotions.

Because of the mutual influence among the mind, emotion and behaviour, 'B' (behaviour) was later added to RET to be known as REBT (rational emotive behavioural therapy).

❐ Activity 1

Think and Discuss

Q. 1: Do you agree with Ellis's criticism on Freud's psychoanalytic view of 'Man as a creature driven by biological instincts'?

Q. 2: Neither does Ellis agree with the existential view of self-actualization. Is his argument well substantiated?

Q. 3: The behaviourists stress the impact of environment on human behaviour. What is Ellis's view on this? Do you agree with him?

❐ Activity 2

Reflection

1. Ellis assumes that Man possesses both rational and irrational behaviour. Based on your own experience, what kind of obvious irrational behaviour do you exhibit?

2. Ellis points out that irrational thinking originates from illogical learning in the earlier stages of one's life, of which parental and cultural influence is the most significant contributor. Following the previous question, can you point

(continued on page 123)

Activity 2 *(continued)*

> out which of your illogical thinking was learnt from your parents? And which
> illogical thinking is a result of cultural indoctrination?
> 3. As a (prospective) teacher, how would you face the irrational thinking and
>   behaviour of pupils, colleagues and parents?

The ABC Theory

Beliefs hold a very significant position in the REBT theory of personality. This
theory is also known as the ABC theory. In Figure 6.1 below, A stands for activating
event, B for Beliefs, and C for emotional consequences.

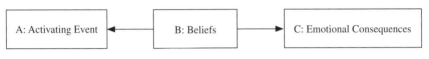

Figure 6.1 ABC theory

In the ABC theory, the activating event or the individual's personal experience
(A) causes emotional consequences (C) only through the effect of the individual's
beliefs (B). A and C are not directly related, with B being the mediating force. Since
human beings have both rational beliefs (rBs) and irrational beliefs (iBs), iBs are
often the cause of problems for C. While many believe that activating events are
the direct causes for behavioural and emotional consequences, Ellis maintains that
thinking and beliefs instead are the direct causes for the individual's emotions and
feelings. In the figure, B is the focus for counselling and therapy. If the person's
belief system renders a rational view of A, the C thus arising will also be rational.
However, if his/her belief system produces irrational and impractical views, they
could possibly lead to emotional disturbance or neurotic symptoms, rendering
C irrational. The persistence of emotional obstacles is the result of the persistent
irrational thinking arising from continual internalized self-talking.

People's Irrational Beliefs and Ellis's Respective Interpretations

**iBs (I):   It is absolutely necessary for one to be loved and lauded by the
             people around**

Interpretation: This is a goal hard to attain. If a person is committed to this goal,
                he/she would lose his/her own stance as he/she tries hard to satisfy

others' expectations, and become 'others-oriented' and over-developed in 'interpersonal skills'. As a result he/she would feel insecure, exhibit many self-inflicting behaviours, and lack the ability to nurture a healthy self-concept and social adaptation. It is not imperative for a person to be loved albeit the feeling being a good one. A rational person would not direct all his/her energy towards this goal but would express love and become a lovable individual.

iBs (II):   A person's worth is as much as his capabilities and achievements

Interpretation: This is not reasonable. If committed to this goal, the individual will experience frustration and distress. A rational person should work hard for his/her own sake, derive pleasure and satisfaction from the process and not overstretching himself/herself by concentrating purely on the result. In other words, the process is more important than the outcome.

iBs: (III): Bad or evil people must be reprimanded or punished

Interpretation: There is no absolute standard of right and wrong. Reprimand and punishments cannot bring about behaviour improvement. Being too stubborn on punishment for the bad will only bring further emotional disturbance. Rational people would not be too severe upon himself or others.

iBs (IV):   It would be catastrophic if things do not turn out the way anticipated or wanted

Interpretation: This is also unreasonable. Frustration and failure are very normal experience. Rational people would accept unfavourable circumstances and avoid exaggerating unpleasant experiences.

iBs (V):   Misfortune and unhappiness are caused by the external environment. The individual cannot overcome or control this.

Interpretation: External difficulties may exist but the pressure usually stems from the psyche. It depends completely on how the individual deals with the problem, so internal factors have a far stronger influence than external ones.

iRb (VI): A person must be wary of possible danger or misfortune

Interpretation: There is bound to be some kind of problems in our life. Feeling anxious and worried would only make things worse. A rational person understands that anxiety will not prevent danger while taking actions to face the danger would prove that the matter is not as terrible as perceived.

iBs (VII): It is easier to evade difficulties and responsibilities than to face them

Interpretation: Escape would only trigger future problems, creating even more frustration and disappointment. An easy life is not a happy life; a rational person understands that a happy and fruitful life means facing challenges and taking up the responsibility to solve problems.

iBs (VIII): One should find a 'strong man' (a capable person) to depend on

Interpretation: A dependent person stops learning, loses his/her self and his/her sense of security. A rational person is independent, takes initiatives and assumes responsibilities. He/she only seeks help when necessary and is not dependent on a long-term basis.

iBs (IX): Past experiences determine present behaviour and circumstances and their effects cannot be eradicated or changed

Interpretation: A rational person sees the importance of the past and learns from it. He/she analyses the effects of past experiences to change present circumstances but is not mired in the past.

iBs (X): A person should pay close attention to others' problems or disturbance

Interpretation: Others' problems belong to others and do not concern us. There is no need to get too involved. A rational person would consider offering direct assistance to change others' circumstances but would not beleaguer himself/herself.

iBs (XI): There is a suitable and perfect solution to every problem

Interpretation: Things do not necessarily have a perfect answer or solution. A rational person would only try various plausible methods and pick the best one. It is not catastrophic not to be able to find the best solution.

Distinguishing between Rational and Irrational Beliefs

It is not difficult to see from the above eleven irrational beliefs that many of them are 'absolute beliefs', expressed in language and notions such as 'have to', 'must', 'need to' and 'definitely'. These absolute social beliefs have a strong negative impact on people's irrational thinking and maladjustment. We have to rectify them to diminish their effects. The self-talk in Table 6.1 may constitute an effective tool for distinguishing between rational and irrational beliefs:

Table 6.1 Irrational beliefs vs. rational beliefs

	Irrational beliefs	Rational beliefs
Belief	Absolute and obsessed pursuit (I must have . . .)	Hope; expect (It would be good if . . . could)
Self-talk	It's so terrible (It's the end of the world; total failure)	It's not too bad (It's a failure, but one can always try again and succeed)
Resilience	Low adversity tolerance (I cannot stand it anymore!)	High adversity tolerance (It's painful, but I still can . . .)
Behaviour	Blame, depression, self-deprecation (I feel too ashamed to face other people!)	Acceptance of the poor result (Try harder next time!)

❐ **Activity 3**

Role-play

Try to play the role of the primary or secondary pupil, and list at least ten common irrational beliefs in their learning or daily life.

The Goal and Role of the Counsellor

Ellis maintains that most people's emotional disturbance originates from irrational thinking because the 'musts' and 'shoulds' in absolute notions take away people's confidence and drive them to depression and self-pity or even aggression and hostility towards others. Thus, when we feel uneased, we can examine the 'musts' and 'shoulds' behind the emotion as they stand in the way of people going after their goals and lead to all sorts of emotive or behavioural problems. Hence, the counselling goals for REBT include:

1. Encourage the client to learn to accept and face himself/herself and stop blaming himself/herself and others.
2. Find his/her own direction and not to live up only to the 'absolute social beliefs' such as the 'musts' and the 'shoulds'. Modify and control one's own emotion and situation through self-introspection, observation and assessment of one's own goals and intentions.
3. Accept the fact that the world is unpredictable and imperfect. REBT counsellors help people examine and change some of their most basic values, especially the eradication of the clients' inelegant goals, and enable them to think in a rational and scientific manner.
4. Require the client to be more concerned about his/her own and society's interests, not to be dependent, be more flexible and more adventurous, and to be more involved in his/her own life and more adaptable to the environment.

In order to attain the above goals, the counsellor has to build a good relationship with the client. However, a good relationship is a necessary but not sufficient condition for a change in the client's behaviour. The counsellor has also to achieve the following:

1. Point out that the client's problem originates from irrational beliefs.
2. Identify and demonstrate the particular irrational beliefs which are disturbing the client.
3. Challenge the client's irrational thinking.
4. Encourage the client to correct his beliefs and discard irrational thinking.
5. Stimulate the client to develop a rational philosophy of life to replace the irrational beliefs and attitudes.

Counselling Strategies and Techniques

There are many strategies and techniques in REBT therapy, which can be categorized as teaching and disputing. Teaching is to acquaint the client with the basic notions of REBT and the relationship between thinking, emotion and behaviour, so that he/she would understand his/her cognition and beliefs and the fact that self-talk, rather than the issue itself, is the cause of emotional disturbance. The client will also learn that he/she has the ability to dispute irrational thinking and to establish a more rational way of thinking. The process is illustrated in Figure 6.2:

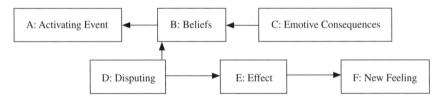

Figure 6.2 Theory of dispute

As for disputing, there are three main ways to dispute, distinguish, analyse and challenge irrational beliefs and thinking. They are in the form of cognition, imagination and behaviour, which aim to help the client discern the emotional disturbance caused by his irrational beliefs and thinking. The disputing process will shed new light upon his/her beliefs and thinking, giving rise to new emotions and feelings, and hence diminishing the earlier emotional disturbance. The therapeutic strategies and techniques of REBT will be expounded on three levels: cognitive, imaginative and behavioural.

Strategies on the cognitive level

Disputing irrational beliefs

This method involves the counsellor actively disputing the client's irrational beliefs, and guiding him/her to challenge his/her own beliefs. The counsellor would tell the client that what is troubling him/her is not an issue or a circumstance but rather his/her cognition and views. Through a series of disputing, the client will be led to examine his/her beliefs, especially absolute and irrational beliefs such as 'must', 'best' and 'definitely', and learn to dispute them with interrogative or narrative phrases such as 'Why should people treat me fairly?'; 'If I don't get the job, I'd be disappointed, but I could stand it'; 'If things don't go my way, it is not a big deal, it is just not too pleasant'. The client's consciousness is brought to a more rational level with these phrases, which would diminish the emotional disturbance, and in the end he will be free from the control of irrational beliefs.

There are three kinds of disputation of irrational beliefs. Here are the examples:

1. Logical disputing

   The main purpose of this kind of disputing is to allow the clients to realize that even though they would love to or prefer to get some kinds of qualities of life, it does not mean that these qualities have to logically exist in our life.

   Example: 'The boss must treat each and every employee equally.'
   Disputation: 'True. It would be ideal if the boss would treat you (the client) and other staff in a fairer way; however, it is not an absolute requisite. Is there any legislation that requires a boss to act this way?'

2. Empirical disputing

   The purpose of this kind of disputation is to reveal to the client that almost all of the thinking and feelings derived from their absolute beliefs do not tally with reality.

   Example: 'I have to be successful in the exam.'
   Disputation: 'According to your past exam results, what evidence is there to indicate that you will not fail in this one?'

3. Pragmatic disputing

   The purpose of this disputation is to tell the client distinctly that as long as he/she agrees with the irrational beliefs, he/she would always be stuck in (negative) emotions.

   Example: 'If you continue to believe you have to succeed in the exam, what would happen to you?'
   Disputation: 'I think I'd be very worried and anxious!'

Homework in cognition and change in self-talk

The client is required to list his/her problems, identify the absolute beliefs and question them. The homework is to track the 'shoulds' and 'musts' in the client's internalized self-talk. A part of the homework is to apply the ABC theory of REBT to the problems encountered in their daily life. The counsellor strongly recommends that the client put himself/herself in an adventurous context and challenge the self-limiting belief. For example, in the case of a person talented in performing who dare not perform for fear of failure, the counsellor may ask him/her to play a minor role on stage and teach him/her to abandon such self-talk as 'I'll fail, I'll look awkward and nobody will like me' and replace it with positive messages such as 'I may look awkward, but I'm not stupid. I can perform, I'll do my best. It'll be nice being liked. But not everyone will like me and it's not the end of the world.' The theory behind this homework is that people often have a kind of self-fulfilling prophecy; if it was negative, in reality it would often lead to failure because they already told themselves they would fail. During the counselling process, the counsellor keeps encouraging the client to complete this kind of homework in his/her daily life and change the content of his/her self-talk, so that he/she would challenge the basic irrational beliefs and think and act in different ways. As a result, the client eventually learns to deal with his/her anxiety and starts to feel differently.

Strategies on an emotive level

This involves unconditional acceptance, rational role-play, demonstration, rational-emotive imagery, and shame-attacking exercises.

Unconditional acceptance and demonstration

The counsellor will teach the client the value of unconditional acceptance: even if his/her behaviour is unacceptable, he/she is still a valuable person. The counsellor will also make the client understand that to sink into self-denial will simply lead to greater damage to his/her life. The counsellor teaches the client to accept himself/ herself through demonstration and portrays the life of not embracing such beliefs as 'should' and 'must'. When the counsellor challenges the client, he/she will reveal his own adventurous spirit and that he/she would still show total acceptance even when the client is in a poor and miserable state.

Rational-emotive imagery

The client imagines the most terrible situation happening to him/her and faces the disturbance and agitation aroused in that situation. He/she has to focus on experiencing these feelings and turns them into appropriate ones. If he/she can turn the unease into appropriate feelings and reactions, it will be possible for him/her to modify his/her behaviour in these scenarios. Ellis once points out that if people practise rational-emotive imagery several times a week for several weeks, they will be free from distress in the face of these scenarios. For instance, a man feels anxious and fearful of taunts whenever he greets the ladies; after several such imagery practices, the scenario changes into the ladies not responding, and he only feels a little disappointed but not devastated. This is the effect of rational-emotive imagery.

Role-play

There are emotive and behavioural elements in role-play. When a client derives a feeling from a scenario through the playing certain designated behaviour, the counsellor will demonstrate to him/her what changes can be made to replace inappropriate emotions with correct ones. For example, a university student may refrain from applying to graduate school for fear of being rejected and hence feeling 'I'm stupid'. Through role-playing the interview with the dean of graduate school, he/she will be shown his/her anxiety and irrational beliefs, followed by a challenge of such irrational beliefs as 'absolute necessity to be accepted by others' and 'non-acceptance means I'm stupid and incapable'.

Shame-attacking exercises

People may exhibit irrational shame in certain aspects. Ellis (1988) maintains that as long as we tell ourselves it is no big deal even if we are deemed a fool, it would be all right. The main point of this exercise is that the client does not feel a bit ashamed even if all others indicate disapproval with him. Very often these exercises involve minor breaches of social conventions, which usually turn out to be highly effective methods for overcoming the sense of shame, e.g. wearing highly 'avant-garde' clothes to catch others' attention in public, singing at the top of one's voice, asking a stupid question in a seminar, not leaving any tip to waiters, etc. Through these exercises, the client will realize that the feeling of shame is created by himself/herself while the others do not care as much as he/she has imagined. In the end he/she would realize that there is no reason to stop doing what he/she wants to do just because of others' reaction or possible disapproval.

Strategies on the behavioural level

Apart from changing the client's irrational beliefs on the cognitive level, REBT also involves actions. Only the actions arising from thinking can bring in real change. The following are the three most common methods in REBT.

Self-management procedures

This mainly refers to operant conditioning. It is not easy for the client to change his/ her long-established way of thinking, emotions, reactions and behaviours and to persevere in practising new modes of behaviour based on rational beliefs. Hence, when counsellors design cognitive or emotive homework for the client, they would ask him/her to reward himself/herself upon completion of the homework, and conversely, mete out punishment as agreed upon by the client and the counsellors. For instance, if the client likes listening to music best and hates doing the dishes, he/she would be allowed to listen to music on completion of the homework, and conversely, made to do the dishes.

Relaxation methods

The counsellor teaches the client some relaxation methods, such as deep breathing and muscle relaxation exercises, which they can practise when confronted with situations that cause fear and anxiety. This way the client can take the focus off his/ her irrational beliefs, thus minimizing the emotional disturbance.

Skills training

REBT holds that if clients learn more skills for dealing with different kinds of problems, their emotional disturbance would diminish, which would help them change their irrational beliefs. The training includes assertiveness training, problem-solving, and social skills training. The arrangement for training is contingent upon the circumstances of the individual client and can be conducted on an individual or group basis.

Reading and listening therapy

This is a characteristic feature of rational-emotive therapy. By means of reading and studying RET psychological literature, the client learns to establish for himself/ herself rational-emotive principles and foundations to help internalize a rational philosophy of life, which would also facilitate the progress of the counselling process. Also, to assist clients with reading difficulties (due to low level of education or young age), the RET counsellor will make use of audio or videotapes to compensate for their deficiencies in this aspect.

Moreover, as RET tends to be educative, a limited number of interviews may not be sufficient for making an impact. Hence, the counsellor will ask the client to listen to the recorded interviews on audio or video tapes to maximize the progress of counselling.

□ **Activity 4**

Application of Techniques

Study the following case carefully. Using the REBT technique for disputing irrational beliefs, help the client in question understand the cause of her emotions and behaviours, followed by counselling.

The Case

Yim Kwan-sum (pseudonym) is an S. 2 student with below-average academic performance. She often runs into problems with family members and teachers but is on good terms with Miss Chow, the social worker. She often talks to Miss Chow at recess and after class. One day, before recess, Kwan-sum dashed into the social worker's office and yelled at the top of her voice, 'The teachers are all mad dogs; they are always picking on me! Everybody talks in class, but they never punish the top student, those who've got good grades or the prefects! They only punish me and yell at me . . . They say I don't obey school rules, that I'm a scourge in the class. They tell the others not to follow my example or to befriend me . . . They had already punished me by making me stand, now they want to meet the parents, like I'm not already getting enough fists from mum and sis! Actually if my mum is not getting a divorce from dad, I wouldn't have felt so disturbed as to pour my heart out in class to my classmate, Kuen!'

Dealing with the Case

Apparently Kwan-sum is very unhappy with and has a lot of misunderstanding towards the way her teachers have dealt with her talking in class. If you were Miss Chow, the social worker, or a teacher Kwan-sum trusts, how would you make use of the techniques mentioned in this chapter to try to discuss with Kwan-sum why her teachers had 'treated' her like this?

Furthermore, apart from the disputing techniques, what other counselling strategies in this theory do you think can help Kwan-sum? Discuss this case in small groups and cite two or three techniques to illustrate.

Conclusion

The essence of REBT is to encourage people to overcome emotional disturbances with rational thinking and to establish a positive and rational philosophy of life so as to avoid being controlled by irrational thinking in one's behaviour and everyday life. It stresses that rational thinking can be learnt and the counsellor should direct the client, through various means, to acquire the new rational thinking and discard the old irrational one. Thus, REBT is a highly directive therapeutic method which requires the client to do homework to practise and consolidate the rational thinking and life skills learnt. Despite being directive, the counsellor does not adopt a cool and rigid demeanour. Instead, the counsellor works together with the client with great patience to analyse and clarify in detail his/her irrational thinking and help him/her with care and encouragement to resolve his/her problems and to establish a healthier mode of rational thinking.

The young people of today are living in a pluralistic society in an age of information explosion. Their thinking and behaviour are all the time bombarded by the family, peers and social trends. Being at a crucial stage of personal growth, they may appear aloof towards other people's comments and stick to their own way. In reality they care very much about how they are perceived by their family and friends. This often gives rise to emotional disturbance for many young people. As a teacher, if you can use this theory appropriately to encourage pupils to develop a rational philosophy of life, when they encounter problems in their lives, they may be able to deal with them with a rational and scientific mindset, so their tolerance level will be higher and their emotional disturbances would be minimized. Therefore, not only can REBT be used for individual, small-group or family counselling, it can also play a preventive role in the personal growth of young people.

Questions for Discussion

1. Discuss the characteristics of the REBT theory and analyse its feasibility in primary and secondary schools.
2. Distinguish between logical disputing and empirical disputing. Please cite three examples each to illustrate.
3. Client-centred therapy stresses genuineness, respect and empathy; behaviour modification techniques stress environment, behaviour and outcome. How would you summarize REBT's content?
4. Are there only eleven irrational beliefs as mentioned in the chapter? Have you encountered problems or disturbance caused by irrational beliefs other than these eleven? Please elaborate.
5. Do you think REBT is suitable for application by (prospective) teachers? Why?
6. There are quite a number of REBT-based personal growth or developmental teaching material/guidance activities/teaching plans available on the market. Try to collect some and evaluate them.

Relevant Websites

1. 認知行為治療 cognitive behavioural therapy
   http://www.nurse.org.hk/pdf/union/6109.pdf
2. 情緒困擾：認知治療在香港的應用及成效
   http://www.hku.hk/socsc/news/press/Cognitive%20Therapy/Cognitive%20
   therapy%20press%20conference_jul%2014.pdf
3. 校本資優情意教育課程教案示例十：ABC 情緒睇真 D
   http://prod1.e1.com.hk/education2/090-096.html
4. 尋常，尋夢想：情緒 ABC
   http://www.editworkshop.com/information_think_3.htm
5. 「人生過山車」棋盤遊戲
   http://www.edb.gov.hk/FileManager/TC/Content_6293/327%20boardgame%20
   training.pdf
6. 艾理斯學術思想
   http://article.aedocenter.com/OldBook/G-09.htm
7. 理性情緒行為治療於恐慌症伴隨憂鬱症個案之應用
   http://www.ceps.com.tw/ec/ecjnlarticleView.aspx?jnlcattype=1&jnlptype=5&jn
   ltype=44&jnliid=1455&issueiid=22836&atliid=272906
8. 理情治療法與圖書館館員之情緒管理（陳書梅）
   http://www.ntl.gov.tw/publish/suyan/52/1.htm
9. Cognitive Behavioural Therapy: The ABCs of Emotions—How Our Emotions
   Actually Work
   http://www.youtube.com/watch?v=1AYAJcOcXFE

Extended Readings

Chu, M. L., Tung, M. S., and Shu, Y. H. (2005). Application of Rational-Emotive Behavior Therapy in a Patient with Panic and Depressive Disorder. *Taiwanese Journal of Psychiatry*, 19(4).

Dryden, W. (1994). *Invitation to Rational-Emotive Psychology.* London: Whurr Publishers Ltd.

Dryden, W., and Neenan, M. (2004). *Counselling Individuals: A Rational Emotive Behavioural Handbook.* London; Philadelphia: Whurr Publishers Ltd.

Ellis, A., and Blau, S. (eds.) (1998). *The Albert Ellis Reader: A Guide to Well-Being Using Rational Emotive Behavior Therapy.* New York: Citadel Press.

Ellis, A., and Wilde, J. (2002). *Case Studies in Rational Emotive Behavior Therapy with Children and Adolescents.* Upper Saddle River, NJ: Merrill/Prentice Hall.

何長珠（1987）：《合理情緒治療法進階》。台北：大洋出版社。

盧靜芬譯（2005）：《理性情緒行為治療：抗拒的處理》。台北：心理出版社。

吳麗娟（1987）：《讓我們更快樂：理性情緒教育課程》。台北：心理出版社。

香港家庭福利會（1997）：《以小組形式促進家庭精神健康實驗計劃——認知行為小組治療法之小組工作員手冊》（第 2 版）。香港：香港家庭福利會。

References

Corey, G. (1991). *Theory and Practice of Counselling and Psychotherapy* (4th ed.). New York: Pacific Grove, Book/Cole.

Corsini, R. J., and Wedding, D. (eds.) (1995). *Current Psychotherapies* (5th ed.). Itasca, IL: F. E. Peacock Publishers, Inc.

Dryden, W. (ed.) (2006). *Rational Emotive Behaviour Therapy in a Nutshell*. London: SAGE.

Gibson, R. L., and Mitchell, M. H. (1999). *Introduction to Counselling and Guidance* (5th ed.). Upper Saddle River, NJ: Prentice Hall.

Ivey, A. E., Ivey, M. B., and Simek, Mogan (1993). *Counseling and Psychotherapy: An Multicultural Perspective* (3rd ed.). London: Allyn and Bacon.

McLeod, J. (1997). *An Introduction to Counselling* (2nd ed.). Hong Kong: Open University Press.

郭正、李文玉清、陳譚美顏（2001）：《輔導與諮商：多媒體自學教材學習指南》。香港：香港教育學院。

郭正、李文玉清（主編）（2006）：《輔導個案：示例與啟迪》。星加坡：McGraw Hill Education (Asia)。

姜忠信、洪福建（譯）（2000）：《認知治療的實務手冊：以處理憂鬱與焦慮為例》。台灣：揚智文化。

李茂興（譯）（1997）：《諮商與心理治療的理論與實務：學習手冊》。台北：揚智文化。

魏麗敏、黃德祥（2000）：《諮商理論與忌諱》。台北：五南圖書公司。

張安玲、王文瑛（譯）（1995）：《兒童與青少年團體工作》。台北：心理出版社。

7

Behaviour Modification Theory
From Research to Student Behaviour Guidance

Yuk Ching Lee-Man

Your proximity to either red or black ink decides your colour.
Like white silk, one turns blue or yellow depending on the colour of the dye.
Mencius's mother moved three times for her son, and (she) cut the shuttle
threads to remonstrate with her child.

(Chinese maxims)

Abstract

This chapter aims to introduce the development and the key ideas of B. F. Skinner's
behaviour therapy, including the theory of conditioning, its approach to human nature,
behavioural function analysis, behaviour modification techniques, the counselling
strategies and the various techniques that are employed by teachers. The chapter will
also clarify and correct many people's misconceptions about this theory, such as over-
conditioning and the negligence of emotions and feelings.

Objectives

This chapter will help you:
- understand the development and the key ideas of the theory of behaviourism;
- master the nature of human behaviour and the ABC behavioural function analysis;
- understand the relationship between individual behaviour and its environment,
  so as to influence and modify behavioural inclinations by means of tools such
  as reward and punishment; and
- apply the theory to everyday teaching and counselling through the study and
  familiarization of it.

Before You Start: Think and Discuss

1.   How do you think human behaviour is shaped? Can the shaped behaviour be modified?
2.   To the best of your knowledge, construct the notions of reward and punishment. Between reward and punishment, which one is more effective?
3.   What are the limitations in the suitability of behaviour therapy? Will it vary with the gender, age, education level and socio-economic background of the client?
4.   As a (prospective) teacher, would you adopt behaviour therapy as the main guiding theory for student counselling?

Introduction

The leading advocate of behaviour therapy was B. F. Skinner, one of the most influential psychologists of our time. Born in 1904 and deceased in 1990, he was hailed by many as the father of behaviourism. Behaviour therapy has been widely used in educational and clinical psychology, sharing its dominance with psychoanalysis and person-centred therapy and having immense impacts on the development of psychology. He designed the Skinner Box to study animal behaviour, from which he developed the theory of operant conditioning and applied it on the prediction and control of human behaviour.

Developments of Behaviourism

Classical conditioning

Early behaviourists, such as I. Pavlov in Russia, experimented on dogs to investigate the relationship between stimulus and response.
*   unconditioned stimulus (food) → unconditioned response (saliva)
*   unconditioned stimulus (food) + neutral stimulus (bell) → unconditioned response (saliva)
*   conditioned stimulus (bell) → conditioned response (saliva)

Operant conditioning

Skinner held the view that the above classical conditioning theory did not give a full picture of learning. Hence, he focused on the study of the effect of the consequence brought by the behaviour on the learning process. He found that the provision of a specific stimulus had the consequence of increasing or decreasing the frequency of repetition in the individual's behaviour.

- rat presses lever (behaviour) → gets food pellet (consequence) → repeats/ increases behaviour (reinforcement)
- rat presses lever (behaviour) → gets electric shock (consequence) → does not repeat/ decreases behaviour (punishment)

Skinner spent tremendous effort to present his ideals in his novel *Walden Two* (1948), which describes the operation of a utopian society based on the principle of behaviour reinforcement and weakening. This novel managed to rouse much controversy. His supporters regarded it as a model for establishing regional autonomies, while opponents saw it as the means an autocratic government would use to control people. In 1971, another book of his, *Beyond Freedom and Dignity*, again gave rise to widespread discussions. In this book, he challenges the traditional notions of self and dignity and considers them outdated. He boldly argues that there is no individual choice in human society and it has only been an illusion. The choices we make are based on our experience in the environment, which is to say our behaviour is a result of our earlier responses being reinforced or weakened. Thus, we must examine what kind of environmental factors can reinforce behaviour that is beneficial to individual development; the society can only improve in this way.

In the field of education, many teachers have been inspired by Skinner's research. They use reinforcement to increase students' motivation for learning and behaviour adaptation and to weaken undesirable behaviour.

❐ **Activity 1**

Think

Try to apply (a) classical conditioning and (b) operant conditioning to explain some common behavioural problems of students.

Key Ideas

View on human nature

According to the theory of behaviour therapy, human nature is neither good nor evil but neutral. The baby is a tabula rasa: paint it blue, and it will be blue; paint it yellow, and it will be yellow. In the course of personal development, the behaviour of the individual is shaped by environmental, social, religious and cultural influences. Through the modification and control of these factors, good behaviour can be developed and strengthened while undesirable behaviour can be modified. Besides, as this theory stresses scientific evidence and holds that behaviour can be observed and measured, the focus is placed on observable behaviour. Hence, for every problem there is a specific intervention target, process and outcome assessment. The goal of behaviour modification is achieved through systematic process design and implementation. The idea is to maintain or reinforce desirable behaviour and weaken or extinguish undesirable behaviour (for the individual or society), so as to achieve the goal of self-restraint and self-control.

Personality traits and behaviour

Unlike other schools of psychology, behaviourism does not assume the existence of personality traits for human beings and considers it unscientific. To understand human mind and emotion, one should begin with observable behaviour. With systematic tuning of the relationship between environment and behaviour, desirable behaviour can be reinforced and undesirable behaviour weakened. The main concepts are set out as follows:

1. Behaviour is shaped by its consequence, which means it depends on what happens to the individual upon the completion of a behaviour.
2. If a behaviour is followed immediately by reinforcer, the behaviour will be strengthened.
3. If a behaviour is not followed immediately by reinforcer, it will be weakened.
4. If a behaviour is followed immediately by punishment, the behaviour will also be weakened.
5. During the early stages of learning new behaviour, continuous reinforcement gives the best results.

6. When the learning reaches a certain target, it is best to maintain intermittent reinforcement during which reinforcement is given at variable or unexpected intervals.
7. Pay attention to the situational contexts of an appropriate behaviour. Human beings learn to manifest certain behaviour in a certain situation because this will lead to certain goals.
8. Most behaviours come from 'learning' and they can also be 'unlearnt'.
9. Human beings would repeat rewarded behaviour and avoid unrewarded behaviour. We have to reward agreeable behaviour if we want to modify nasty behaviour.

Behavioural problems and emotional disturbances

From the above introduction, it can be seen that the behaviour modification approach believes that most behaviour is acquired from learning. In the course of personal development, if an individual's appropriate behaviours are rewarded, his/her cognitive and emotional development as well as socialization will also be facilitated. On the contrary, if his/her appropriate behaviours are neglected while undesirable behaviours unduly reinforced, it will become the root of emotional and behavioural problems.

Behavioural function analysis

This process involves the gathering of information on the behaviour, analysing the causes of the problem behaviour, how the individual's adaptation has been hampered and the way the problem has been formed. This process can be summarized in three letters: A (antecedents), B (behaviour) and C (consequence), and hence is known as the ABC Behavioural Function Analysis.

A—Antecedent refers to the events or environmental factors that led to the target behaviour.

B—Behaviour manifestation refers to the target behaviour that needs dealing with.

C—Behavioural consequence is the consequence that befalls the individual after the manifestation of the target behaviour.

The respondents for the ABC Behavioural Function Analysis can be the student or people who know the student well (e.g. parents, teachers, classmates, etc.). The content has to be the environmental details related to the individual's problem behaviours.

❏ **Activity 2**

Contextual Analysis

During recess, when Tai-keung, an S. 3 student, and a group of students are playing football, their ball hits a prefect. The latter asks Tai-keung to present his student card so he can record the incident. Not only does Tai-keung refuse, he also strikes a defiant pose and yells at the prefect, using foul language. When the discipline teacher arrives at the scene, Tai-keung, in a cheeky manner, accuses the discipline teacher of allowing prefects to bully students. Behind him a crowd of students have gathered; several students are adding oil to the fire and criticizing school rules . . .

Based on the above situation, discuss the following questions:
1. What is Tai-keung's problem behaviour?
2. What happens before the manifestation of the behaviour? What are the situational contexts?
3. Which of the behavioural consequences in the situation would support his problem behaviour?
4. What changes in the environment does it take to give rise to a change in the behavioural consequences?
5. How does Tai-keung's behaviour inspire you as a (prospective) teacher?

As one analyses the above event with 'ABC', it is not difficult to see that Tai-keung's defiance stems from the group of 'on-lookers' behind him (the support of the crowd). His undesirable behaviour has been applauded and reinforced: he considers himself a 'hero' among the crowd and musters up his courage to further challenge the discipline teacher. At this moment, the discipline teacher should keep calm and avoid a confrontation as it would not only damage teacher-student relationship and the teacher's image, but also spur Tai-keung on to up the ante. It is better, therefore, for the teacher to first send the other students back to the classroom so as to isolate Tai-keung from his peers and their support. Only then the teacher can deal with the issue and avoid the pitfall of a teacher-student tussle!

Behaviour modification

Behaviour modification involves mainly the study of operant behaviour, i.e. the explanation of the relationship between the individual (including animals and humans) and the environment. Environmental factors could be the stimulus that controls the occurrence of a behaviour or they could also be the consequence that follows a behaviour—upon the appearance of a behaviour, its consequence is sufficient to affect the probability of the behaviour recurring. The consequence of behaviour modification could be reinforcement, punishment, time-out and extinction. In the school setting, behaviour modification involves simply the use of the above fundamental behavioural theories and techniques to influence students' behavioural inclination in a systematic and purposeful way. Of course, the teacher's purpose of doing so is only to achieve educational targets, complete classroom duties, or provide students with a suitable learning environment, but not to control the students.

Counselling Objectives

The following are the general objectives of student counselling with behaviour modification approach:
1.   Assist the individual in learning new and appropriate behaviour, and extinguish the old and undesirable one.
2.   The counsellor helps the client understand the relationship between his/her environment, his/her behaviour and the behavioural consequence.
3.   Help the client raise new learning requests to improve on existing conditions.
4.   Assess whether the client's resources and abilities will enable him/her to reach his/her targets.
5.   To be directly involved in the modification programme to change the client.

Counselling Strategies

As behaviour modification upholds scientific experiment as its basis, it stresses the logical approach in its counselling strategies. Figure 7.1 illustrates the steps in behaviour modification:

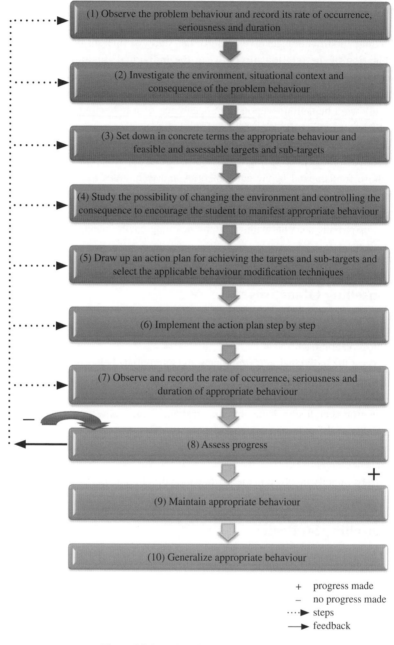

Figure 7.1 Steps in behavioural modification

Cautions for applying the above steps:

1. Observe the client (student): be objective, list the problem behaviours in concrete terms, their frequency of occurrence (the interval between occurrences), seriousness (the number of times they appear) and the duration of each occurrence. It is advisable to keep a record sheet.

2. Investigate the environment where the problem behaviour takes place (such as playground, classroom, or library), the student's purpose of performing that behaviour, and the actual consequence that befalls the student.

3. Discuss the problem behaviour with the student based on the information in 1 and 2, and draw up appropriate behaviour to replace the problem behaviour. Care must be taken to ensure that the appropriate behaviour is attainable by the student and assessable (observable) by the counsellor. Then write down the appropriate behaviour in the form of a target. If necessary, the target can be divided into several sub-targets to be attained step by step until all the targets have been reached.

4. Study how to change the environment and control the consequences so as to weaken and extinguish the problem behaviour and encourage the student to develop appropriate behaviour.

5. Draw up a concrete programme, like a contract, to attain the target. Use techniques such as reinforcers, extinction, and punishments appropriately, as well as setting up of models, role-play and self-control.

6. Implement the counselling/intervention programmes step by step.

7. After the intervention programme, observe and record the frequency of student's appropriate and undesirable behaviour, the intensity, and time of occurrence.

8. Compare the records of Step 1 and Step 7 (before and after intervention) to assess the effectiveness and progress of the programme.

9. If improvement is shown, encourage the student to maintain the appropriate behaviour and gradually reduce the reinforcers to enable the development of self-control.

10. If the individual keeps showing improvement, he/she can be guided to perform the same appropriate behaviour in similar or different situations. This is a 'generalization' of the appropriate behaviour. For instance, if the student can hold back the behaviour of 'leaving his seat' in the classroom, then advise him to do the same in the Music Room (or other special purposes rooms).

11. One thing that should be noted: if the student does not show any progress in the assessment in Step 8, it is necessary to re-examine the procedures from Step 1 to Step 7 and check if anything has gone wrong, so that rectification and improvement can be made.

☐ **Activity 3**

Application

It is necessary to be objective when applying behaviour modification techniques to deal with student problems. But very often when teachers criticize or berate students' problem behaviour, they inevitably resort to vague adjectives to describe subjectively the students' behaviour in the absence of objective supporting evidence. Now proceed to apply steps #1 and #2 above to describe concretely and objectively the situations of the three students below:

A.   Mung-ching does not care about his studies.
B.   Tai-sing disrupts classroom order.
C.   Ah Fan disturbs his classmates in class.

Counselling Techniques

Behaviour modification emphasizes the training and application of techniques. The following is a brief account of the techniques counsellors and teachers can employ:

Formulation of a behavioural contract

The counsellor and client work together to discuss the appropriate behaviour. After an agreement is reached, they set down the targets and sub-targets, and design the action plan towards these targets. Then the client is requested to write down in contractual terms the method and procedures to achieve the targets; he is encouraged to follow the terms in the contract and evaluate the progress regularly. The content of the contract comprises the following:

1.   A clear description of the target behaviour
2.   Method for gathering evidence (data)
3.   Kinds of reinforcers, when to be dispensed and by whom (clauses for reward and punishment)
4.   Timetable for evaluation
5.   Names and signatures of the signatories to the contract
6.   Date of signing of the contract
7.   Witness (if necessary)

The strength of this technique is that it enables the client to know clearly his/ her commitment, which facilitates its implementation and the evaluation of progress. Besides, the wording of the contract can be adjusted according to the client's literacy level. This can also be made into an important event by inviting a significant figure to be the witness, so the client will take the programme seriously and be more motivated to see it through. Most important of all, the formulation of the contract is mutually agreed and negotiated by both parties instead of being dictated by only one party (authoritative party such as the teacher or the parents) as in the signing of 'unequal treaties', otherwise it will lose its effectiveness.

❏ **Activity 4**

Formulating a Contract

Formulate a behavioural contract for a student's behavioural problem (such as missing homework or assignments) and describe briefly the time and detail of its execution. Show it in class.

The application of reinforcement

The counsellor has to first find out about the client's interests and likings in order to decide what reinforcement to use. Reinforcers can be primary or secondary. Primary reinforcers refer to necessities for survival, such as food, warm clothing and security. Secondary reinforcers are learnt, such as praise, encouragement, care, or even money and power. Reinforcers are also categorized as either positive or negative, the former referring to the consequence presented upon the performing of the appropriate behaviour so as to reinforce further performing of it. The latter, easily misinterpreted as punishment, actually achieves the same end through the removal of aversive stimuli. According to behaviour modification theory, both are able to encourage appropriate behaviour, although positive reinforcers are more effective.

Reinforcers can be further divided into:

(a) Social reinforcers—verbal: 'very good', 'keep going', 'I like it'; non-verbal: a smile, thumbs-up, applause. This kind of reinforcers can be delivered fast and easily, their interference with the learning behaviour is minimal, and they can be paired up with other reinforcers. The more variations there are in the language, facial expression and voice pitch, the more thorough the effect.

(b) Tangible reinforcers—stickers, stationery, candy and books. The gratification saturates quite easily and hence they are only suitable for relatively short-term programmes.

(c) Token reinforcers—stamps, token coins (tokens/coupon stamps).

(d) Activity reinforcers—privilege or favoured activities such as games, leisure reading and painting. This kind of reinforcers has their inherent limitations: e.g. impossible to be presented right after a behaviour; some activities may interfere with other students' learning; and less flexible.

Application of extinction and punishment

Extinction refers to the removal or termination of the reinforcing effect of undesirable behaviour and ending the reinforcing process. When a student manifests undesirable behaviour and the teacher and other students ignore him, he/she will lose interest and the behaviour will be weakened or extinguished. However, the following should be noted if extinction is to be used properly:

1. The behaviour is neither dangerous nor serious.
2. When the extinction procedures start, there is a chance that the student may augment his/her undesirable behaviour to reach his/her goal. The teacher may experience more trouble than before and hence must persevere.
3. If the extinction is not thorough, the wavering response may strengthen the undesirable behaviour which will become more difficult to change.

As for punishment, common sense tells us that it is effective in stopping undesirable behaviour on the spot. Yet we have found that using aversive or unpleasant consequences to suppress undesirable behaviour may also produce negative effects:

1. It leads to negative sentiments and affects interpersonal (especially teacher-student) relationships.
2. It leads to lying and escape behaviour (for fear of being punished).
3. Students will eventually believe that it is acceptable/or even effective to cause aversion in others.
4. Because of its ready effect, teachers' meting out punishment is reinforced (an increased inclination to use punishment as an easy resort).
5. The student may stop his/her undesirable behaviour to avoid unpleasantness without truly understanding how to establish good behaviour.
6. If improperly handled, the undesirable behaviour can rebound drastically. If punishment is unfortunately used by teachers as a means to vent their frustration, the situation may turn into a scenario of power struggle and revenge. Not only will it fail to modify students' problem behaviour, it will also aggravate the situation, disrupt learning and damage relations.

□ **Activity 5**

Complete the Following Table

Fill in the diagram with the respective means which the teacher uses to achieve the various consequences:

Positive reinforcement   Negative reinforcement   Punishment   Extinction

		Consequence	
		Increase behaviour	Decrease behaviour
Methods of application	Administer certain consequences		
	Remove certain consequences		

Factors affecting the effect of reinforcement and punishment

Many behaviour modification techniques may appear simple, but to be able to apply them properly, one must know their key points, practise continuously, and accumulate experience, in order for them to be effective. It is also true for the application of reinforcement and punishment. The following are points that deserve teachers' attention:

1. Timing

In order for the reinforcement and the punishment to be effective, the reinforcers or punishment have to be administered right after the behaviour; delayed or late administration would dampen their effect or even reinforce non-target behaviour. For example, Ming-fai has done well in maths exercise in class and warrants a reward. He should be praised right away (verbal reinforcement) or rewarded with a small gift (tangible reinforcement). Do not wait until the next day to administer the reinforcer, as Ming-fai and his classmates may have forgotten what happened the day before, and fail to connect the reinforcer and the behaviour; or he may mistake the teacher's praise as referring to other behaviour. Similarly, if Siu-lai has ripped her classmate's pictures, the teacher should punish her on the spot, otherwise, with the lapse in time, it may fail to modify her undesirable behaviour.

2.   Quantity and strength of the reinforcers

Not only must reinforcement or punishment be administered immediately; they should also be sufficient and strong enough to be effective. For instance, if Ling-ling talks in class and the teacher only reprimands her lightly and continues with the teaching, Ling-ling may only talk more, and it will be much more difficult for the teacher to stop her. If at the beginning the teacher had treated the matter sternly to show its seriousness, Ling-ling would have quieted down immediately and the undesirable behaviour would have been effectively stopped with one stern warning.

3.   The cause and effect relationship

Reinforcement or punishment (effect) follows the emergence of behaviour (cause). If there was no such behaviour in the first place, there would not be any reinforcement or punishment. In our daily life, however, adults often overlook the cause and effect relationship so the children have no frame of reference to follow. For example, Shiu-yip's father promises to buy him French fries if he gets three consecutive passes in dictation; Shiu-yip gets only two passes but because Dad is in a good mood, he buys him French fries anyway. In another school term, Shiu-yip gets four consecutive passes in dictation, but because Dad is too busy, he does not buy French fries for him. As a result, Shiu-yip doubts the sincerity of his father's promises and dampens the effect of behaviour modification.

4.   Individual differences

The effectiveness of reinforcement and punishment is relative; they work differently on different people and very much depend on the respective interests of the students. For the sweet-tooth Fattie, chocolates are effective reinforcers, but for the athletic Ko-sing, the opportunity to play basketball is more attractive. Hence, we have to take into account the students' own preferences when choosing the reinforcement or punishment in order to solve the problem.

Modelling

A lot of human behaviour is learnt by imitation, especially regarding social behaviour. Behaviour models can be found among significant others (such as parents and teachers), celebrities (such as movie stars and great men), and peers. The following principles govern the use of modelling:
1.   The level of the student's behaviour has to match that of the model.
2.   The model's attributes have to be similar to those of the student's or to his/her liking—gender, age and activity.

3. Let the student start from modelling more attainable behaviours.
4. Guide the student to study the model's behaviour in detail and with precision.
5. Reinforce his/her modelled behaviour.
6. Pick a model preferably from real life (in his/her immediate surroundings).
7. Pick various models to demonstrate the same behaviour target.

□ **Activity 6**

Picking a Model

Draw up an emulation target for a student (such as bicycle training). Then, based on the principles above, pick three to five models for him/her. Share your selection results in class with classmates.

Self-management

Self-management is both an effective technique to modify behaviour and a desired target of behaviour modification: even if the counsellor/teacher is not around, the client can still manifest appropriate behaviour. The best way to learn self-management is to let the client participate in the formulation, implementation and assessment of the programme so that he/she would feel he/she is heavily involved in the programme and not only fulfilling a passive role. When the appropriate behaviour becomes habitual, he/she will not need constant rewarding and will still be able to behave well in similar or different situations. Then it will be time to help him/her establish and expand the scope of self-management.

The strategies and procedures of self-management are similar to those of behaviour modification discussed in Figure 7.1 which readers can refer to directly. The only difference is that the client is taking greater initiative and capable of managing himself/herself without the outsider's—counsellor/teacher's help.

The Roles and Functions of the Counsellor

The counselling strategies derived from behaviour modification theory require the counsellor to lead and to instruct. The counsellor has to rid himself/herself of any subjective ideas and bias, take the scientific approach to carefully study the relationship between environment, behaviour and consequence, and then point out the client's problem and make recommendations for improvement.

During the counselling process, the counsellor has to apply different strategies and techniques and provide encouragement and support for the client to make improvement and progress. It is a rigorous and scientific undertaking. To a certain extent, the counsellor plays the roles of a 'scientist' and 'researcher'; he/she uses control measures in the programme to reach the expected goals. It is for this that some have criticized behaviour modification theory for being too mechanical and the relationship of counsellor and client as skewed. However, I do not agree with this criticism. Behaviour modification stresses the flexibility and changeability of behaviour. The gist of the approach is to use the environment, behaviour consequence and reinforcement to shape behaviour and the client will go on to internalize the shaped behaviour so that he/she will be able to control and improve himself/herself, a goal beneficial to both the self and others. From being controlled to self-control, from being disciplined to self-discipline—it is a process of personal growth, one which is far from being mechanical. Regarding the counselling relationship, with the role of giving direction, the counsellor easily gives an impression of being superior. Nevertheless, during the entire process, he/she has to respect the client's choice and let the client participate in underlining the improvement targets. Therefore, behaviour modification does not involve imposing the behaviour modification programme on the client; otherwise the guidance programme would have a very low chance of success.

Conclusion

Behaviour modification is widely used, covering nearly every aspect of society, in which education, clinical psychology, correctional services, vocational training and psychiatric rehabilitation are particularly relevant. Its strength comes from its ability in facilitating learning, helping the individual modify undesirable behaviour, and establishing appropriate behaviour with clearly defined targets and outstanding effectiveness. After training, counsellors or teachers are able to help those in need in a systematic manner. With more and more research on human behaviour, behaviour modification theory now put more effort to study the individual's cognition and emotions. Hence, the voice against this school for targeting only observable behaviour and neglecting emotions and the inner world of the client is gradually losing ground. Of course, it still has its limitations, which is why when applying this method, counsellors/teachers should take more consideration of the client's psychological factors other than environmental ones in order to achieve a more thorough result in the counselling.

Questions for Discussion

1. Do you agree with the rationale behind behaviour modification theory? Why?
2. Behaviour modification emphasizes the application of reinforcement, extinction and punishment. Try to define them and give examples for each. On the other hand, what could be the consequences if reinforcement and punishment are inappropriately used? Please elaborate.
3. Bullying is prevalent nowadays in primary and secondary schools. Try using behaviour modification to help:
   (a) those who bully; (b) the victim; (c) the on-lookers
4. Do you agree that once the individual's behaviour is changed, the problem is solved?
5. Reflect on your own experience in the process of growing up and personal development and find modes of behaviour which illustrate and support the ideas of behaviour modification theory.
6. Behaviour modification theory tends to give the counsellor a dominant and instructional role. Do you think it is good or bad for the teacher? What needs to be taken into consideration in its application?

Related Websites

1. Behaviour Modification Strategies in Education
   http://www.ehow.com/way_5245903_behavior-modification-strategies-education.html
2. Behaviour Modification in the Classroom
   http://www.ldonline.org/article/6030
3. Behaviour Management
   http://specialed.about.com/od/behavioremotional/a/5step.htm
4. Lesson Plan for Behaviour Modification
   http://www.ehow.com/way_5465273_lesson-plan-behavior-modification.html
5. How to Use a Behaviour Modification Program for Kids
   http://www.ehow.com/how_4852425_use-behavior-modification-program-kids.html
6. Behaviour Modification - Child Behaviour Problems - Out of Control Teens - Behaviour Modification Schools
   http://www.nationalyouth.com/behaviormodification.html
7. Behaviour Management for ADHD Children
   http://add.about.com/od/treatmentoptions/a/Behavioralmodi.htm
8. Behaviour Modifications for Autistic Students
   http://specialed.about.com/cs/devdelay/a/autistic1.htm

9. How to Create a Behaviour Modification Plan for Students With Behavioural Disabilities
   http://www.ehow.com/how_13758_create-behavior-modification.html

Extended Readings

Rachman, S., and Eysenck, H. J. (1997). *The Best of Behaviour Research and Therapy*. Oxford: Pergarnon.

Spiegler, M. D., and Guevremont, D. C. (2010). *Contemporary Behavior Therapy* (5th ed.). Belmont, CA: Wadsworth, Cengage Learning.

蕭寧波（2000）：〈五個印花可以換甚麼？〉。《亞洲輔導學報》，第 7 期，頁 53–63。

蕭寧波（2002）：〈懲罰以外〉。《亞洲輔導學報》，第 1 及 2 卷第 9 期，頁 68–78。

蕭寧波（2003）：〈適得其反：論消減與塑形〉。《亞洲輔導學報》，第 2 卷第 10 期，頁 215–233。

References

Bergin, A. E., and Garfield, S. L. (1994). *Handbook of Psychotherapy and Behavior Change* (4th ed.). New York: John Wiley and Sons, Inc.

Corey, G. (1991). *Theory and Practice of Counselling and Psychotherapy* (4th ed.) New York: Pacific Grove, Book/Cale.

Corsini, R. J., and Wedding, D. (Ed.) (1995). *Current Psychotherapies* (5th ed.). Itasca, IL: F. E. Peacock Publishers, Inc.

Gibson, R. L., and Mitchell, M. H. (1999). *Introduction to Counselling and Guidance* (5th ed.). Upper Saddle River, NJ: Prentice Hall.

Ivery, A. E., Ivery, M. B., and Simek, Mogan (1993). *Counselling and Psychotherapy: An Multicultural Perspective* (3rd ed.) London: Allyn and Bacon.

McLeod, J. (1997). *An Introduction to Counselling* (2nd ed.) Hong Kong: Open University Press.

郭正、李文玉清（主編）（2006）：《輔導個案：示例與啟迪》。新加坡：McGraw Hill Education (Asia)。

郭正、李文玉清、陳譚美顏（2001）：《輔導與諮商：多媒體自學教材學習指南》。香港：香港教育學院。

何中廉、梁展鵬（2000）：《課室行為改造 ABC》。香港：文林出版有限公司。

樂國安（1999）：《從行為研究到社會改造：斯金鈉的新行為主義》。武漢：湖北教育出版社。

李茂興（譯）（1997）：《諮商與心理治療的理論與實務：學習手冊》。台北：揚智文化。

林孟平（2000）：《輔導與心理治療》（第 11 版）。香港：商務印書館。

8

Roles and Functions of the Class Teacher

Guidance for Pupils' Personal Growth on an Individual and Class Basis

Ching Leung Lung

I have come that they may have life, and have it to the full.

(*John* 10:10)

Abstract

This chapter discusses guidance for pupils in their whole person development on individual as well as class bases, and describes the guidance roles and functions of class teachers in Hong Kong. On the individual level, it holds that the personal attributes and attitudes of the class teacher facilitate the development of a personal teacher-pupil relationship which will help the pupils enhance their self-esteem and serve as a basis for initial counselling. On the class level, the class teacher facilitates the collective growth and development of the whole class by establishing a positive class culture, showing care for maladjusted pupils, and planning and carrying out year-long whole person development programmes.

Objectives

This chapter will help you:
- ascertain the guidance roles and functions of the class teacher;
- offer guidance to pupils in their personal growth on an individual level;
- understand the special nature and stages of development of the class community;
- establish a positive classroom culture;
- care for maladjusted pupils in the class; and
- plan and carry out year-long whole-class development programmes.

Before You Start: Think and Discuss

1. What do you think are the roles and functions of the teacher?
2. What is the guidance role for class teachers in Hong Kong? Is there a difference between class teachers in primary and secondary schools?

3. Do you have any experience in receiving individual guidance or guiding others? How has the experience inspired you in caring for your pupils?
4. What kind of preparations do you think the class teacher should make at his/her first meeting with pupils?
5. How can a class teacher establish a positive classroom culture?
6. What methods and strategies can the class teacher use in caring for maladjusted pupils?

Introduction

As the ancient Chinese writer Han Yu said, 'In ancient times, all scholars had a teacher. The teacher passes on the right way, imparts knowledge and resolves problems.' The position of 'teacher' comprises different roles and functions, and the impact of Han Yu's interpretation of the duties of a teacher is still being felt today. In Hong Kong, new recruits are often assigned by the school to take up the duty of a class teacher. They have to face a myriad of challenges such as full-time teaching, taking care of the pupils, taking up administrative duties on the way, and organizing extra-curricular activities. In Case Study 1, the new class teacher Miss Lam can finally return to her desk after a day's teaching. Let us have a look at Miss Lam's situation. Can you point out Miss Lam's roles and functions?

Case Study 1

School finishes for Miss Lam who is into the fifth day on her new job. She has just hung up the phone and returned to her desk. She finds on her desks all sorts of documents and work schedules, e.g. The XXX School Guideline for New Teachers, a list of pupils of special learning needs, and circulars to parents. Added to them are rolls of notice board paper, piles of student workbooks, sheets of extra-curricular activities application forms, minutes of meetings, pupils' journals, half-finished subject worksheets . . . there are loads of work for her to finish. It is only the fifth day and Miss Lam is feeling tired out.

Roles and Functions of the Class Teacher

Wu (1987) argues that the teacher plays the role of the parent (strict father and gentle mother) who provides for the various needs and offers social support, the evaluator who grades the pupils and assesses the learning outcomes, as well as the guide who helps the pupils realize their potential. Alongside the social advancements and the emergence of the knowledge-based economy, the roles and functions of the teacher are continuously evolving and becoming ever more complex. Wang et al. (2005: 81–83) hold that the roles of the teacher are now concentrated in the two main areas of education and administration. Table 8.1 lists in detail the various roles and functions of the teacher.

Table 8.1 Roles and functions of the teacher

Areas	Roles	Functions
Education	1. Teacher	Imparts knowledge; facilitates student learning
	2. Evaluator	Enhances teaching outcomes; responsible for the selection of talent for society
	3. Socializing agent	Helps pupils learn the rules of adult society to prepare for the future
	4. Parent	Helps pupils grow in the family-like school community; feels the warmth, security, sense of belonging to this community and self-respect
	5. Counsellor	Helps pupils attain a balanced state of emotions, concentrate on school work, and develop a healthy personality
	6. Mentor	Passes on the right 'way' and virtuous conduct in a natural and pleasant environment
	7. Doctor	Treats problem pupils, e.g. pathological behaviour, psychological problems, defective value system and lack of moral soundness
Administration	8. Facilitator	Achieves educational goals, and assists the principal and other personnel in school duties
	9. Bridge	Helps pupils understand, accepts and carries out the school's policies, curriculum and rules; lets the school authority know the pupils' reactions and opinions
	10. Follower	Follows the lead of the principal and assumes the rights and responsibilities of participation in and execution of various administrative measures.

Although Wang et al. (2005) have given quite a comprehensive overview of the teacher's diverse roles and complex functions, they have not delineated, portrayed or highlighted the teacher's roles and functions from the guidance perspective.

Guidance roles and functions of class teachers in primary and secondary schools in Hong Kong

Most schools in Hong Kong use the class system, where 30 to 40 students are assigned to a class, and the school assigns teachers to be class teachers responsible for the moral education, social development and the various needs of the pupils (Lung 2000). Hong Kong society has undergone rapid changes in recent years such as a reduction in family size and an increase in the number of working parents. With a decrease in parent-child contact and a rising divorce rate, together with the negative influence brought about by the media and the peers, schools have become more and more important for pupils' development. Schools have to support and partner with the family, and help pupils adapt to changes and face the many challenges and difficulties (Lam 1995; Luk-Fong 2005; Ng 2008). As parents, employers and society expect more from schools, the demands on teachers and class teachers in nurturing students' whole person development have also increased (Education and Manpower Bureau 2001; Curriculum Development Council 2002). Hence, class teachers have to know the unique character of each of his/her pupils in the class to establish a good teacher-pupil relationship; he/she has to communicate with the pupils and understand their needs; he/she has to make good use of the form period to help his/her pupils develop and solve their problems.

After free compulsory education was introduced in 1978 in Hong Kong, the problem of school pupils flouting school rules in and out of school came to the fore. Thus the Education Department issued in 1986 *Guidance Work in Secondary Schools: A Suggested Guide for Principals and Teachers*, which defines for the first time the duties of the class teacher.

A guideline is of course welcome, but when examined more closely, one discovers that this guideline tended towards a rather passive approach in dealing with pupil behavioural problems, which is a pity. It had not taken into account pupils' moral, physiological, vocational and social development, nor did it care about their whole person development. In view of this, the Education and Manpower Bureau published a new school guidance guideline in 2004, which stated that as the class teacher is the front-line person in closest contact with the pupils, he/she is crucial in the prevention of disruptive behaviour and the identification of problem pupils. The guideline pointed out several important issues that class teachers should pay attention to (Education and Manpower Bureau 2004), viz.:

1. Facilitate the implementation of guidance programmes.
2. Encourage pupils to organize class activities to enhance class morale and the sense of belonging.
3. Pay attention to the pupils' needs, and identify problem behaviour in its early stages, with a view to offering guidance before the behaviour worsens.
4. Meet the parents or guardians to exchange information on the pupil and find out about the family members' perception of the pupil.
5. Attend case meetings, and evaluate pupils' needs and coordinate related services together with school administrators and professionals such as school social workers and education psychologists.
6. Assist in dealing with cases through long-term observation of the pupils and their progress.

The above official documents have emphasized and confirmed the guidance role of the class teacher, and the 2004 guideline is an improvement over the 1986 one by giving more weight to pupils' social development and home-school collaboration, as well as introducing the developmental and preventive guidance.

Regarding the consultative and guidance roles and functions of teachers, the opinions varied among scholars. The author believes the guidance role of the class teacher should focus on guidance and initial counselling contact. Costar (1980), McIntyre and O'Hair (1996), and Kottler and Kottler (2004) also argue that teachers should participate in these two aspects.

Regarding guidance, the scope of guidance work for the teacher in the classroom is wide, which includes assessing pupils' needs, and organizing, implementing and reviewing guidance activities and programmes of the class. The class teacher has more opportunities and room to design guidance activities and programmes which target pupils' needs and to help them develop a positive self-concept, e.g. the use of 'Riding on the Train of Growth' (新成長列車) (Kwok 2004) in the Primary Personal Growth Curriculum and the use of 'We're in the Same Class' series (同班系列) (Cheung et al. 1998) in form periods in secondary schools to promote a comprehensive personal growth of the students.

As for initial counselling contact, Kottler and Kottler (2004) hold that as teachers are not professional counsellors, they are not responsible for counselling work, not least because they have not received full training in counselling. Nevertheless, teachers spend a lot of contact hours with their pupils; they understand them more than the parents or the professional counsellors in the school, know their needs better, can learn about their problem at the first instance, and are therefore suitable for short-term initial counselling contact. Gibson and Mitchell (2008) suggest that teachers build on the trust and respect between teachers and pupils to establish a good and therapeutic teacher-pupil relationship, listen to their needs and help them solve their problems. In this way, even though the teacher may not be 'counselling' the pupil in the conventional sense, they can still play the role of the initial 'counsellor' in the school. Because of this, Costar (1980) argues that for the general students, the teacher may offer better guidance and initial counselling than the counsellor, psychologist or social worker. McIntyre and O'Hair (1996) are of the view that many schools, especially primary and secondary schools, may not have the professional counsellor at hand, nor is there often the need to call for his/her emergency service. So teachers and class teachers are responsible for guidance or initial counselling contact with the pupils, providing them with support and advice especially in the following areas (Costar, 1980; Kottler and Kottler, 2004; Gibson and Mitchell, 2008):

1. career development
2. educational planning
3. social development

4. home-school co-operation
5. general school adjustment

☐ **Activity 1**

Try to recall your experience of personal growth education in primary school or in secondary school, and share what you think you have gained from them and areas that need improvement.

Helping Students on an Individual Level

Enhance pupil's self-esteem

Scholars and educationists (Lam 1995; Sheldon, Elliot, Kim and Kasser, 2001; Lung and Chan-Tam 2004; Bracken, 2009) generally agree that among the many psychological traits, self-esteem is the most crucial. Self-esteem can affirm an individual's worth and confidence, the latter of which is instrumental in strengthening one's resilience, increasing adaptability to life, and helping one face the hardships and challenges in life. Self-esteem is an individual's self-evaluation, which can be high or low. The scope of self-evaluation can cover academic, interpersonal, emotional, physical, familial and competence aspects (Bracken 2009). People with high self-esteem believe in their competence and potential, and hence enjoy a greater chance of success: higher grades at school, a greater chance of achievements at work, and, more likely, a satisfying and happy marriage and family life. This is why the class teacher has to help pupils raise their self-esteem, the strategies for which are listed below (Lung and Chan-Tam 2004: 108):

Table 8.2 Educationists' strategies for raising pupils' self-esteem

Approach	Educational Psychology	Psychological Counselling
Aims	Promote learning (emphasis on academic pursuit)	Help people help themselves (emphasis on social skills, emotion and physical development)
Targets	Emphasis on the whole school and the class community	Emphasis on care for small groups and individuals
Strategies	1. Principles and missions of education 2. Teacher's attitude and how learning is organized	1. Help pupils establish the right attitude and direction of personal growth 2. Guide pupils towards enhanced self-esteem by means of self-coaching

If the teacher can incorporate educational psychology theory, education principles and missions with the right attitude in class and careful planning of pupils' learning process, he/she will be able to facilitate learning among individuals as well as the class community, and help the pupils establish a sound learning foundation and master the correct attitude and direction of study. Using a psychological counselling approach, and through form periods, extra-curricular activities, and small group guidance, the class teacher can help the whole class and those with special needs to help themselves by establishing the right attitude and value system, and encourage them to perform self-reflection on their own to raise their self-esteem.

Major factors for establishing personalized teacher-pupil relationships

A teacher's personal attributes and attitudes are very important for raising pupils' self-esteem (Lawrence 1996). Kao (2008) holds that certain personality attributes and attitudes are required of a teacher, namely positive thinking, a mild and bright personality, being optimistic and possessing a sense of humour. He/she also has to create an ambience of warmth in the classroom, sustain the learning ethos, and establish personalized relationships with the pupils in a genuine, accepting and respectful manner, in order to raise the pupils' self-esteem and develop them as whole persons. Actually, this idea is in line with what Lam (1984; 2000) and Rogers (1983) believe to be the basic requirements of a counsellor: empathy, positive regard and genuineness. The class teacher has to establish a certain degree of rapport with the pupils before he/she can help them open up and solve problems. 'Empathy' means the class teacher has to put him/her in the pupils' shoes to understand their feelings and inner world, and to feel and think from their perspectives, so that he/she will understand them better and avoid unnecessary misunderstanding and conflict. 'Positive regard' means the teacher is willing to respect and accept the pupils' nature, affirms that each one of them is a unique individual, and believes that they can be changed and shaped. In this way, the teacher will be able to appreciate the pupils' achievements and strengths, and accommodate and accept their shortcomings and weaknesses, so that the latter will lower their defences and have the courage to be responsible for their own actions. 'Genuineness' means that the teacher holds dialogues with the pupils on an equal basis, and expresses appropriately and sincerely his/her own feelings and experiences, actively inviting the pupils to exchange and share with him/her their inner worlds and difficulties and establishing mutual trust.

❏ **Activity 2**

Teacher's Attitude in Counselling and Practice of Skills in Initial Counselling Contact

Based on the three fundamental attitudes in counselling (genuineness, respect and acceptance), rank the following teacher responses to the pupil in order of quality, 1 being the highest.

Chow Siu-mei of 6A says indignantly, 'If I have done wrong, you can punish me, but why am I not allowed to bring a cell phone to school? My grandfather is in hospital. What can we do if my family wants to ring me in an emergency? Besides, I've turned the phone off and haven't used it in class. Why can't I bring a cell phone to school? It's so unreasonable!'

Teacher A: The school doesn't allow cell phones because it doesn't want you to lose your belongings. Your criticism of the school has gone too far!

Teacher B: I understand that you're very unhappy about this school rule. You're angry because you think it's unreasonable.

Teacher C: You're unhappy about the school's prohibition of cell phones. Do you think this rule is unreasonable?

Teacher D: Do you think that as long as you haven't used the cell phone in class, you can bring one to school?

Teacher E: School rules have been laid down after careful consideration. How can you be so radical?

Teacher F: Say no more. You've already broken the school rules ten times this month! You must've brought your cell phone to school to show off before your classmates.

Initial counselling contact with individual pupils

Initial counselling contact is made when a teacher intervenes actively on finding out a pupil's special needs, difficulties or personal growth problems. He/she approaches the pupil to solve the problem. In this process, teacher and pupil face the problem together and look for a solution. Kottler and Kottler (2004) and Chou (2003) point out that the counsellor (the teacher) should in the helping and counselling process facilitate the client's (the pupil) personal growth. The whole process consists of seven stages: establishing the context, building the relationship, exploration, evaluation and diagnosis, drawing up a plan, taking actions, and completion of the counselling.

Helping Students' Personal Growth on a Class Basis

Preparations for first meeting with students

When a new class teacher first practises classroom management, apart from learning from experience, he/she must take care to establish a unique and positive teacher image in front of the pupils. This cannot be attained by being friendly; rather, the professional image of a teacher is established through the teacher's professional knowledge of the subject, lively modes of instruction, diverse teaching techniques and systematic classroom management. The first impression he/she gives to the pupils is also very important. Hence a new class teacher can make the following preparations:

1. The setting: check that the classroom is clean, the desks and chairs are neatly arranged, the passageways are unobstructed, and there are enough desks and chairs for the class.
2. The information: learn the names of all the pupils in advance, read their personal files to gain an understanding of their interests, character, family background and academic profile. If necessary, consult the pupils' former class teacher.
3. Psychological preparation: prepare an outline of the initial address to the class, e.g. a brief introduction of oneself, a welcome note to the class, the new collective goals and modes of interaction to be proposed to the students, etc.

The attributes of the class community and its stages of development

Scholars (Kong and Ho 2006; Qi 2006; Zhong 1995) believe class communities may possess the following characteristics:

1. It is a community in which pupils spend most of the day for over a year.
2. It is set up with school education in mind; its goal, content, and methodology framework have to match pedagogic principles and the educational missions of the school.
3. Its main purpose is to help pupils in their personal growth, particularly their whole person development, which differs from production-oriented business groups.
4. In order to realize its goals, the class community has to accept the teacher's purposeful and conscious influence, and not according to the pupils' preferences.
5. For the pupils, the class community was formed on a random and mandatory basis. Thus, even though they are of the same age, their needs, ability, and personality can be entirely different, which can easily lead to conflicts and disagreements.

In view of the above five characteristics, the class teacher has to take great care in managing the development of the class community so as to ensure its coherence and unity. In general, a class community goes through three development stages:

Stage 1: Conflicts between individuals

For the pupils, in a newly-formed class community, they would explore and develop the possibilities, which may give rise to the gradual formation of small circles, each having its own turf, leading to conflicts.

Stage 2: Conflicts between the demands of the community and the individual

This is the initial stage of the conflicts between the teacher and the pupils. Individual pupils disregard, or even resist, the teacher's instruction; disagreements may also arise among the teacher, class committee members, and the pupils, leading to conflicts.

Stage 3: Gradual dissipation of internal conflicts by demand of the community

The success of this stage depends on the cooperation and understanding between the teacher and the pupils. They work together to build a positive classroom culture, so that the disagreements among the small circles will dissipate and the potential of individual pupils can be realized.

❐ Activity 3

Role-play

Split the class into two groups. One group drafts an address by the new class teacher to the pupils on the first day of school. The other suggests what the teacher can say to the pupils (e.g. a story, a brief lecture or a personal note) or do when small circles emerge in class.

A Positive Classroom Culture

Regarding the establishment of a positive classroom culture, many views have been proposed by researchers (Cheng 2002; Gao and Xia 2006; Kong and Ho 2006; Qi 2006; Cheng 2008), some exploring the concepts and directions for development, while others proposing practical courses of action.

Among the many proposals, Cheng (2007; 2008) stresses the need for the class teacher to initiate and apply guidance skills to establish a positive classroom culture; in other words, it is to combine management and group counselling skills to unleash the positive energy of the class and alleviate the pupils' negative and deviant behaviour. On the other hand, Kong and Ho (2006), and Cheng (2002) focus on action and application. The following are some examples of their management strategies for initiating a positive classroom culture:

Visionary leadership strategy

'Visionary leadership' means that the teacher leads discussion on class development with the pupils to forge and pursue a higher goal which is then sloganized (e.g. 'A Healthy Lifestyle Brings a Rainbow Life') (Kong and Ho 2006: 16). This will become the joint endeavour of the whole class and the teacher.

The visionary leader can use the following as starting points:

(I)   Design a name and an emblem for the class.

(II) Pin the class name and class goals in big print on the front and back walls of the classroom to enhance the effect of contextual teaching. For instance, if the class goal is to cultivate a sense of belonging, the theme for classroom decoration could be '1D is my home' (Kong and Ho 2006: 15).

(III) If resources are plenty, T-shirts and class badges can be made to enhance the sense of class unity.

(IV) Set achievement targets for inter-class competitions in the school.

(V) Set performance targets for academic subjects and instil a disciplined approach to realizing them, e.g. the slogan for learning objectives can be 'Always finish the day's homework and everyone will get promoted', or 'Diligence and practice make a scholar and a sportsman'.

Class ethos forging strategy

'Class ethos' refers to the cultural ambience of a class which embodies its activity, culture, spirit, and orientation. The forging of the class ethos depends on the class teacher's leadership, professional demonstration and practice. Based on the pupils' disposition, needs and existing modes of interaction, the teacher will make adjustments and create a positive learning environment, leading the members of the class to love and help one another in their whole person development (Cheng 2007).

The main steps in forging a positive class ethos are as follows:

(I)   The class teacher discusses with the pupils to establish goals for learning, living and service.

(II) Point out the main methods for reaching these goals and remind pupils to cooperate with one another.

(III) The class teacher has to set a good example and abide by the conditions laid down to reach the common goals.

(IV) The class teacher joins the pupils to participate in inter-class and inter-school activities to promote a sense of belonging within the class, and, from there, cultivate a unique ambience to forge a positive, united and mutual-aid class ethos.

Universal participation strategy

In classroom management, the class teacher should readily accommodate different opinions and needs of the pupils and let all of them participate in open discussions, laying down class rules, designing class activities and electing representatives of class affairs. Decisions made along democratic lines would inspire the pupils to place their trust in their teacher and feel a sense of belonging to the class.

The main points for promoting democratic participation in classroom management are as follows:

(I)   During the form period, the class teacher discusses with the pupils to establish learning goals, class rules and the allocation of class duties, e.g. for class rules, establishing whether it is permissible to run around the classroom.

(II) Welcome suggestions and proposals from all pupils, allow suggestions to be discussed and passed, e.g. the establishment of a reading club in the class (Cheng 2002: 24).

(III) Important issues have to be open for consultation in class and agreed upon using the one-person-one-vote system.

(IV) Ready volunteers can be given priority in assuming class duties.

Empowerment strategy

In management theory, empowerment means the enhancement of the function of an organization. When applied to classroom management, it means the class teacher delegates to a suitable degree leadership work and duties to the pupils and encourages them to do the job well, thereby raising the positive energy of the class.

Empowerment in classroom management can begin as follows:

(I)   Establish a specialty service system and a learning service system. For example, the 'little IT agents' will be responsible for helping the teacher turn on the computer, and the 'little poets' responsible for leading the class in reading aloud texts between classes.

(II) Allocate, when appropriate, duty posts according to pupils' performance to promote positive competition among them and spur them on in their work.

(III) Present rewards and honours to pupils who render services.

(IV) Provide a title for every pupil in the class who leads or provides services, such as class monitor, lunch coordinator, environment officer, hygiene prefect, and school uniform supervisor. Alternatively, they can serve as leaders or become members of various groups, such as the academic group, recreation group, notice board group, library group, and audio-visual group.

Encouragement and recognition strategy

Under the encouragement and recognition strategy, the class teacher continues to give pupils positive encouragement, to sustain their good behaviour. In terms of classroom management, this can also enhance the pupils' identification, satisfaction and solidarity with the class.

As for the pedagogic activities and classroom management strategies, the class teacher can adopt the following encouragement measures:

(I)   Share his/her positive expectations with the pupils to produce a self-fulfilling effect on their part.

(II) Implement a reward programme, e.g. Good Pupil Reward Programme—'Star of the Month', to let pupils discover their merits as stimuli for further learning achievements (Kong and Ho 2006: 16).

(III) Let the pupils affirm their own merits with the teacher's encouragement, so they will aspire to further learning achievements.

(IV) Celebrate the pupils' progress so that they will feel the satisfaction of their learning outcomes and sustain their effective study.

(V) Describe at times the roads to success of famous people to motivate pupils to learn and study diligently.

(VI) Study the pupils' background and help them get rid of factors not conducive to learning.

❐ Activity 4

Case Study

There were five classes last year. When the classes were regrouped this year, 3A was made up of one-fifth of the pupils from each previous class. At the beginning of term, every pupil was cautious. They would wait and see the reactions of others before giving their own opinions. The class teacher has observed the pupils for some time and taken special note of some of them:

*   'Big Mouth' loves talking and chatting with classmates.
*   'Critic' often disparages classmates and points out others' shortcomings or mistakes.
*   'Nanny' likes helping others, keen on class duties, albeit a bit too aggressive at times.
*   'Taciturn' rarely expresses his opinion, but has his own way of doing things.
*   'Joker' likes to joke whether in class or at recess, and likes to tease others as well.
*   'Aggressor', burly and strong, often threatens classmates with physical strength.
*   'Participator' participates in all sorts of extra-curricular activities, is proactive, but his/her academic performance is not up to par.

With such an eclectic mix of pupils, there is little cohesiveness among them. Try to apply the five strategies for positive class culture and suggest how you can help unify this class and instil in them a sense of belonging, so they will be able to realize their own potential.

Strategy for the care of maladjusted pupils

When pupils encounter adaptation problems in learning, emotion, and social relationships, or exhibit deviant behaviour, apart from giving them personal help, the class teacher can make use of the following strategies (Cheng 2008; Lo 2009):
1. 'Peer group support strategy' which includes the following:
    (I)   Study groups for academic subjects: within each small group, the pupils learn and discuss the subject together, the more competent pupils helping the less ones.
    (II)   Homework discussion groups: upon completion of homework, the pupils exchange and mark their own work, followed by discussion and corrections.
    (III) Collaboration in class duties: the more experienced pupils lead the less experienced to complete class duties.
    (IV)   Group-based growth programme: each group has the right to establish short-term learning goals and monitor one another in their personal growth.
    (V)   Group trouble-shooting: when a group member encounters social, emotional or learning problems, other members of the group have to actively offer assistance, facing the difficulties and solving the problems together.
2. 'Class learning support strategy' mainly targets the pupils who lag behind in their studies. It works on three levels:
    (I)   Reciprocal consultative learning: set aside weekly support hours for each academic subject, when the more competent pupils lead discussions, answer questions and solve problems posed by the less competent ones.
    (II)   Remedial learning: in small groups, discuss and correct common errors in exercises; consult the teacher only when the problem cannot be solved among the pupils.
    (III) Learning support for crucial knowledge: subject teachers preside at the weekly after-school classes to help pupils' whose performance is not up to par acquire the crucial knowledge.
3. 'One-to-one mentorship strategy' is a mentorship scheme implemented in the class to target pupils with clear learning problems or deviant behaviour. The school's discipline and guidance team pairs the pupils with mentors who are either their favourite teachers or volunteering parent. They will provide the pupils with extended one-to-one special care and support.

☐ **Activity 5**

Case Study

In the 'Peer group support scheme', Lai-fong, whose English competence is very high, often uses vocabulary that other classmates have not learnt to show her linguistic prowess. On the other hand, Chi-yuen, whose English ability is weaker, does not like English lessons and answering questions. They have been assigned to the same group by the teacher to study together. What problems may such an arrangement create? What kind of guidance and instructions should Miss Chan give to the participating pupils in the scheme before and during the process?

Planning and implementing 'year-long whole person development' activities

After the teacher has laid down the class goals with the pupils, in order to promote the pupils' whole person development, he/she has to prepare a draft of the year-long development programme. He/she can divide the goals into short, medium and long terms, plan the year-long implementation schedule, and invite pupils and parents to collaborate. The following is a class teacher's draft for the year-long whole person programme with headings and activities, with the focus on learning guidance (academic) and class community guidance (social relationship, personal growth, and vocational development) (Student Affairs Committee, Ministry of Education 1993: Cheung et al. 1998; Kong and Ho 2006):

Table 8.3 Key guidance activities for the first term

	Learning Guidance	**Class Community Guidance**
Sep.	1. Review and evaluate summer vacation assignments 2. Decorate the classroom and the notice board in concerted effort	• Get to know new classmates • Election of class committees and the allocation of duties
Oct.	1. Announce checking out procedures and management methods of the class library 2. 'Smart Reading': personal reading programme	• 'Rule of Law': laying down class rules • Individual guidance for maladjusted or misbehaving pupils
Nov.	1. 'Little Encyclopedia of Memory': sharing memorization and reading skills	• 'Little Angels Scheme': promoting mutual help and care among classmates • Strengthen discipline in everyday life and nurture good habits
Dec.	1. 'Secret Learning Weapons': setting study timetables and starting revision groups 2. Learn about the meaning of district elections	• 'Integrity': steering pupils towards honesty and integrity during examinations and away from cheating
Jan.	1. 'Gold in Books': showcasing and rewarding academic achievements	• Review one's own conduct and behaviour for the current term

❏ **Activity 6**

Designing Activities

Divide the class into groups and design a year-long whole person development programme for P. 1/P. 3/P. 6, or S. 1/S. 3/S. 5.

Conclusion

This chapter begins by pointing out that apart from being an educator, an evaluator, an executer of school education policy, the teacher is also a guidance provider who assists in the pupils' whole person development. The teacher needs to possess personal attributes and attitudes, such as respect, empathy and genuineness, to be able to help his/her pupils grow and enhance their self-esteem so that they will be more confident and capable of facing difficulties and challenges. Although teachers are not professional counsellors, they are often required to provide initial counselling contact with the pupils during their day-to-day interaction in the classroom. The entire counselling process consists of seven stages: establishing the context, building the relationship, exploration, evaluation and diagnosis, drawing up a plan, taking actions, and completion of the counselling session.

For his/her first meeting with the pupils, the class teacher has to make contextual, informational as well as psychological preparations, as the first meeting is crucial in determining the kind of relationship to be forged between the teacher and the pupils. Every class community has its characteristics and stages of development, namely conflicts between individuals, conflicts between the individual and the demands of the community, and the gradual dissipation of internal conflicts by demand of the community.

This chapter emphasizes that the class teacher has at his/her disposal five strategies for promoting a positive class culture, namely: visionary leadership strategy, class ethos forging strategy, universal participation strategy, empowerment strategy, and encouragement and recognition strategy, all of which have an immense impact on the pupils' positive learning and personal growth. In helping those who have adaptation problems, the class teacher can make use of the peer group support strategy, class learning support strategy, and one-to-one mentorship strategy. In order to foster the whole person development in class, the class teacher has to plan a year-long whole person development programme.

Questions for Discussion

1. Among the many roles of the teacher, which ones do you play best? Why? Which ones do you not play very well? Why? How can you improve it?

2. Against what background and under what circumstances have the guidance roles and functions of the class teacher evolved in Hong Kong? What are your views on these roles and functions?

3. When the class teacher offers personal growth guidance to individual pupils, he/she has to know how to make the initial counselling contact. In this counselling process, the teacher's genuineness, respect and acceptance are three essential conditions. Which one do you think is the most easily attainable, and which one the most difficult to attain? Why?

4. When applying the strategies for the establishment of a positive class culture, what difficulties do you expect to encounter during their implementation? Suggest corresponding solutions.

5. For pupils with low motivation for learning, which strategies among those for helping maladjusted pupils are more feasible? Why?

6. What are the principles and directions for planning and implementing a year-long whole-class development programme?

Related Websites

1. Guide to curriculum for maladjusted children
   https://cd.edb.gov.hk/la_03/chi/curr_guides/Maladjusted/index-ema.htm
2. 班主任之友
   www.bzrzy.com
3. 教協班主任資料冊
   http://www.hkptu.org/profession/html/classteacher/html/content.htm
4. 班級經營策略
   http://www.zlips.hlc.edu.tw/home/002/new_page_8.htm
5. 訓輔人員專業手冊
   http://www.hkdca.org/handbook/index2.html

Extended Readings

皮愛民（主編）(2000)：《首席教師的思考：新世紀班主任工作藝術》。長沙：湖南人民出版社。

齊學紅（主編）(2006)：《今天，我們怎樣做班主任》。上海：華東師範大學出版社。

王曉嵐 (2000)：《班主任：愛的藝術家》。上海：學林出版社。

鄭學志（主編）(2005)：《班主任工作招招鮮》。長沙：湖南師範大學出版社。

References

Bracken, B. A. (2009). Positive Self-Concepts. In R. Gilman, E. S. Huebner, and M. J. Furlong (eds.), *Handbook of Positive Psychology in Schools* (pp. 89–106). New York: Routledge.

Costar, J. W. (1980). Classroom Teachers in the School Guidance Program. *International Journal for the Advancement of Counseling*, 3(2): 147–59.

Gibson, R. L., and Mitchell, M. H. (2008). *Introduction to Counseling and Guidance* (7th ed.). Upper Saddle River, NJ: Merrill.

Lawrence, D. (1996). *Enhancing Self-esteem in the Classroom* (2nd ed.). London: Paul Chapman.

McIntyre, D. J., and O'Hair, M. J. (1996). *The Reflective Roles of the Classroom Teacher*. Belmont, CA: Wadsworth.

Rogers, C. R. (1983). *Freedom to Learn for the 80s*. Columbus, OH: Charles E. Merrill.

Sheldon, K. M., Elliot, A. J., Kim, Y., and Kasser, T. (2001). What is Satisfying about Satisfying Events? Testing 10 Candidate Psychological Needs. *Journal of Personality and Social Psychology*, 80: 325–39.

Kottler, J. A., and Kottler, E. 著，孫守湉、林秀玲譯 (2004)：《教師諮商技巧》。台北：心理出版社。

高鴻怡 (2008)：〈高效能導師心情故事寫真：從成功經驗中探尋正向管教策略的基本元素〉，《學生輔導季刊》，第 105 卷，頁 100–119。

高謙民、夏青峰 (2006)：《今天，我們怎樣做班主任·小學卷》。上海：華東師範大學出版社。

郭志丕總編 (2004)：《新成長列車：小學生命成長課程》。香港：文林出版有限公司。

江哲光、何碧愉 (2006)：《學校改進行動：用「心」的班級經營》。香港：香港中文大學教育學院：香港教育研究所。

教育部訓育委員會 (1993)：《領航明燈：國民小學導師手冊》。台北：張老師出版社。

教育署 (1986)：《中學學生輔導工作：給校長和教師參考的指引》。香港：政府印刷局。

教育統籌局 (2001)：《香港教育制度改革簡介：終身學習，全人發展》。香港：政府印務局。

教育統籌局 (2004)：《中學輔導》，瀏覽日期：2004 年 10 月 23 日，http://www.emb. gov.hk/FileManager/TC/Content_2264/role4_c.pdf

課程發展議會 (2002)：《基礎教育課程指引：各盡所能，發揮所長（小一至中三）》。香港：課程發展議會。

林孟平 (1984)：〈師生關係：學校教育的關鍵〉。《香港中文大學教育學報》，第 12 卷第 2 期，頁 18–23。

林孟平 (1995)：〈以健康自我形象為核心的全校參與活動〉，《教育質素：不同卓識之匯集》，頁 148–171。

林孟平 (2000)：《輔導與心理治療》。香港：商務印書館。

羅慧燕 (2009)：〈香港融合教育的發展與「融合」式的校長領導〉，載於吳迅榮、黃炳文主編：《廿一世紀的學校領導》（頁 45–60）。香港：學術專業圖書中心。

龍精亮 (2000)：〈促進學生成長和愉快學習：班主任角色〉。《學與教喜悅》。香港：朗文出版社。

龍精亮、陳譚美顏 (2004)：〈教育工作者如何提升學生的自尊感〉。《教育曙光》，第 50 期，頁 106–114。

陸方鈺儀 (2005)：從系統理念看家庭與小學輔。《基礎教育學報》，第 14 卷第 1 期，頁 101–120。

齊學紅 (2006)：《今天，我們怎樣做班主任‧優秀班主任成長之路》。上海：華東師範大學出版社。

王以仁、陳芳玲、林本喬 (2005)：《教師心理衛生（第二版）》。台北：心理出版社。

吳靜吉 (1987)：〈教師角色〉。《張老師月刊》，第 19 卷第 4 期，頁 69–71。

吳迅榮 (2008)：《家庭、學校及社區協作：理論、模式與實踐—香港的經驗與啟示》。香港：香港專業圖書中心。

張儉成、龍精亮、陳潔貞等 (1998)：《同班幾分親》。香港：香港教育圖書公司。

鄭崇趁 (2007)：《台北縣卓越學校經營手冊：指標系統》。台北：北縣中小學校長協會。

鄭崇趁 (2008)：〈正向管教理念中的班級經營策略〉。《學生輔導季刊》，第 105 卷，頁 30–41。

鄭麗玉 (2002)：《班級經營：致勝實招與實習心情故事》。台北：五南圖書出版社。

鍾啟泉 (1995)：《班級經營》。台北：五南圖書出版公司。

周甘逢、徐西森、龔心怡等 (2003)：《輔導原理與實務》。台北：高雄復文圖書出版社。

9

Roles and Functions of the Class Teacher

Guidance for Pupils' Personal Growth on a School Basis

Ching Leung Lung

The Master said, 'When I walk along with two others, they may serve me as my teachers. I will select their good qualities and follow them, their bad qualities and avoid them.'

—*The Analects*, Confucius (551–479 BCE), tr. James Legge

Abstract

This chapter discusses how the class teacher can foster pupils' whole person development within a school context, and describes his/her roles and functions within the larger framework of whole school guidance work. The class teacher works under the principal's leadership, collaborates with the discipline and guidance team, communicates with parents, and makes good use of the support from the professional sectors and the community at large. He/she must be able to adopt the appropriate attitude, skills and strategies in interacting with parents of varying backgrounds and temperaments. Where a parent displays threatening or challenging tendencies, the class teacher can apply the conflict resolution approach effectively, in order to win the parent's support towards helping his/her child's growth.

Objectives

This chapter will help you:
- understand the roles and functions of the class teacher within the framework of whole school guidance work;
- enhance collaboration and communication within the discipline and guidance team;
- understand the mode of collaboration and channels for communication between the class teacher and parents;
- identify the four main types of parents and manage their requests in general; and
- apply the conflict resolution approach in resolving the conflicts arising in parent-teacher conferences.

Before You Start: Think and Discuss

1.   What are the roles and functions of the class teacher in whole school guidance work?
2.   How does the class teacher achieve effective collaboration with the discipline and guidance team?
3.   Normally, under what circumstances will the class teacher confer directly with parents? During the interview, what are parents' general expectations and fears?
4.   What kind(s) of parents will the class teacher commonly encounter in parent-teacher conferences? What kind(s) of parents do you fear most? Why?
5.   What strategies can you use when dealing with challenging and threatening parents?
6.   What forms of professional and community support are there in and outside the school to assist the class teacher in solving problems involving students and parents?

Introduction

Guidance for pupils is not the sole responsibility of the class teacher, and therefore he/she needs to understand the positioning of his/her guidance role, and collaborate with the principal, the senior teachers, the entire teaching staff and parents to support students in their development (Lung 2010). Case Study 1 describes what Miss Cheung sees in the corridor. If you were Miss Cheung, what would your reaction be? What is your view of the discipline teacher's way of dealing with the incident? What would you have done? How would you deal with a possible complaint by the parents?

Case Study 1

Miss Cheung is 2B's class teacher. As a novice teacher, she is not familiar with the discipline and guidance policy of the school and its application. One day, she was walking along the corridor and saw several pupils fighting in the 2B classroom. It was clear that Chi-keung was the one being beaten up, and his eyes were sending out a distress signal when they met with Miss Cheung's. His parents once complained to the school about his classmates, who called their son derogatory names and taunted him. By then the discipline teacher had rushed into the 2B classroom and announced that the whole class would be punished.

Whole School Counselling: The Functions of the Class Teacher

In 1990, the Education and Manpower Bureau suggested in Report No. 4 (Education and Manpower Bureau 1990) that schools should adopt a 'whole school approach to guidance' to raise the quality of education. The approach stresses the collaboration of the entire staff of the school under the leadership of the principal to create a learning environment characterized by care, trust and mutual respect. This would help pupils realize their potential and enhance their self-esteem, thus embracing the education ideal of 'whole person development'. Since then, the Education Department has adopted this approach as the main direction in school guidance.

Apart from being responsible for individual and class guidance, the class teacher has also to assist in the whole school guidance programme (Figure 9.1).

In the division of labour in school guidance, the principal assumes the multiple responsibilities of leading, supporting, supervising and coordinating guidance and discipline, career guidance, extra-curricular activities and other related functional groups. The guidance teacher, responsible for drawing up the whole guidance programme, has to collaborate with the various systems in the school, especially the discipline teacher, to implement the school discipline and guidance initiatives. The entire teaching staff can make suggestions on their own initiative, and assist in carrying out activities which promote pupils' personal growth, while the in-house social worker and educational psychologist provide professional support for teachers and pupils.

The class teacher has to communicate with the principal frequently to report the conditions, needs, progress and achievements of the class in a professional exchange. In case of a crisis or a special incident, such as drug abuse by pupils in the class, or repeated complaints from controlling parents about school administration or management, the class teacher has to confer with the principal for instruction and support.

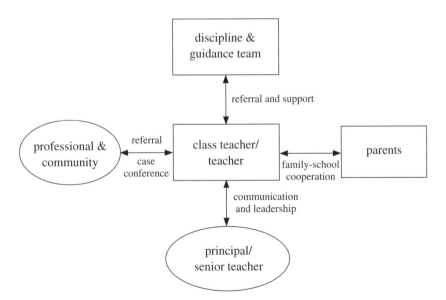

Figure 9.1 A class teacher's participation in whole school guidance

Collaboration between the Class Teacher and the Discipline and Guidance Team

Integrating discipline and guidance

Within the school's discipline and guidance system, the senior management—including the guidance and the discipline coordinators—has to work together with the teachers in drawing up guidance and discipline policies, so that the latter identifies with the ideals and goals laid out. The whole school would then be in a position to systematically implement developmental measures in discipline and guidance. Being on the front line of the implementation, the class teacher has to work closely with the discipline and guidance team to facilitate the various activities, such as guidance for personal growth and leadership training.

Discipline and guidance are complementary, but not conflicting or contradictory. Lam (2008) points out that they are two processes leading to the same outcome, and each has its own functions but they are essentially complementary in nature, in fostering students' whole person development.

Internal referral and collaboration

When a pupil is troubled and encounters serious difficulties relating to learning, emotions, health, family and behaviour, the class teacher has to seek assistance and support from the discipline and guidance team, especially if the case: (I) is beyond the scope of the teacher, such as criminal or legal matters; (II) involves professional support, such as a pupil having suicidal tendencies; (III) is beyond the duty of the teacher, such as a family problem requiring long-term follow-up; and (IV) causes emotional distress for the teacher due to its urgency or sensitive nature, such as a pupil's crush on the teacher. In these cases, the class teacher will have to make a referral, as shown in Figure 9.2.

In the 'whole school' approach to discipline and guidance, every school has to discuss with its entire teaching staff the following four questions regarding policy-making:
A. What are the criteria and examples for referral?
B. How to make effective referrals?
C. How teachers teaching the same class can collaborate effectively?
D. How to collaborate effectively with guidance teachers/ the social worker?

❐ **Activity 1**

Miss Ma has found out that her pupil Chun-kit once slit his own wrist, and recently he has had mood swings, accompanied by frequent squabbles with his classmates, at times leading to physical violence.

If you were Miss Ma, how would you work together with the discipline and guidance team to help this student?

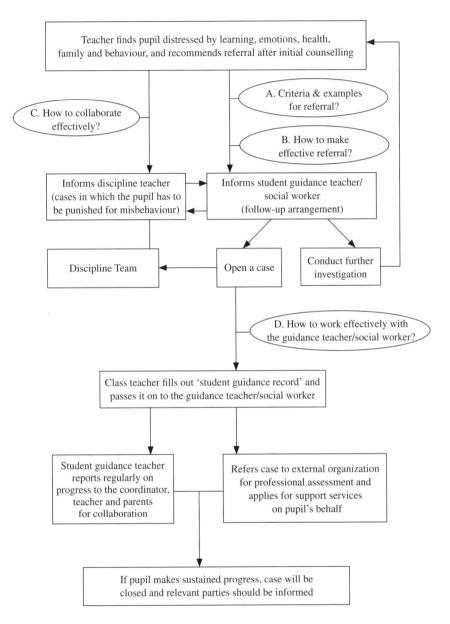

Figure 9.2 The mechanism of pupil referral by the class teacher for guidance services

Collaboration and Communication between the Class Teacher and Parents

Mode of collaboration between the class teacher and parents

As parent participation is the key to a successful guidance policy, the class teacher serves an important communicating role in the home-school cooperation. The mode of cooperation is generally categorized as either 'separate responsibility' or 'shared responsibility' (Pong 1999). 'Separate responsibility' is a more backward mode of cooperation, in which the school is responsible for imparting knowledge and supervising pupils' daytime activities, while the parent is responsible for providing resources and supervising the pupil in the evening. Only when the pupil encounters problems will the two parties confer and exchange information to attempt resolution. It is 'problem-based', rather than 'development-based'. On the other hand, most schools adopt 'shared responsibility' nowadays, where family and school complement each other in a unified approach to cultivate the pupil. Undoubtedly, parents know their child's personality and developmental history better than teachers, while the latter, equipped with professional training, are more informed regarding the pupils' psychological development and the nurturing of cognitive abilities. Therefore, both parties have to communicate and collaborate in a systematic and regular manner, in order to gain a comprehensive understanding of the pupil. Parents have the right of access to the information, accountability and education obligations regarding their child's learning and development at school. They have to join hands with the school in the education of their child, and hence home-school cooperation is necessary.

Communication modes between the class teacher and parents

It is a fact that 'shared responsibility' creates a greater link between home and school, and the frequency of contact and communication between parent and teacher increases. In his study on collaborations among the family, school and community, Ng (2008: 160) suggests a list of areas of communication between the parent and teacher, and the respective feasible actions to take:

Table 9.1 Areas and actions for developing the parent-class teacher link

Area	Action (example)
1. Conduct bilateral communication	A greeting, circular, letter, telephone call, or Parents' Day at the commencement of an academic year or term
2. Support or help with the child's learning	Parent-child study projects, parent-teacher meetings, volunteering in school activities, and workshops on parents' supervision skills
3. Participate in school activities	Invite parents to become members of the parent-teacher association or participate in its activities; attend parenting workshops, parent seminars, and courses for parents
4. Assist with the running of the school	Invite parents to become school volunteers, classroom assistants, library assistants, lunch assistants, and part of the home-school communication network
5. Offer views on school policies	Invite parents to participate in school policy consultative committees, parent consultative meetings, and school regulations consultative meetings
6. Participate in school policy-making	Invite parent representatives to join the school's policy-making group and become members of the school council

Ng (2008) believes that to forge a good collaborative relationship between the parents and teacher, bridging activities promoting bilateral communication is particularly important. If the teacher can follow up systematically and establish regular contact with parents to enhance communication, understanding and mutual trust, misunderstanding and conflicts will be reduced.

Strategies for a Class Teacher in Dealing with Parents

Factors of consideration in interviews between the class teacher and parents in general

Among the many ways of communicating and collaborating, the most direct and challenging type of contact between the class teacher and the parents is the parent-teacher meeting on Parents' Day. If a class teacher desires to see a child's development through concerted effort with the parents, he/she must be aware of the drawbacks and residual effects of the previously popular mode of 'separate responsibility'; and also, avoid a 'problem-oriented' approach. He/she must be acquainted with a number of factors of consideration which come into play in parent-teacher interaction, including: discrepancy between parents and the teacher in their roles and beliefs, parents' expectations and fears, the keys to seeking parent cooperation, and the main points for the meeting on Parents' Day.

1. Discrepancies between the parents and teacher in their roles and beliefs

    Discrepancies in roles and beliefs may emerge when parents and teachers attempt to work in collaboration. Both need to respect the uniqueness and contribution of the other party, and complement each other. Table 9.2 is a brief description of the aforementioned discrepancies:

Table 9.2 Discrepancies in roles and beliefs between parents and teacher

Parents	Teacher/Class teacher
Emotionally-charged, fully involved	Dispassionate, professional and objective
Care about child's needs on all fronts	Sees child as a member of a group
Thorough understanding of the child's character and personal growth	Professional knowledge in children and teaching
All-inclusive round-the-clock responsibility	Fixed working hours and fixed duties
Hope to give the child the best	Hopes to give all pupils the best

2. Parents' expectations and fears

    Because of their differing roles, the beliefs held by parents and teachers may also differ. Parents often have certain expectations of a teacher in a meeting. They hope the teacher recognizes and respects that they love their children and have done the best for them; that the teacher trusts and acknowledges their competence and efforts made; and, above all, they hope the teacher can provide more information and observations of their child's performance at school. On the other hand, parents are afraid of the teacher's criticisms of their child, of direct or indirect accusations at themselves, and of any negative impact brought about by the exposure of incidents relating to their child or to the family.

3. Keys to seeking parents' collaboration

    In order to facilitate collaboration with parents, the teacher has to bear in mind the following in interviews:
    (a) Emphasize the pupils' positive performance in school, their progress, contributions and potential.
    (b) Show understanding of the parents' love for their child and the efforts made.
    (c) Let the parents express their opinions, and (i) listen with empathy; (ii) respond and identify with genuineness; (iii) encourage and acknowledge parents' actions and efforts.
    (d) Work with the parents in a positive way to seek feasible solutions.
    (e) Guarantee full support from the school.

4. Main points for interview on Parents' Day

    The interview with parents on Parents' Day can be divided into four stages. The main points for each are as follows:

    (a) The preparation stage

    The teacher prepares the students' learning records, such as report cards and homework samples. He/she can also make a simple list of all the questions or issues to be discussed as a reminder.

    (b) The interview stage

    The teacher needs to show his/her amicability towards the parents, for instance, by shaking hands and maintaining eye contact. Before the interview begins, he/she should also make positive comments about the pupil regarding the pupil's behaviour in class, his/her conduct and academic performance, highlighting strong subject areas and progress. The teacher can begin the interview by asking open-ended questions to find out more about the pupil, especially information known only to the parents. In reporting the pupil's problems, the teacher should adopt a consultative and communicative approach, inviting the parents for their views and working out a plan together to help the pupil improve.

    (c) The closing stage

    The teacher can invite parents to summarize what they have gleaned from the interview and what actions they will take. He/she can also take this opportunity to ask the parents' opinion on what he/she can do to help.

    (d) The review and reflection stage

    The teacher can review and reflect on the following after the interview: (I) Have the parents been reassured? (II) Have the pupil's strengths and weaknesses, as well as the direction for improvement, been identified in the interview? (III) Was the discussion focused on the pupil and not on the parents or the school?

❏ **Activity 2**

Apart from the discrepancies in beliefs between parents and teachers, and parents' expectations and fears, what other factors do you think stand in the way between the two parties in terms of effective communication and collaboration?

Strategies for dealing with four main types of parents

Apart from an awareness of the general parental perspectives, when it comes to certain types of parents—the worried parent, the disappointed parent, the angry parent, the silent parent, the parent who shows up unexpectedly and the manipulative parent (Kottler and Kottler; Gorman 2004)—the teacher needs to be prepared psychologically and have the appropriate attitude and skills. He/she must be open and adjust his/her mind-set, and should not label and stereotype parents. The following section describes four common types of parents that one may meet on Parents' Day, and the respective communicative strategies that the class teacher can draw reference from:

Parent I: The worried parent who feels helpless about his/her child

Description: This type of parents may have a relatively low socio-economic status or his/her education level. He/she may have tried to show care towards the child, and has attempted different methods to improve a less-than-ideal situation, but with little success. He/she feels helpless despite having great concern for his/her child.

Example: 'I know Mei-sum needs me a lot, but I've just arrived in Hong Kong and don't know much about the place and where to seek help. Mei-sum is getting more and more rebellious! As I have to work, I don't know how to teach her. She's not bad by nature! Please help her. Your words are ten times more effective than mine!'

During the interview, the parent appears uneasy, shows a lack of self-confidence and has little eye contact with the teacher. However, he/she has a lot of respect for the teacher's opinion, and is willing to co-operate with the school.

The teacher's corresponding strategy: Be attentive to the parent's worries and gain an understanding of the various measures for improvement the parent has tried before. Begin by acknowledging the parent's previous efforts, and point out the actions which may have had an effect. Enhance his/her confidence with the assurance that the efforts were not in vain, and encourage perseverance while indicating full support from the school and teachers.

> 'You are the one who knows Mei-sum best. You have mentioned that when she was young and was living on the Mainland, you helped her with her revision and she was among the top of her class. Your relocation to Hong Kong is already a big challenge. This place is new to you, and you have to work to support the family while taking care of your daughter; it is already quite a handful! Mei-sum has mentioned to me before that you are a very capable person who can stand up for yourself. Let's think of some ways to help her together. You'll help her at home, and I'll do what I can here at school.'

Parent II: The disappointed parent who does not understand his/her child

Description: This type of parents has certain expectations for his/her child. He/she would make all the arrangements for the child's daily schedule, revision time and extra-curricular activities, taking little account of the child's interests and talents, and often forcing the child to realize the parent's own dreams. He/she does not quite know what is on his/her child's mind.

Example: 'Every day I help Kai-mei with revision, checking homework, and accompany her to running and swimming practice. She always gets full marks for her rehearsal dictations at home. Why has she got only a B for her overall grade? She's a really good girl, and we have high expectations for her. We hope she'll do well in schoolwork as well as in sports, as her father was once swimming captain at university and we are hoping to send her abroad for further studies and training. But she doesn't seem to care very much about schoolwork. I always have to coax and cajole before she finishes the work. She doesn't seem a bit fazed by such results this time. Teacher, can you tell me how else should I be raising her?'

During the interview, the parent never stops talking, and wishes the teacher could collaborate with them to raise their children's academic results and performance.

The teacher's corresponding strategy: This type of parents needs someone to listen to them from beginning to end. The teacher should listen attentively and help them see the discrepancies between 'their own expectations' and the 'real situation'. Appreciate the meticulous arrangements they make for their children but at the same time make them understand their children's interests, abilities and feelings, as the latter have their own limits, hopes and plans for their lives.

'Kai-mei is fortunate to be able to engage in so many extra-curricular activities, and to have parents that take time out to supervise her homework and revisions. But wouldn't she feel a bit tired and short of time for work if she engages in so many extra-curricular activities? As far as I know, Kai-mei has never revealed in class that she can swim, that she practises swimming and competes in swimming events. She reveals in her journals that she feels the pressure of studies because she's afraid of disappointing her parents with poor results and not being picked for the swimming team. Here they are. (Show the journals.) When you said she has little initiative for studying, it may have to do with the kind of subjects. You were right: her English teacher has told me that Kai-mei has a lot of initiative in answering questions in class, but her maths and science teachers told me she is rather passive in class and is unwilling to do the reports. As we're all here to help her, I suggest we try to understand Kai-mei more, you at home and me at school, regarding her feelings and wishes, let her express her feelings and thoughts, and let us study her interests and aspirations to nurture her appropriately and in a focused way!'

Parent III: The angry parent who covers for his/her child

Description: During the interview, this type of parents may become rude or resort to violent language. The teacher must observe and recognize that the anger usually comes from setbacks and being wronged. In such a situation, it is best for the teacher to assume an understanding, empathetic and accepting attitude. Most importantly, recognize their love for their children and the fact that they have done the best for their children.

Example: 'I told you last time: we're rich and Yiu-cho would not steal his classmate's cheap stationery. This time it's even more ridiculous: you accuse him of stealing his classmate's wallet! I give him $2,000 a week; he can't possibly steal from his classmates! He's got everything: his schoolbag is an expensive one, his phone is the latest model, and his stationery and notebooks are all brand new. It's unthinkable that he should steal from his classmates. It's either you are trying to wrong him, or the other classmates are trying to frame him. You should investigate properly!'

During the interview, the parent's emotions are volatile. He/she may stand up, point his/her finger at the teacher and scold nonstop, or even bang the desk.

The teacher's corresponding strategy: It is best for the teacher to assume a calm, polite and accepting manner, and allow the parents to release their anger. Use the technique of emotion reflection and active listening to first calm them down and understand the causes for their infuriation. During the interview, the teacher's personal integrity and professionalism may be called into question. The teacher's self-control and avoidance of a heated argument will benefit both parties. Of course, the teacher should draw a bottom-line: when the situation gets out of control or the parent fails to calm down, another teacher or the coordinator should intervene or take over, or another appointment should be made, as the parent also needs some time to calm down and regain his reason.

'We're not trying to mete out severe punishment for Yiu-cho; we want to give him a chance. We just want to report what has happened today to his parents. We would very much want to understand Yiu-cho's life at home, that's why we have this appointment today. What's happened to Yiu-cho has made us teachers very sad, let alone his parents! I totally understand your feelings at the moment. I think Yiu-cho is blessed to have been born into a well-to-do family. We have the evidence for today's incident: his classmates witnessed it, Yiu-cho himself has admitted it, and so the school wants to know why. What we emphasize is not punishment, but how to help him right the wrong and get him back on the right track in his personal growth. We do not want to see him re-offend. There's an adage that 'the boy steals the needle; the man steals the gold'. Theft is a criminal offence—once convicted, it is punishable with criminal record and a custodial sentence. At that point, it would not be just a small entry on the school record. We would like to see with you his recent condition, whether he's been acting in an unusual manner, and who he has been seeing so as to understand the causes for this action and discuss how to help him. We're all here for his well-being!'

Parent IV: The manipulative parent who complains and confronts

Description: This type of parents has more confidence and are better educated; they understand, to a certain extent, how the school is run, but they are unhappy with it; they may even be socially privileged or in authority positions. These parents would complain to the teacher directly, or through the complaints expressed in an indirect way what they want the teacher to do to have things their way.

Example: 'Ka-him was already very strong in English back in Canada. I believe he must be among the top ten here. But his score this time round is such that I really think it must be due to poor teaching or it's a clerical error. I know your director Mr. Chan very well. Do I need to talk to him about hiring native speakers to teach them English? Or would you want to double-check if it's a marking error? Or is the paper just too difficult? I'm not sure if you local teachers here have all passed the English benchmark test.'

During the interview, the parents look apparently cool-headed and rational, and keep an alienation stance with apparently no personal feelings involved. They rationalize a lot in an unremitting and aggressive way.

The teacher's corresponding strategy: The teacher has to remain calm, level-headed and confident; follow professional standards and refuse to succumb to manipulative means. At this moment the teacher has to listen carefully at the parents' requests, distinguish between the reasonable and the unreasonable, clarify the disagreements between points of view and try to reach a consensus, agree to disagree, pay attention to and follow-up on reasonable requests, and discuss with the school authority the more dubious and unreasonable requests before giving any response, least of all making hasty promises. The teacher needs support from others such as the principal, the coordinator and senior teachers to discuss strategies.

'Ka-him's English performance is quite good. This is something both of us know. The many teachers who have taught Ka-him all think very highly of him. Perhaps this time it's just a hiccup on his part, or it could be due to some other factors, as many in his class have said they misread the questions. Why don't we talk to him individually and find out what he feels about this exam and the reason why? Just now you mentioned there might have been a marking error, but let me say this is very unlikely. As for the exam questions that are pitched too high, we'll follow up and review. As regards assigning another teacher, I'll also discuss this with the principal. Why don't we make another appointment to discuss these further? The crucial thing to do now is for us to talk to Ka-him independently to understand how he's adapting to Hong Kong and what his needs are. This is how we can help him grow.'

The above are the four main types of parents. They will give teachers differing experiences in interviews. From the helpless parents to the manipulative ones, the teacher will experience a rising sense of being threatened and pressured. The teacher should, therefore, make corresponding adjustments to the goals of interview according to parents, but the direction the interview should be the same, that is, to win the parents' collaboration. See Table 9.3.

Table 9.3 Goals and direction of discussion between class teacher and the four main types of parents

Parent type	Feel helpless about children (worried parent)	Do not understand children (disappointed parent)	Cover for children (angry parent)	Complain and confront (manipulative parent)
Teacher's feeling towards parents	————————————————————————————> Being threatened and pressured			
Goal of interview (helping parents)	Affirm parent's own competence	Let parents understand students' feelings	Let parents be self-determining and accountable for own actions	Find room for collaboration
Direction of interview	————————————————————————————> Win parents' collaboration			

❑ **Activity 3**

Role-play

In groups of three, play the roles of parent, class teacher and observer respectively and practise the strategies with references to cases under the four main types of parents.

Modes for Resolution of Conflict between the Class Teacher and Parents

The most feared parents for new recruits are perhaps the angry and the manipulative, i.e. those who cover for their children and those who complain and confront. To obtain a cooperative stance from these parents, teachers have to make ample preparations and adopt appropriate attitudes and techniques.

Educationists and scholars (Klempner and Jones, 1992; Kauffman, Mostert, Trent, and Hallahan, 2002; Kottler and Kottler 2004) point out that in an interview with these types of parents, the conflict resolution mode can be used (Table 9.4). It comprises the following stages, steps and main points.

Table 9.4 Steps and main points in the application of the conflict resolution mode

Processes	Main points
Stage I: Preparation before interview	Information gathering/ decoration of setting/ interview agenda
Stage II: During the interview	
Step (1) Starting amicably	Start with a friendly greeting and handshake Introduce yourself
Step (2) Sharing information	Ask question in a friendly manner Listen carefully; express acceptance and empathy Make genuine responses Clarify main mutual concerns
Step (3) Seeking consensus	Clarify crux of problem Avoid jumping to conclusions Re-organize existing ideas
Step (4) Finding solution	Collaborate in discussion and analysis Identify and affirm feasible solutions Examine details
Step (5) Drawing up a plan	Suggest detailed planning Set out each party's responsibilities
Stage III: Actions and post-interview follow-up	Review/take action/continue discussion

Stage I: Preparation before the interview

After informing the parent in an appropriate way the purpose, time and place of the interview, the teacher should gather information about the child's strengths, interests and abilities, such as the student's work albums, report cards and class work to serve as supporting evidence for the discussion; collect especially the student's best work samples to start the interview on a positive note.

The teacher should also consider the time and place of the interview, its duration, who the attendees are (other teachers and students), etc. the most important is the ambience, such as the way the desks and chairs are arranged, and the creation of a warm and harmonious atmosphere. Other necessary items are a list of questions about the student in question and a draft of the main points to be discussed.

Stage II: During the interview

Step 1: An amicable start

The teacher can greet the parent in a friendly manner with a handshake and appropriate eye contact. Then he/she introduces himself/herself briefly and welcomes the parent, shows appreciation for his/her attendance in the midst of a busy schedule, and shows concern by asking whether the traffic has been smooth on the way.

Step 2: Information sharing

The best way to start the meeting is to go straight to the point, i.e. the purpose of the interview. The teacher can start by asking open questions in a friendly way, such as: 'What has Kwan-hung told you about the school?'

When the parent speaks, the teacher needs to listen carefully, and clarify issues of mutual concern to ascertain he/she understands the purpose of the interview. Listen first for the student's behaviour at home and his/her interaction with family members, show acceptance and empathy and make genuine responses, and jot down any clues that might explain the child's behaviour in question. If the student is present, he/she can also speak his/her mind.

Step 3: Seeking consensus

The teacher can describe the pupil's behaviour and performance in class, and point out his/her strengths and weaknesses. The teacher should also clarify the pupil's problem for the parent. Avoid using education jargon or jumping to conclusions. Conduct the discussion in a language that is comprehensible to the parent in order to seek consensus on the way the problem is understood. At the same time, the teacher should have an open mind regarding the pupil, re-organize existing views and use the new information or a new perspective to approach the problem. Crude categorization must be avoided.

Step 4: Finding a solution

Both parties should work together to explore and make suggestions to find feasible solutions. Details have to be examined and the interview should focus on strategies that can help the child. It is not easy to ask for collaboration from these types of parents. The teacher has to be psychologically prepared for a difference in perspective and a lack of consensus. He/She should approach and understand the parent's anger and dejection in a positive way. He/she has to listen carefully, soothe the parent's emotions and make positive assessments of the pupils and their parents, such as showing appreciation of the parents for making efforts for their children, understanding the parents' feelings and viewing the pupils' behaviour from their perspective. On the other hand, the teacher needs to respond to the parents in a level-headed and professional manner, using language that is concrete and refined. Avoid blaming the parents, and let them know that you want very much their collaboration in caring for their children.

Step 5: Drawing up a plan

The teacher collaborates with the parent to reach the goal agreed by both parties. The teacher helps formulate a detailed plan, and decide together what the pupil's and parent's responsibilities should be, as well as the role to be played by the teacher. When the respective responsibilities have been set out, the content for each item should be clearly and aptly defined, and the channel for future communication between the teacher and the parent determined.

Stage III: Actions to be taken and post-interview follow-up

After the interview, the teacher should first quiet down. After reviewing and recording what improvements can be made, he/she should take timely actions and ring the parent to learn about the pupil's progress and condition, and maintain continued discussion with the parent.

❒ **Activity 4**

Study and Role-play

Kin-keung is a famous 'chatterbox' among the second-year students. All teachers are wary of teaching that class. Miss Wong is Kin-keung's class teacher and maths teacher. Kin-keung often complains about his neighbour making noises while playing with stationery, which affects the learning atmosphere of the class. Kin-keung's parents are doubtful of Miss Wong's descriptions of Kin keung's behaviour in class, and maintains that he is a good boy at home, and so must be a good pupil at school. Recently, Kin-keung has been walking brazenly back and forth in class to attract his classmates' attention, seriously disrupting classroom order. Miss Wong decides to make an appointment with his parents to let them know.

Professional and Community Support

There is a Chinese saying that 'every family has its own problems to handle'. Students' family backgrounds differ, and the problems they face can be of various types, such as low-income family, domestic violence, teenage pregnancies, and drug abuse. One class teacher is responsible for thirty-odd unique cases. He/she cannot do it alone. This is why teachers have to consult other professionals and understand the relationship between the school and the community so as to make use of the resources wisely (Lin and Huang 2005; Yuen 2009).

Professional support within the school

Just as the teacher giving consultation to his/her pupils' and their parents, he/she should seek the opinions and services provided by other professionals when he/she is himself in need. The advantages are that the teacher can obtain professional opinions outside his/her own expertise; use other professionals' objective perspective to examine his/her own experience; find a new and innovative solution; and receive external help to handle cases that are beyond his/her capability, or that he/she has no time or desire to finish.

There are three kinds of professionals within the school whom the teacher can consult. The first is other subject teachers. Teachers of other subjects have different contact with the pupils, and from the perspective of that particular subject, they may have a better idea of the pupils' strengths, interests and the kind of activities that suit them, and so they can offer valuable opinions for the pupils' positive and whole person development. The teacher can thus learn about and assess the pupils from various perspectives based on his/her participation and performance in the various subjects. The second kind is the teaching staff in the administrative coordinator grade, whose rich experience makes them experts in problem-solving strategies. Both the coordinator and the principal have gone through the difficulties and setbacks now confronting the new recruit, and can hence understand the feelings and problems of a new teacher. You must remember to let them know at which point you need their help. The third kind of professionals are the guidance teachers and the social workers: their guidance skills and their secure and confidential support system can help teachers tackle problems pertaining to psychological well-being or find corresponding professional opinions (Kottler and Kottler 2004).

External referral and professional support

If the support within the school fails to help the teacher resolve effectively the problem faced by the pupil, he/she can seek assistance from external professionals and organizations. When the teacher asks for such assistance, he/she needs to pay attention to the referral process and the route through which the case is referred, and offer help and participate in case meetings where appropriate. The process may take the following form: the teacher and the coordinator, social worker, or the principal discuss the need for a referral → contact professionals or organizations → case received by professionals or organizations → professionals conduct a preliminary assessment → case accepted or referred to other organizations → organizations to provide services or interventions → professionals or organizations to monitor services and assess progress → close the case when appropriate → case recorded.

At the early stage of the referral, the class teacher has to aid the professionals and organizations, for instance, by providing the pupil's information such as family background, academic performance, behaviour at school and social relationships, as well as the kind of contact made with the parents. During the whole process, the class teacher should offer the best help for the pupil through continued communication, exchange of views, reaching consensus, re-organization of knowledge, and exchange of experience with the helping professionals (Lim and Huang 2005: 577–78).

The class teacher can also consult with education psychologists and local university professors. Traditionally, educational psychologists emphasize helping pupils with tests and assessment, but nowadays, they are providing a much wider array of support and information, including taking care of individual differences between pupils in their studies, and proposing multi-facet class dynamics as well as more effective strategies for pupil behaviour modification. Not only do they solve individual problems of the pupils from a professional point of view; they also promote developmental and preventive programmes and activities at the school level, such as 'Be an expert in managing your emotions', 'Project C.A.R.E' and 'Know more about character and emotions'. For high-risk pupils, educational psychologists would also draw up personalized counselling plans for them according to their circumstances and needs.

With the principal's permission, the teacher can invite university professors in the related disciplines to give talks, conduct workshops, give demonstrations or make class observation to help teachers reflect on pupils' needs and problems and their own attitudes, in order to enhance their guidance skills and improve their teaching styles. Teacher can even invite professors to be consultants or consult them on special cases.

Counselling resources in the community

Many non-governmental organizations in the community provide support for pupils and their families confronted with hardships and challenges, e.g. Hong

Kong Federation of Youth Groups runs the 'Youthline' in which professional social workers offer instant and appropriate crisis intervention counselling to young people to help with their immediate problems and crises. As for young people's whole person development, many organizations, such as The Boys' and Girls' Clubs Association of Hong Kong, Yang Memorial Methodist Social Service and Hong Kong Christian Service, organize long-running multi-faceted youth programmes, like emotion management, resilience in the face of adversity, making friends and love relationships, with a view to nurturing the physical and psychological development of youngster and steer them away from bad habits. With regards to family problems, organizations such as Caritas Hong Kong and Family Welfare Society of Hong Kong offer help to families to prevent, confront, intervene and deal with problems such as unemployment, domestic violence and sex abuse. The class teacher can provide parents with the information of these organizations and encourage them to seek help on their own accord; or he/she can, with the parents' consent, inform the relevant organizations of their problem and make the referral.

❐ **Activity 5**

Web Search

Search on the Internet for professional support organizations in your district (including the types of service, address, fees, and application details) that can help the class teacher facilitate the pupils' whole person development, solve their problems or support their parents. Share them in the next lesson.

Conclusion

The class teacher is an important link and important executer for the whole school guidance work. Under the leadership of the principal and in collaboration with the discipline and guidance team, he/she maintains communication with the parents and makes good use of professional support in the community to facilitate the pupils' growth and help them overcome their problems in a comprehensive manner. In the collaboration between the class teacher and the discipline and guidance team, the teacher has to recognize the importance of the oneness of discipline and guidance, and that timely and appropriate in-house collaboration and referral will help reduce student misbehaviour and solve problems. The principal, discipline and guidance teachers, class teachers and the entire teaching staff should reach a consensus regarding the discipline and guidance policy and the principles for counselling referrals, and take corresponding actions to collaborate effectively to ensure the whole personal development of the pupils.

Nowadays, as home-school collaboration is getting stronger, the communication between the class teacher and the parents is becoming more frequent. In order to ensure an effective collaboration, the class teacher has to understand the respective roles and beliefs of the teacher and the parents; make contact with the parents in various ways, e.g. Parents' Day, parent-teacher conference, and joint efforts in organizing activities; and be constantly aware of parents' expectations and fears, recognize their efforts, and respond to the parents with genuineness and sincerity. When facing the four main types of parents mentioned above (helpless towards their children, lacking understanding of their children, covering for their children, and complaining and confrontational), it is doubly important for the class teacher to prepare himself/herself psychologically, adopting strategies to fine tune the discussion to suit the different goals and seeking more rooms for collaboration with the parents. When conflict with parents arises, the class teacher needs to empathize and accept them, or he/she can use the conflict resolution approach to try to resolve the conflict. When necessary, he/she can seek support from external professionals to solve the problem.

Questions for Discussion

1. Which of the roles and duties of the class teacher are the most important in terms of whole school guidance?
2. What are the difficulties that may arise from the collaboration between the class teacher and the discipline and guidance team? How can they be resolved?
3. When a parent does not want to co-operate with the class teacher, how will you deal with it?
4. What are the factors that the class teacher has to pay attention to when interviewing parents? Why?
5. What are the points that the class teacher has to pay attention to when interviewing the four main types of parents? How can he/she win their respect and collaboration?
6. How can the class teacher make use of the in-house and external professional and community support appropriately? What are the priorities?

Related Websites

1. Hong Kong Christian Service
    http://www.hkcs.org/index-e.html
2. The Hong Kong Federation of Youth Groups
    http://www.hkfyg.org.hk/eng/index.html

3. 小童群益會
   http://www.bgca.org.hk/bgca06/main/home.asp?id=302&lang=C
4. 家庭福利會
   http://www.hkfws.org.hk
5. 循道衛理楊震社會服務處
   http://www.methodist.org.hk/locations/socialservices/5/
6. 香港明愛家庭服務
   http://family.caritas.org.hk/ser/family.html
7. 學校與家長溝通合作
   http://www.hkedcity.net/article/education_issue/050321-004/page4.phtml

Extended Readings

Gestwicki, C. (2007). *Home, School, and Community Relations*. Clifton Park, NY: Thomson Delmar Learning.

謝淑賢 (2003)。《有效與家長溝通 70 式》。香港：香港教育圖書公司。

References

Gorman, J. C. (2004). *Working with Challenging Parents of Students with Special Needs*. Thousand Oaks, CA: Corwin Press.

Kauffman, J. M., Mostert, M. P. Trent, S. C., and Hallahan, D. P. (2002). *Managing Classroom Behavior: A Reflective Case-Based Approach* (3rd ed.). Boston: Allyn and Bacon.

Klempner, Y., and Jones, D. (1992). *Parent-Teacher Conference:* resolving conflicts *[video recording]: Resolving Conflicts*. Evanston, IL: Altschul Group Corporation.

Kottler, J. A., and Kottler, E. 著，孫守湉、林秀玲譯 (2004)。《教師諮商技巧》。台北：心理出版社。

教育統籌委員會 (1990)：《教育統籌委員會第四號報告書》。香港：政府印務局。

林孟平 (2008)：《輔導與心理治療》。香港：商務印書館。

林萬億、黃韻如 (2005)：《學校輔導團隊工作：學校社會工作師、輔導教師與心理師的合作》。台北：五南圖書公司。

龍精亮 (2010)：〈全方位學生輔導服務：建構學校關顧文化之初探〉。《教育曙光》，第 58 卷，頁 43–53。

龐憶華 (1999)：〈邁向共同責任的家校社區協作〉。《基礎教育學報》，第 8 卷，頁 83–89。

阮衛華 (2009)：〈學校與社區關係〉，載於吳迅榮、黃炳文主編：《廿一世紀的學校領導》(頁 307–322)。香港：學術專業圖書中心。

吳迅榮 (2008)：《家庭、學校及社區協作：理論、模式與實踐：香港的經驗與啟示》。香港：學術專業圖書中心。

10

Crisis Management and Its Application to School Guidance

Ming Tak Hue

The scourge of life is usually hidden in unnoticeable places, and crops up when people are off guard.

(Sir Francis Bacon)

Abstract

This chapter discusses possible crises that may occur in the classroom or at school, and suggests solutions for dealing with the issue of crisis management from a macro point of view, focusing on the positive effect it may have on school guidance. From the point of view of the 'crisis management cycle', the government's proposal for setting up a crisis management committee in every school presents a good opportunity to examine the related theoretical framework, and to cite two different instances of 'crises' for analysis. The cases will be approached separately at the individual level as well as the group/school level. Discussions on the use of different intervention strategies and the intended improvement will also be included.

Objectives

This chapter will help you:
- define a 'crisis' and 'crisis management', and enable you to recognize students' various responses in the face of a crisis;
- apply the concept of the crisis management cycle while drawing up an action plan for school crisis management;
- recognize the functions of the school crisis management team and the respective roles and functions of the team members; and
- understand various intervention strategies at the group/school and individual level.

Before You Start: Think and Discuss

1.   What do you understand by a 'crisis'?
2.   What kind of relationship exists between a 'personal crisis' faced by students and an 'organizational crisis' encountered by the school?
3.   What kinds of 'crises' might students encounter? What are their causes?
4.   In the course of assisting students to cope with their 'crises', what role should school guidance play?
5.   As a teacher, how do you render effective support to the students who are facing a 'crisis' so as to help them recover from the trauma of it?

Introduction

In order to meet the expectations of parents and society on the school and teachers, present-day teachers need to get prepared and be ready to give appropriate response and reaction to different crises that were rarely heard of some ten years ago. The following headlines in a local newspaper, *South China Morning Post*, provide good examples of the kind of crises that schools and teachers may have to face: 'One Child in Six Suffers Abuse by Family Member' (6 July 2009),[1] 'A Quarter of Teenagers Have Considered Suicide, Survey Finds' (17 October 2008),[2] 'Schoolboys Collapse after Snorting Drugs' (5 June 2009),[3] 'Student Fined for Shoplifting While under Exam Pressure' (4 September 2009),[4] 'Police Saddened as Young Girls Lured into "Compensated Dating"' (5 September 2009),[5] and 'Schoolgirls' Bullying Uncivilized Behaviour, Magistrate Says' (11 September 2009).[6] We can understand why the teacher may feel unable to withstand the blow when the crisis comes, especially when the majority of teachers have never received any training in crisis management. The situation is aggravated because it is not easy for the school management to get resources for crisis management or acquire relevant professional skills. Nevertheless, the school management and teachers cannot refrain from taking on the responsibility for crisis management, mitigation and prevention. Unless a crisis could be dealt with appropriately in a timely manner, the staff and students of the school would be adversely affected both physically and psychologically. This does not only disrupt students' studies, but can also damage a school's reputation. Therefore, it is in the best interest of the school for the management personnel to adequately prepare the school and its staff for the possible crises.

This chapter will describe the general characteristics of crises and explore further the distinct features specific to school crises, with the introduction of the school crisis management plan and the school crisis management team (SCMT). It will also discuss various points of intervention in crisis management, namely at the school, class and individual levels, as well as rendering suitable assistance to the students being affected. Finally, the chapter will suggest suitable strategies for the prevention and mitigation of school crises with reference to two specific types of incidents, namely suicide and campus violence.

Crisis Management

In the school setting, teachers and students are accustomed to orderly campus life and they can follow the regulations and procedures to resolve problems. However, unanticipated events do happen: e.g. somebody getting seriously hurt, or a female student falling victim to sexual abuse. Such incidents are not only shocking, they could also put the school in dire straits if they were not handled properly. Unpredictable incidents and emergency situations which adversely affect the individual or the school community are referred to as 'crises' by our definition. In psychological terms, a crisis occurs when an individual facing a certain change in the external environment cannot cope with it by means of the information and knowledge accumulated from his/her past experience and is thus trapped in a state of mental stress, with the formation of negative sentiments. From the educational perspective, the occurrence of a school crisis may provide an opportunity for furthering the personal growth of students. The school can grasp the opportunity to educate students on the coping skills at different conceptual levels such as knowing, thinking, feeling and behaving so that a 'crisis' can be resolved effectively by such strategies as mitigation, prevention and positive response. However, we must not overlook the adverse effects that a crisis may have on school administration as it is likely to cause temporary disruption and 'malfunctioning' in the individual or the school. Besides, it is not always possible to resolve the crisis simply by means of the customary practice or current procedure available to the school. Since a crisis simply happens without any prior warning, and is usually not taken into consideration by the routine regulations and normal administrative procedures, it is therefore usually beyond the capability and experience of an individual to handle the situation properly and efficiently.

❐ **Activity 1**

- The term 'crisis' (危機) in Chinese consists of two characters, meaning 'threat' and 'opportunity'. How do you understand the double meanings in this term? And how can we possibly turn a crisis from a threat to an opportunity?
- What kinds of crises have you encountered at school? Did these incidents have any impacts on you and your colleagues at school?

Responding to crises

Different kinds of crises will have different impacts on people; even when different people encounter a similar crisis, they may not have the same kind of reaction. The actual impact that can be wrought on the person by a crisis depends on two deciding factors: the nature of the crisis and the characteristics of the person (Heath and Sheen 2005). The former refers to the characteristics of the crisis situation and its specific environmental setting, for instance, the distinct features of the incident, the duration of the crisis and the impacts on the daily routines and habits that the crisis has on the individual. The latter refers to the individual's characteristics, social background, personality and ability, including such personal aspects as age, sex, life experience, support network and temperament.

The reactions of students towards personal crises may be somewhat different depending on what stage of schooling they are at, as shown in Table 10.1. It must be noted that the table only provides descriptions of the students' general reactions when they come face to face with a crisis. If students are found to display such reactions, the teacher should also consider their other psychological, behavioural and mental symptoms which may adversely affect the students' social and career development and hinder their normal functioning in other important areas of life. When this stressful situation is allowed to persist, it may eventually lead to mental disorder (Lerner, Volpe, and Lindell 2003). Therefore, a crisis may affect a student's ability to learn in the short term; and if the crisis is not managed properly, the resulting mental stress may in the long run cause lasting damage to his/her physical and mental health.

Table 10.1 Students' reactions to crises

General reactions of students when facing crises:		
• Revert to immature behaviour • Complain about stomachaches or headaches • Over-react, act, become jumpy, or lose temper easily • Have sleep problems, such as nightmares or insomnia • Change eating habits suddenly • Have angry outbursts of aggressive behaviour		
Kindergarten	**Elementary school**	**Middle and high school**
• Shivering • Crying, becoming irritable and acting in discontent • Sucking thumb • Wetting, suffering from incontinence • Feeling insecure and becoming over-dependent • Being hyperactive • Getting gruff and overreacting	• Being irritable and complaining • Excessive fear and anxiety • Sadness, crying • Guilt and self-blaming Incessant demands • Attention seeking • Distractible and day dreamy • Difficulty in concentrating	• Withdrawn and isolated • Excessive fear and anxiety • Sadness and depression • Shame and guilt • Careless, risky behaviours • Acting out, rebelling • Declining grades • Change in personality • Avoidance to talk about feelings • Self-absorption • Grotesque humour

Source: Heath and Sheen 2005: 11.

The crisis management cycle

Although we cannot predict when a crisis will occur, it does not mean that it is not manageable. Prior to the onset of any crisis, the school should carry out forward planning and make reasonable preparations for any unexpected incidents. The school can draw up a school-based strategic plan for crisis management, which will give details about the coordinated deployment of manpower and other resources, the allocation of duties among the members of staff concerned, and the guidelines on communication and coordination procedures should a crisis occur. Besides, the plan should also include information on how to cope with the intense and confused situation in a crisis, and what can be done to dampen the undesirable impacts (Heath and Sheen 2005). The benefits of a school-based crisis management plan are evident, for it does not only cater for the unique background, ethos and sub-systems of the school, but also take care of the needs of individual students, while making good use of the special skills and professional knowledge of the staff members.

When making the crisis management plan, one can refer to the 'crisis management cycle' introduced by the US Department of Education. As shown in Figure 10.1, the crisis management cycle can be divided into four phases, namely mitigation and prevention, preparedness, response and recovery. The proposed work cycle outlines a systematic approach. Whenever a crisis occurs, the school should continuously take part in the situation while the school management should constantly assess the situation so as to make necessary modifications based on recent developments in the crisis or newly gained experience.

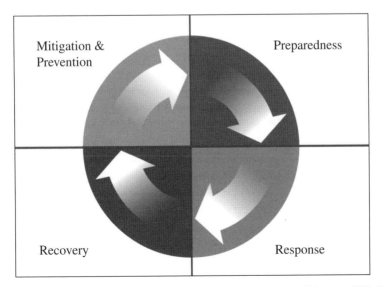

Figure 10.1 The crisis management cycle. Source: The US Department of Education 2007: 12.

Specifically speaking, the phase of mitigation and prevention is mainly concerned with identifying the hidden threats to the school through collaboration with the community's emergency services departments, like the problems of campus violence and drug abuse, so that the current safety measures and procedures can be reassessed with a view to reducing the likely impact of a crisis or even the chance of its occurrence. The preparedness phase is concerned with devising measures and procedures to cope with different types of crises, and establishing channels of communication and decision-making mechanisms in readiness for any crisis. To achieve this goal, it is necessary to draw up a crisis management plan, and conduct the relevant education and training activities to brief the school staff and students about the details of the plan. The response phase is concerned with identifying the existence of threats, and choosing a logical course of action so as to ensure the safety of students during the crisis. It is necessary for the school to execute the crisis management plan with flexibility so that students are kept away from danger as far as possible, the affected students are able to receive suitable care and support, and smooth contact is constantly maintained with all the stakeholders throughout the crisis. The goal of the recovery phase is to enable the students to return to normal school life and to render emotional support to the students in need.

The school crisis management team

In Hong Kong, every school is required to set up a school crisis management team. The crisis management cycle is most suited for this team in its forward planning. More specifically, the aim of the team is to ensure the safety of all teachers and students in the school, the normal and stable operation of the school, and the efficient flow of information without interference to prevent further injuries to people. The team also provides individuals with contact information and remedial support, strengthen home-school cooperation, and make provisions for support to classrooms and groups. The school management should invite staff members with crisis management knowledge or experience to join the team. Whenever a crisis occurs, the team members must make sure that they can be contacted easily and promptly, and are on call for help for as long as needed. According to the Education Bureau (2005), it is recommended that the crisis management team comprise a team leader, a staff liaison member, a parent liaison member, a community liaison member, a school social worker/guidance teacher and an educational psychologist. Table 10.2 shows the allocation of duties among the team members.

Table 10.2 Composition of the crisis management team

Key member	Role
Team leader	• supervises the crisis management team • convenes the team to plan response • coordinates the crisis response • makes important decisions in the handling of the crisis • conducts evaluations of the crisis management plan
Staff liaison member	• coordinates support for staff in the crisis • keeps a phone contact list and record forms for emergency needs • arranges and assists in conducting staff debriefing meetings
Parent liaison member	• coordinates communication with parents • coordinates assistance and support to the affected family
Community liaison member	• coordinates outside resources to provide support to the school, staff and students
School social worker/ guidance teacher	• conducts individual or group meetings with the students or staff as needed • helps screen students at risk, and identifies other helping resources for students and staff • assists teachers in conducting special class periods
Educational psychologist	• assists school in managing the psychological impact of a crisis and developing a crisis intervention plan • provides individual or group debriefing sessions to students or teachers in need
Other team members	• designates rooms for different uses and makes this known to all staff • assists other team members to smoothen the crisis management when necessary

Source: Education Bureau 2005: 7.

❏ **Activity 2**

- What are the functions of the crisis management team in your school?
- What types of crises does the crisis management plan of your school envisage?
- As a teacher, how do you determine your own specific role and responsibility in the crisis management plan drawn up by the crisis management team?

Intervention

The crisis management team may employ intervention strategies or procedures to alleviate the impacts of a crisis and to enable the students to return to normal school life. Whenever a crisis occurs, the crisis management team should immediately formulate a crisis management plan and make the necessary announcements on behalf of the team. Thereupon, the team should mobilize resources, activate the support network in and outside the school, contact staff members to handle the situation, and render support to all stakeholders involved. The Education Bureau (2005) has outlined for the members of the crisis management team their different intervention duties (see Table 10.3). These duties must be carried out in coordination with the crisis intervention procedures/tasks conducted by the crisis management team as soon as a crisis is known to occur. Teachers are also required to perform crisis intervention procedures/tasks at the group or individual level. Their important roles and responsibilities will be described in detail below. Of course, the teachers assigned with intervention duties should be healthy and stable mentally, psychologically and emotionally in the first place. Should any teachers be overcome with negative emotions as a result of the crisis, they are not fit to take part in the intervention measures. Instead, they should be promptly referred to professional counsellors for timely treatment.

Table 10.3 Crisis management procedures/tasks

Procedure/Task	Person-in-charge
Verify the information	Team leader
Notify the school and regional education office	School principal
Convene an urgent crisis management team meeting	Team leader
Liaise with outside agencies for support	Community liaison member and school social worker
Call an all-staff meeting and conduct debriefing	Staff liaison member and school principal
Support to students • announce the case to students • conduct special class periods • arrange for counselling to students in need	School principal • class teacher, staff liaison member • school social worker, educational psychologist
Prepare for media enquiries	School principal
Contact and support to parents	Parent liaison member
Review the crisis plan and devise follow-up actions	Team leader
Conduct an evaluation of the effectiveness of the crisis management	Team leader

Source: Education Bureau 2005: 8–9.

Group intervention

In the school environment, group intervention is one of the intervention strategies that will cause relatively little disruption to the normal school life of students. In an environment where students can feel safe and secure, they are enabled to enjoy normalcy again in their school life. As students who go through the same crisis often experience similar reactions and emotions, the students in the group are more ready for mutual sharing. More importantly, when they exchange their views on the crisis through group interaction and listen to other people's opinions, they create an environment for mutual support and acceptance. The teacher may make use of class sharing to initiate the group intervention.

Class sharing

After the crisis emerges, teachers can immediately conduct a special class sharing session before the school day ends. This arrangement is able to help restore class discipline, assess the need for and possible goal of individual intervention measures, keep the students' reaction in check and make preparations for future group intervention. The sharing session would require the involvement of the students who have gone through a similar crisis.

During the class sharing session, the teacher ought not to be the only speaker. Rather, he/she should first foster an orderly and mutually supportive environment and then encourage students to express their views on the incident and the people involved in it, their reactions to the incident, as well as their concern for its possible development in the future.

At the start of the sharing session, the teacher should first explain the procedures and rules governing the discussion, so as to reduce anxiety and worries. The teacher also needs to make clear the purpose of the sharing and his/her expectations for the discussion, while expressing his/her sincere wish to listen to the opinions of students. The guiding principle is on fostering mutual respect, acceptance and compassion. The teacher should prepare him/herself adequately for the debriefing so that he/she can initiate the discussion and provide the class with possible directions for discussion. Next, the teacher can provide students with relevant information about the crisis, and give an authentic account of the incident so as to dispel any doubts that the students may have. After that, he/she can let students revisit the crisis from their point of view, by describing the crisis, the order in which the events take place, and explaining their roles in the incident as well as the things they have done. This is to enable the students to talk about the time frame of their participation in the incident. When the narration is over, students should come to a consensus about the order of the events taken place, become aware of the group feeling regarding the incident, and gradually form a common view towards the crisis.

During the sharing, the teacher should guide students to recollect their thoughts while the crisis was taking place, to make connections between their views and their own feelings towards the crisis, as well as to listen to other people and reflect on the different interpretations that people may have on the same incident. After that, the teacher can ask students to further explore and reflect on what they are thinking, and see if they will come to some new interpretations and conclusions about their own experience.

The teacher guide students to explore how their feelings and reactions should also have changed, and share their personal recollections with fellow students. The teacher may invite students to describe their reactions to the incident, and guide them to give emotional expressions to these reactions. The students who take part in the discussion should never make judgements about other people's feelings. Instead, they should understand that these reactions are just human nature, and well within our expectations. No matter what thoughts and feelings they might have about the incident, those are just residues of their traumatic experience. Provided the students could understand more deeply about their own as well as other people's reactions, they would be more capable of coping with the post-crisis reactions.

During the class sharing activity, the teacher should do his/her utmost to foster a positive, supportive and secure atmosphere. To attain this goal, the teacher may follow these procedures:

1. Lead the discussion with the right attitude, showing calmness, total involvement and willingness to listen, and set a good example for students.
2. Allow students to express their worries, but try not to let the feeling of anxiety spread and adversely affect their peers.
3. Provide comprehensive and accurate information in a timely manner so as to enable students to understand the situation.
4. Be on the alert for self-reproaching students and be firm in pointing out where their thinking is erroneous.
5. Watch carefully the body language of the students, so as to quickly detect their reactions and struggles.
6. Recognize the feelings of students.
7. Focus on the exchange with students, responding empathetically towards their feelings and taking their words with trust.
8. Prevent students from coming into contact with anything that might remind them of the crisis.
9. Encourage students to give one another mutual support, and, if necessary, assist students in setting up a peer support group (source: Johnson 2000: 6).

Individualized intervention

Individualized intervention refers to the strategies used to help individual students understand the situation and conduct self-evaluation. Individualized intervention is generally performed on a one-to-one basis, with the ultimate goals of raising the individual's self-esteem, lessening his/her sense of guilt, restoring productivity, and maintaining continued personal safety. Generally speaking, as individualized intervention requires the use of a variety of counselling and therapeutic skills, it is usually made the responsibility of the social worker or the teacher who has received training in guidance and counselling. Throughout the intervention process, the teacher or social worker must take care to assess the needs of individual students so as to help them understand the situation as well as how they would be affected by the events. The students will be given a chance to express their emotional responses to the crisis before deciding the next course of actions. In most cases, the teacher or social worker concerned will help students learn the problem-solving methods as well as the skills of stress management, and provide them with information on available resources. Finally, the teacher and the students can draw up a specific plan to help the latter cast away the victim's role and gradually regain control of what is happening around them. In order to enable students to execute the plan effectively, the teacher concerned can negotiate with the other teachers to reduce academic workload such as homework, tests, and study projects. Besides, it may be necessary to lower the expectation on their academic performance in order to increase the chance of success.

In regard to individualized intervention, the school can provide guidance to the students in need. Bibliotherapy is one of the intervention strategies (Heath and Sheen 2005). To begin with, the teacher can read the same book or story that the student had read, and through sharing assist the latter in thinking about his/her personal problems and healing the scars of emotional trauma. If some characters in the story also have similar difficulties or experiences, they will echo with the students, increasing the effectiveness of the strategy. The students will perceive the ways in which the characters in the book cope with their problems, and revisit their own experience. During the process they will learn to express their emotions more effectively. Bibliotherapy can also help students alleviate the sense of isolation, develop healthier expectations and hope for the future, and gain the necessary life skills to cope with the many challenges and problems confronting them in the future. In brief, bibliotherapy may go through six stages, as shown in Table 10.4.

Table 10.4 Stages of bibliotherapy

Stage One: Involvement
• Students' motivation and interest in the story are aroused.

Stage Two: Identification
• Students find out the similarities between themselves and the characters in the story, as well as the similarities between the story and reality.
• Students identify themselves with the protagonist of the story.

Stage Three: Catharsis
• Students empathize with the protagonist.
• Students experience the feelings of the protagonist.
• When resolution to the characters' dilemma is found, students also release their emotional tension.

Stage Four: Insight
• As they see how someone in similar circumstances solve their problems, they may find it easier to cope with their own problems.
• Students recollect what happens in the story and apply it to their own situations.
• Students resolve their problems.

Stage Five: Universalization
• Students realize that others have similar struggles.
• A sense of connection replaces isolation as students recognize that they are not alone.

Stage Six: Post-reading Discussion
• Students retell the plot and discuss the characters' emotions.
• Students reflect on their feelings and identify with the characters and events in the story.

Source: Heath and Sheen 2005: 66.

Examples of School Crisis Management in Hong Kong

The introduction of group and individualized intervention has brought up another issue: Under what circumstances should the teacher or crisis management team intervene? Some scholars point out that intervention action should be taken when any of the following four scenarios or events occur (Schonfeld and Newgass 2003), namely (a) environmental hazards such as chemical leaks or outbreaks of fire; (b) death of a staff member or student; (c) a situation in which the students' personal safety is endangered, even though nobody is actually hurt; and (d) a threatening situation that keeps students emotionally unstable. In the following section, we will focus our discussions on two types of crises: suicide and campus violence, and make suggestions on how to manage and resolve them.

A suicide case

Daily News (19 October 2007)[7] reported that an eighteen-year-old S. 7 student jumped from his flat and died from the injuries on 18 October. The deceased had excellent academic results, and studied in a band 1 school from S. 1 to S. 5. However, he was only able to get an aggregate score of 14 points in HKCEE and was therefore not admitted to S. 6 by his school. Even though his family did not give him any pressure, the deceased had very high expectations of himself and always tried hard to get good results. He was soon diagnosed with depression and psychosis disorder. Although his family brought him to psychiatric treatment, it was already too late.

How serious is the problem of suicide in Hong Kong? As shown in Table 10.5[8] and Table 10.6,[9] suicide is not a serious problem among students under fifteen and we can see a decreasing trend in this group. However, educators should be aware that there is a higher rate of attempted suicides among female students. In comparison, as shown in Table 10.7[10] and Table 10.8,[11] the suicide rate is higher among students aged between fifteen to twenty-four. Although we can see no apparent trend in the figures of suicides, there is an increasing trend in attempted suicides among male students and a decreasing trend among female students in this group. To sum up, we can say that more female students tend to attempt suicide, but more male students committed suicide, with the implication that they generally employ more deadly means to kill themselves.

Table 10.5 Rates of suicides among persons aged under 15

	1997	1998	1999	2000	2001	2002	2003	2004	2005	2006
All	0.5	0.3	0.9	1	0.5	0.7	0.4	0.1	0.2	0.1
Male	0.8	0.2	0.8	0.9	0.4	0.5	0.2	0.2	0.4	0
Female	0.2	0.4	0.9	1.1	0.6	0.9	0.6	0	0	0.2

Years: 1997–2006; per 100,000 persons.
Source: HKJC Centre for Suicide Research and Prevention 2010.

Table 10.6 Rates of attempted suicides among persons aged under 15

	1997	1998	1999	2000	2001	2002	2003
All	5.9	6.6	5.6	5.9	5.5	7.1	4
Male	2.5	2.2	2.2	2.4	1.1	4.1	1.6
Female	9.5	11.3	9.3	9.6	10.3	10.4	6.6

Years: 1997–2003; per 100,000 persons.
Source: HKJC Centre for Suicide Research and Prevention 2010.

Table 10.7 Rates of suicides among persons aged 15–24

	1997	1998	1999	2000	2001	2002	2003	2004	2005	2006
All	8.8	10.4	5.9	7.7	8.9	12.6	10.7	10.5	7.1	8.2
Male	11.9	12.6	7.1	9.5	11	15.8	12.6	12.8	9.9	11.6
Female	5.6	8.1	4.7	5.8	6.8	9.3	8.8	8.3	4.4	5

Years: 1997–2006; per 100,000 persons.
Source: HKJC Centre for Suicide Research and Prevention 2010.

Table 10.8 Rates of attempted suicides among persons aged 15–24

	1997	1998	1999	2000	2001	2002	2003
All	72.1	78.5	68.7	63.6	71.9	76.7	68.8
Male	42.2	49.1	45	37.7	44.6	44.5	52.9
Female	102.3	107.8	92.3	89.3	98.9	109.6	85.2

Years: 1997–2003; per 100,000 persons.
Source: HKJC Centre for Suicide Research and Prevention 2010.

❐ **Activity 3**

Suppose you are the class teacher of Yi-hong and Mei-ling studying in S. 2B. One day after school, Yi-hong rushes into the staff room to tell you that Mei-ling has just split up with her boyfriend, and is loitering on the rooftop of the school building, wanting to do 'something foolish'. He has tried to dissuade her, but to no avail. Yi-hong also urges you not to reveal the incident to anyone.

* Confronted with such a situation, how would you react and respond?
* How would you respond to Yi-hong's request?
* If you were the first person to arrive on the scene, what would you say to Mei-ling?
* What role would you expect the crisis management team and Mei-ling's parents to play in this incident?

Prevention is better than cure. A school's management should consider how to prevent students from attempting to commit suicide. Teachers should learn to be sensitive and perceptive so that they can cope with students who have strong suicidal tendencies. They can make reference to the variables listed in Table 10.9 to help identify the students at risk (Lerner et al. 2003). As soon as the students at risk are identified, the school should pay special attention to them and initiate intervention actions at the group and individual levels respectively. More importantly, whenever students are found to be thinking seriously about suicide or making plans for it, the school must render immediate support and guidance. The teachers must activate all support networks available, including the family members of the students, their peers as well as the social worker, and make full use of available resources to help the students overcome their difficulties.

Table 10.9 Variables related to high suicidal risk

Family variables	• Family discord/conflict (i.e. lack of cohesion) • Family history of depression and/or mental illness • Lack of emotional support • Illicit drug or alcohol abuse among family members • Sexual and/or physical abuse, or neglect within the family • Family stress including parental unemployment, divorce and family relocation • Family history of suicide
Individual variables	• Emotional instability, especially depression • Feelings of hopelessness • Sleep and/or eating problems • Anger, aggressive tendencies and hostility • Behavioural problems, including running away • Substance use and abuse (e.g. alcohol and illicit drugs) • Poor problem-solving skills • More negative life events (e.g. recent loss of family member) • School problems (e.g. academic failure, behavioural problems) • Prior psychiatric hospitalization • History of self-destructive behaviour/suicide attempt(s) • Difficulty promising that they would not harm themselves • Unusual neglect of personal appearance • Impulsivity • Anxiety/Panic-related symptoms • Eating disorders • Sudden tendencies towards isolative and withdrawn behaviour
Suicidal symptoms	• Saying farewell to peers • Giving away prized possessions • Writing essays and/or notes about suicide • Verbalizing to a peer or teacher about 'not wanting to be around any longer' • Excessive fatigue • Sudden changes in personality • Self-destructive behaviour (e.g. self-mutilation)

Source: Lerner et al. 2003: 58–59.

At the group level, we can promote students' social and emotional development, and help them build up a social network for mutual support so as to prevent or reduce the chance of suicide. The teacher can help students build up interpersonal relationships, improve social skills, enhance problem-solving skills and foster the capacity for positive thinking through the organization of group activities. Whenever students lose the sense of security or encounter any trouble, these skills or capacities will help them face the challenges more confidently, figure out where to get the necessary assistance, as well as enhance their capacity for recovery after the problem.

At the individual level, the school must make individual counselling available to students. When talking with the students, the teacher should make it known that he/she is concerned about the problem encountered by the students and indicate that he/she cares and is there to help them through this difficult period. When the students regain their sense of security and are willing to reveal their inner feelings, he/she can ask them directly about their thoughts towards suicide, their actual suicidal attempts as well as their motives. The teacher should then try to evaluate, through their conversations, the students' 'suicidal ideation' and 'suicidal intention' (Lerner et al. 2003: 61). The items to evaluate include: (a) the means or method of suicide; (b) the viability of the stated means; (c) the lethality or likelihood of success given the chosen suicidal method; and (d) the intent or how probable the individual is to follow through on the act. When such information has been gathered, the teacher is then able to determine how serious the problem is, and make a more accurate assessment of the situation so as to take effective measures to deal with it. In the helping process, the teacher must avoid making empty promises or giving false hopes. The ultimate guiding principle is, even though the student refuses to let you seek the assistance of the professionals or requests that you keep it secret, you must try to seek the help of the professionals as soon as possible.

The campus violence case

Sing Tao Daily (30 October 2009)[12] reported that a video clip entitled 'Female Student Bully in Hong Kong School' was in hot circulation on the Internet. At the beginning of the video, a girl aged about thirteen to fifteen is apologizing to another girl. Next, she is being insulted, slapped on the face, and spitted on by four other girls. Then, the attackers take off her top and bra by force and threaten to gang-rape her. Outside the screen come the loud yelling of male students, urging the victim to retaliate. Finally, one of the bullies suggests taking off her pants as well, but another bully persuades her not to. Somehow they decide to let the victim put her clothes back on and leave. When the video concludes, the victim is seen thanking her torturers.

The majority of the victims and witnesses adopt a tolerant and indifferent attitude towards violence at school. Some victims even take revenge on their torturers. These aggressive responses will no doubt worsen school violence and bullying. The students involved will have no choice but to endure more hardship and the school environment becomes intolerable. Therefore, the teacher should encourage the victims and witnesses to come forward and seek help from adults. Apart from taking revenge, the inability to control temper and habitual bullying behaviour are major contributing factors towards bullying. For this reason, teachers must help students learn the necessary emotional management skills.

Similar to the suicide crisis, the best way to manage incidents of school violence or bullying is prevention. Teachers must cultivate the sensitivity in perception so as to readily identify students with violent tendencies. These students have things in common, for instance, having records of attacking other people or animals, wilfully vandalizing public property or other people's belongings, and taking part in gang activities. If they carry weapons with them, have the habit of using words of hatred, or threat to hurt others, it shows that they have the tendency to bully, intimidate, or threaten others. Some students may even make detailed plans for carrying out their violent acts. Teachers should be vigilant for students who have recurrent discipline problems, and those who feel being excluded by their peers, teachers and the school (Lerner et al. 2003), because it is possible that they may give vent to their discontent and anger by resorting to aggressive and violent behaviour. Meanwhile, teachers must also consider feasible ways of preventing students from being bullied. They can refer to the physical and behavioural signs of abuse listed in Table 10.10 to identify the victims of violent behaviour.

Table 10.10 Signs of abuse

Physical	Behavioural
• Bruises in shapes that look like handprints or objects • Black eyes • Bone fractures • Injuries after being absent • Injuries without sufficient explanation • Poor medical or dental care • Low hygiene level • Constant hunger or thirst • Unexplained physical complaints	• Unexpected change in behaviour • Immature behaviour • Shying away when approached by someone • Frequent blank stares/spacing out • Poor sleep or frequent nightmares • Irrational fears • Excessive fear of a specific person • Acting out sexually

Source: Heath and Sheen 2005: 116.

As for intervention at the group level, teachers can organize group activities to enhance solidarity among students and improve their social skills, including emotion management, effective communication, problem-solving, relaxation techniques, and conflict resolution skills. As suggested by the American Academy of Experts in Traumatic Stress (Lerner et al. 2003: 108), students involved in school violence must learn how to articulate their feelings about themselves and others, and replace self-defeating statements with positive attitudes. Besides these social skills, they should make use of their cognitive faculty to become aware of and identify behaviours that generate feelings of frustration and anger in others. It is also necessary to make sure that designated members of the teaching staff are readily available to listen and respond to students in need so that they can provide the necessary help to cope with their students' difficulties.

For intervention at the individual level, when the teacher chats with students involved in acts of violence, he/she must be ready to express appreciation and encouragement for individual differences. There is a general tendency for the teacher to pass negative judgement on students who are known to have bullied and abused their peers, and to remonstrate them for their bullying behaviours. However, if the teacher really want to help students reform, he/she must let them feel that they are no different from others in that they too need to enjoy the sense of love, acceptance and respect of other people. It is through training in integration, acceptance and compassion that we are able to change students' ideas, and teach them to look at things from other people's points of view. They can thus learn to understand other people's feelings, have due respect for others and become more tolerant of individual differences.

Conclusion

In recent years, school crises have become more common. Since the nature of crises and their complexity vary, it is not only the responsibility of the school administrators but also that of the teachers to take part in dealing with or improving the situation as well as to offer the necessary assistance to the staff members affected. This chapter aims to instigate the establishment of a school crisis plan by the school management so as to prevent the occurrence and reduce the risk of crises on the one hand, and on the other to provide the emergency protocol to cope with the crisis situation, so that the school can restore its daily operations and the students return to their normal school life as soon as the crises pass. The school management can set up a crisis management team, with the members' responsibilities and authorities clearly defined. The crisis management team will be responsible for drawing up the school crisis plan, and assume the role of a command centre when a crisis occurs.

For the school management, crisis intervention may be divided into three levels. At the school level, the school can mobilize the majority of its teaching and non-teaching staff to act under the command of the crisis management team at the occurrence of a crisis and during its follow-up. The objective of intervention at the group level is to consolidate the spirit of the group so that the occurrence of crisis may be reduced and the healing process may be hastened. Individualized intervention is targeted at students in need, with provisions for resources, support and referral service. Whenever a crisis occurs, the school management should respond with flexibility. Taking into account the nature of the crisis, the school's available resources and the needs of students, they should also make suitable use of intervention strategies to handle the crisis.

Questions for Discussion

1. If the crisis management team were to require you to tell 'a white lie' to cover up part of the truth of the crisis, what would you think of it? How would you respond?

2. Suppose you happen to spot a female student attempting to jump down from the school building, what should you do?

3. If rumours are spreading in the school about some severe events that could easily precipitate into a crisis, including accusations against a certain teacher for indiscreet behaviour, as a member of the crisis management team, what suggestions will you make on the strategies to stop the rumours from spreading further?

Notes

1. A. Chiu (6 July 2009). One Child in Six Suffers Abuse by Family Member. *South China Morning Post*, p. CITY 1.

2. C. Lee (17 October 2008). A Quarter of Teenagers Have Considered Suicide, Survey Finds. *South China Morning Post*, p. CITY 3.

3. C. Lo, A. Lam, and Y. Tsui (5 June 2009). Schoolboys Collapse after Snorting Drugs. *South China Morning Post*, p. CITY 1.

4. F. Fung (4 September 2009). Student Fined for Shoplifting While under Exam Pressure. *South China Morning Post*, p. CITY 3.

5. J. But (5 September 2009). Police Saddened as Young Girls lured into 'compensated dating'. *South China Morning Post*, p. CITY 3.

6. L. Fong (11 September 2009). Schoolgirls' Bullying Uncivilized Behaviour, Magistrate Says. *South China Morning Post*, p. CITY 3.

7. Rejected by Prestigious School after HKCEE, Depression Leading on to Illusion: S. 7 Student Jumps to Death under Academic Pressure 會考擯出名校 抑鬱致生幻覺 學業壓力中七生跳樓亡 (19 October 2009). *Daily News* 新報, A06.

8. HKJC Centre for Suicide Research and Prevention, HKU. Statistics. Accessed 1 January 2010. http://csrp.hku.hk/WEB/eng/customized.asp

9. Ibid.

10. Ibid.

11. Ibid.

12. Four Evil Female Students Slap Schoolmate and Force Her to Strip: Bullying Video Uploaded to the Internet 校園四魔女掌摑同窗逼脫衣欺凌短片上網 (30 October 2009). *Sing Tao Daily* 星島日報, A08.

Related Websites

1. What Is a School Crisis?
   http://www.davenportdiocese.org/faithform/fflib/FFCrisisschool.pdf
2. School Crisis Guide: Help and healing in a time of crisis
   http://www.neahin.org/crisisguide/
3. School Crisis and School Emergency Plans
   http://www.schoolsecurity.org/resources/crisis.html
4. School Safety and Crisis Resources http://www.nasponline.org/resources/
   crisis_safety/index.aspx
5. The National Child Traumatic Stress Network
   http://www.nctsnet.org/nccts/nav.do?pid=ctr_main

Extended Readings

Educational Psychology Service Section, School Development Division, Education and Manpower Bureau (2005). *School Crisis Management*. Hong Kong: The Bureau.

Kerr, M. M. (2009). *School Crisis Prevention and Intervention*. Upper Saddle River, NJ: Pearson Education.

MacNeil, W., and Topping, K. (2007). Crisis Management in Schools: Evidence-basedPrevention. *Journal of Educational Enquiry*, 7(1), 64–94.

胡潔婷、楊虹、駱慧芳（1999）。《臨危不亂：校園危機處理手冊》（初版）。香港：香港家庭福利會。

香港小童群益會（2004–2009）。《校園危機支援計劃：校園危機資料冊》（初版）。香港：香港小童群益會校園危機支援計劃。

References

Council on Professional Conduct in Education. (1995) Code for the Education Profession of Hong Kong. Accessed 26 October 2009. http://cpc.edb.org.hk/english/download/CPC_Code%20_Eng_1%20July%202007.pdf

Education Bureau. (2005). *School Crisis Management*. Accessed 26 October 2009. http://www.edb.gov.hk/filemanager/EN/content_2348/crisise.pdf

Government Information Centre. (2007). LCQ4: Student Dropout Problem. Accessed 26 October 2009. http://www.info.gov.hk/gia/general/200702/28/P200702280197.htm

Heath, M. A., and Sheen, D. (2005). *School-Based Crisis Intervention: Preparing All Personnel to Assist*. New York: The Guilford Press.

Lerner, M. D., Volpe, J. S., and Lindell, B. (2003). *A Practical Guide for Crisis Response in Our Schools* (5th ed.). New York: The American Academy of Experts in Traumatic Stress.

Johnson, K. (2000). *School Crisis Management: A Hands-on Guide to Training Crisis Response Teams* (2nd ed.). Alameda, CA: Hunter House Publishers.

Schonfeld, D. J., and Newgass, S. (2003). *School Crisis Response Initiative*. Washington: US Department of Justice. Accessed 26 October 2009. http://www.ojp.usdoj.gov/ovc/publications/bulletins/schoolcrisis/ncj197832.pdf

US Department of Education. (2007). *Practical Information on Crisis Planning: A Guide for Schools and Communities*. Accessed 26 October 2009. http://www.ed.gov/admins/lead/safety/crisisplanning.pdf

Virginia Department of Education. (1999). *Model School Crisis Management Plan*. Accessed 26 October 2009. http://www.doe.virginia.gov/VDOE/Instruction/model.pdf

Whitla, M. (2003). Suicide and Schools. In M. Whitla (Ed.), *Crisis Management and the School Community*. Camberwell, Victoria: ACER Press.

11

Ethics in School Counselling

Suk Chun Fung

We are not studying in order to know what virtue is, but to become good, for
otherwise there would be no profit in it.

(Aristotle, NE II.2)

Abstract

This chapter aims to enhance teachers' knowledge of the codes of ethics in
counselling, to heighten their awareness of ethical issues and their competence in
handling them, and to highlight the need for recognizing professional counselling
work. The chapter begins with an exposition of the necessity for teachers to study
counselling ethics, followed by a discussion of the importance and limits of the
ethical codes, covering also significant ethical issues relevant to school counselling.
In the discussions a case study format is adopted. By referring to several typical
school counselling cases, the complicated and contradictory nature of ethical issues
is illustrated. On the basis of the ethical codes laid down by Western and local
professional counselling organizations, methods appropriate to the Hong Kong
school culture and social environment are proposed.

Objectives

This chapter will help you:
- point out the necessity for teachers to understand counselling ethics in school
  counselling;
- explain the importance and limits of ethical codes of counselling;
- list ethical issues in school counselling; and
- apply counselling ethical codes and make optimal decisions for pupil-counsellees
  when dealing with controversial ethical issues.

Before You Start: Think and Discuss

1. Before a counselling relationship starts, what relevant issues does the pupil need to know?
2. Under what circumstances can the teacher break his/her promise of confidentiality to the pupil-counsellee?
3. Who has the access to the information of school counselling cases?
4. How do you respond to the queries from parents, the principal and colleagues regarding the counselling progress of a pupil-counsellee?
5. What are the positive and negative effects of teacher's dual or multiple roles in student guidance work?
6. How do a teacher's values affect the entire counselling process? How do we handle the conflict in values between the teacher and the pupil-counsellee?

Introduction

Counselling is a profession that offers help to people. The maintenance and further development of its professionalism require a set of comprehensive, integral and updated codes of ethics. The presence of such codes of ethics indicates the level of maturity and development of the profession (Leung, Leung, and Chan 2003). At present, primary and secondary teachers in Hong Kong are still short of a set of localized school counselling codes of ethics. The lack of ethical codes, on the one hand, reveals the underdevelopment of school counselling work in Hong Kong; it has also become one of the obstacles that hinders teachers from effectively carrying out counselling practices. In the school system, how should teachers steer their counselling work along the ethical lines? And when they encounter complicated and controversial ethical issues, what principles should they follow when making decisions? This chapter attempts to provide prospective teachers with relevant materials, guiding principles, and directions regarding ethical issues. It is hoped that this chapter can help them better equipped in the area of knowledge, attitude and techniques.

The Necessity of Understanding Ethical Issues in School Counselling

Under the 'whole school' approach of guidance in Hong Kong primary and secondary schools, counselling work is generally carried out under the leadership of professionally trained personnel, namely school social workers, school guidance masters/mistresses and educational psychologists, with the entire teaching staff joining force in the implementation of student guidance. The class teachers among them play the most important role as they are in contact with their pupils on a daily basis. Hence, it is natural that they are expected to be 'sensitive to their students' needs and be able to pin-point early symptoms of problematic behaviours so that these areas can be promptly attended to before minor troubles aggravate' (Education Bureau 2004). As a matter of fact, there are only a limited number of professional counsellors in a school. It is virtually impossible to rely solely on just one or two counsellors to offer consultations to the students. It is therefore necessary for the class teachers to take up the counselling work. For new recruits, apart from being assigned with teaching duties, they are often class teachers as well, who are responsible for the developmental needs of a whole class of pupils. Some schools may even ask the new recruits to join the guidance team. Hence, new teachers have to be prepared for school counselling work, including getting themselves acquainted with the ethical issues in school counselling. Once a counselling relationship starts, the teacher will immediately have to assume ethical responsibilities for the pupil-counsellee and should take the student's rights and interests as the prime concern.

Furthermore, as the counselling targets of primary and secondary teachers are children and youth between the age of six and eighteen, the vast majority would be minors. Compared to adults, they are more protected by the law, but at the same time, the law imposes more restrictions on the behaviour of minors. When dealing with certain controversial ethical problems, e.g. when a male pupil reveals that he has had sexual intercourse with a classmate, or when a pupil who is a minor intends to have an abortion, the teacher would have to carefully consider the legal implications. New teachers, like their veteran colleagues, are likely to encounter problems in counselling that may involve legal liabilities. Hence they need to equip themselves properly with adequate knowledge, awareness, and competence to deal with ethical issues in their work.

The most direct way to learn about ethical issues is to read up on codes of ethics. The codes of ethics of local and Western professional counselling organizations mentioned below are all worthy of note; it is advisable for prospective teachers to study at least one of them and familiarize themselves with the basic principles. At the same time, to prepare themselves psychologically for reading these codes, prospective teachers would do well to first appreciate the limits and characteristics of codes of ethics as set out below.

The Importance and Limits of Codes of Ethics for Counselling

Many professional psychological health organizations, such as American Counseling Association (ACA), American Psychological Association (APA), and American School Counsellor Association (ASCA), compile codes of ethics for their members. Herlihy and Corey (1996) spell out in clear and concrete terms the three uses of codes of ethics.

First, the basic use of a code of ethics is to educate counsellors about reasonable and sensible ethics. Reading and contemplating on various codes would enable counsellors to raise their awareness, clarify their personal values, and find a clear direction for coping with the challenges presented by their work.

Second, a code of ethics provides references and standards for professional accountability, and informs the public clearly of acceptable and unacceptable professional behaviour.

Third, as a code of ethics is a working document that is revised regularly according to real social needs, it facilitates the continuing development of the counselling profession. When there is occasion for counselling practitioners to interpret and apply the relevant code, the problems that emerge can often help them clarify their positions in the dilemma, which may in turn further the profession.

Chen (2003) also points out the importance of abiding by the codes of ethics developed by professional bodies. He believes that when a counsellor identifies with the spirit of a code of ethics, he/she would become more professional when dealing with the behaviour of the client and hence would give the latter the best available care.

However, codes of ethics do not provide a concrete solution for every quandary; it only provides general principles and guidelines (Corey, Corey, & Callanan 2003). The National Association of Social Workers (NASW) expounds on the limits and nature of codes of ethics thus: 'A code of ethics cannot guarantee ethical behavior. Moreover, a code of ethics cannot resolve all ethical issues or disputes or capture the richness and complexity involved in striving to make responsible choices within a moral community. Rather, a code of ethics sets forth values, ethical principles, and ethical standards to which professionals aspire and by which their actions can be judged.' While a code of ethics is deemed an indispensable working document for the counselling profession, the code per se is not sufficient to enable counselling practitioners to work in accordance with ethical standards. Making ethical decisions is actually a process in which the counsellor has to show sensitivity and problem-solving techniques in applying the code to individual contexts, and professional consultation is by all means an indispensable component in such a process.

At present, codes of ethics developed by local professional bodies include guidelines from the Hong Kong Professional Counselling Association (HKPCA), Hong Kong Psychological Society (HKPS) and Hong Kong Social Workers

Association (HKSWA). However, these codes are developed for professional counsellors, psychologists and social workers. Inasmuch as they can be used as a reference by school teachers, they are not geared towards answering the needs of teachers with counselling duties. As for the code of ethics developed by ASCA, it can serve as a useful reference for Hong Kong teachers, especially as most of its content focuses on school counselling. Teachers have to bear in mind that the code's target audience are professional counsellors, and more importantly, there is the question of cultural differences. As pointed out by Chen (2003), the Western codes of ethics are inspired by a strong emphasis on basic human rights and the right of the individual in Western culture; when the teacher applies the Western counselling codes of ethics, he/she should also consider the emphasis on social relationships in the Chinese culture.

Ethical Issues in School Counselling

In order to give beginners a more solid grasp of how to handle ethical issues in school counselling, this section will explore the significance of four ethical issues, namely confidentiality agreement and warning responsibility, informed consent, dual/multiple relationships, and the influence of personal values. By adopting a case study format and with references to the codes of ethics developed by the Western and local professional bodies, this section proposes methods and directions of treatment appropriate to the Hong Kong social context and school culture.

Confidentiality agreement and warning responsibility

Glosoff and Pate (2002) point out that 'confidentiality' is a professional commitment or contract; unless under consensual circumstances, the client's privacy has to be respected, and the counsellor cannot divulge any revelations made by the client during the counselling process. In fact, confidentiality is the foundation of a counselling relationship, and a condition for successful results. During the counselling process, the teacher will come into contact with a lot of the pupil's private information such as personal data, his/her everyday life, and private views and thoughts. The teacher has to keep all this information in strict confidence. The consequences of violating this confidentiality are grave. The pupil engages himself/herself in a counselling relationship based on his/her trust in the teacher, to whom he/she reveals candidly his/her thoughts and feelings, his/her family situation and interpersonal relationships. Once the teacher leaks the information, the pupil will find it difficult to maintain his/her trust, which will lead to a breakdown of the counselling relationship. In a more serious scenario, the pupil may never trust anybody, or any counselling relationship, ever again (Lam 2008). Collins and Knowles (1995) conducted a survey on 557 students aged thirteen to eighteen in Melbourne. The researcher asked the pupils to imagine themselves the counsellees and indicate their opinions on the importance of confidentiality in various counselling contexts. The results show that 53 per cent of the pupils indicated that confidentiality was absolutely necessary, while another 46 per cent thought it was very important. This study underscores the importance of confidentiality in a counselling relationship.

Teachers should by all means protect the pupils' right to privacy. Lam (2008) has made eight concrete suggestions, the first three of which can be viewed as targeting counsellors whose confidentiality awareness is low. They include the avoidance of using the client's information in social chit-chats, in public lectures or talks. Even when it is used for professional training, the client's identity has to be kept confidential. One should also guard against using the cases as examples to show off one's own capabilities or experience. These are all important guidelines for new teachers. The school is a place which emphasizes open communication. Whether it is between pupils, between teachers, between pupils and teachers, and between the school and families, clear and straightforward communication and exchange is always encouraged. This culture of communication in schools pits it against the confidentiality required of counsellors (Welfel 2002). Teachers have to be conscious of the confidentiality at all times. They should not share the information of the pupil-counsellee with other teachers in the staff room like any other topic; nor should they divulge private information of the pupil-counsellee to other pupils. Moreover, Lam (2008) has made four concrete suggestions regarding the storage and the confidentiality of information, which comprise not taking information away from the organization premises, not allowing access to the information by third parties, the setting up of a storage system, and obtaining the permission of the client when the need to share the information arises. These suggestions are also important references for school counselling work. New teachers should take the initiative to familiarize themselves with the system and operating method of information storage in the school. They need to make a conscious effort and take great care to ensure that case data are handled separately from general student assignments, circulars and documents.

The above are basic and important measures to safeguard confidentiality, and are generally uncontroversial. What is more difficult for teachers are probably the inquiries from other teachers, the principal and parents/guardians concerning the pupil-counsellee. Should the teacher disclose the content of the counselling to them? Below are three case scenarios with discussions on how the confidentiality principle is applied. Concrete suggestions are also provided.

Case Study 1

Teacher's Inquiry

Miss Fung, a class teacher and a Chinese teacher, holds a weekly meeting with Wing-keung, a P. 6 pupil. With his parents filing for divorce, Wing-keung's life has been turned upside down and he is emotionally disturbed. The math teacher has also noticed Wing-keung's deteriorating performance in the subject, laxness in class, and that he has become much quieter. Hence the teacher talks to Miss Fung to find out more about Wing-keung. Miss Fung indicates that due to the confidentiality principle, she cannot disclose Wing-keung's personal information.

Analysis and recommendations

According to the code of ethics of ASCA, school counsellors should provide information to relevant school personnel to help the pupil-counsellee. The ACA, on the other hand, does not cover school-based events in its code of ethics, but recognizes that if needs be, the professional members of the 'treatment teams' can share information. The code also requires the counsellor to inform the client when he/she shares information with other professionals. In the above scenario, there is a need for the maths teacher to know about Wing-keung's condition as it is affecting his academic performance. The best action to take would be for Miss Fung to inform Wing-keung that his information has to be disclosed to the maths teacher, and to encourage him to talk to the teacher himself. If Wing-keung refuses to disclose the cause for his angst to the teacher, Miss Fung should provide the teacher with some information on Wing-keung's situation, and reiterate the confidentiality of the information.

Case Study 2

Parents' Inquiries

The class teacher began counselling sessions a month ago with Man-yu, an eight-year-old P. 3 pupil. Quite a number of her teachers have found her very quiet recently. Not only is she not talking to her classmates, she also answers questions in class with an extremely low voice. During counselling, Man-yu tells the class teacher of her newborn little brother: he's noisy and cries very often, and her mother has become very busy. Today the class teacher receives a phone call from Man-yu's mother, who indicates that Man-yu has told her the class teacher often talks to her. Man-yu's mother thanks the teacher for her concern, and asks about the content of the counselling. The class teacher thanks her for her call and explains that the content is confidential, so she cannot disclose what Man-yu has told her. The class teacher also tells the mother that if there is anything she wants to know, she will contact her.

Analysis and recommendations

The class teacher's response falls short of being appropriate. The code of ethics of the ASCA points out clearly that school counsellors have to exercise confidentiality regarding the pupil's information, but at the same time they have to balance it with the legal rights of pupils' parents/guardians. According to the code, school counsellors have to recognize the need for cooperation with the parents/guardians, and should adopt reasonable measures to honour parents/guardians' wishes to gain access to their children's information. The code states that school counsellors have to provide parents/guardians with 'accurate, comprehensive and relevant information' in an objective and caring manner. Regarding the requests for information on counselling progress from parents/guardians of minors, Corey, Corey, and Callanan (2003) also indicate that therapists are expected to provide some response. The ACA further allows the counsellor to suitably incorporate parents or guardians in the counselling process.

In the above situation, it is appropriate for the class teacher to stress the confidentiality of the content of the counselling to the parent, but she should also find a way to exercise her ethical responsibility towards Man-yu and her mother. Feasible options include asking Man-yu to tell her mother about what is happening in the counselling process, inviting her mother to be present in one of the sessions, or providing her with some general information about Man-yu's concerns. But before she provides this information, the class teacher should first inform Man-yu, and let her know what she will tell her mother. The class teacher can also take this opportunity to discuss with Man-yu what she can tell her mother and how to put it; this process itself can be of good therapeutic value.

Case Study 3

The Principal's Inquiry

During a counselling session, an S.5 pupil Yu-ping tells his counselling teacher, Mr. Choi, that he has heard that some classmates have seen a newly recruited teacher going out with an S.6 female pupil. Yu-ping indicates that he has not seen it with his own eyes, but he believes those who have witnessed it as they cannot have fabricated the story. Mr. Choi asks Yu-ping about the details of the story, and believes they are still going out. Yu-ping gives Mr. Choi the names of the three classmates who witnessed the incident, but insists that Mr. Choi must not reveal the source of this information. Mr. Choi agrees that under permissible circumstances, he will keep Yu-ping's identity confidential. Moreover, Mr. Choi informs Yu-ping that he will report this information to the principal, including the identities of the new teacher, the S.6 pupil, and the three classmates who witnessed their going out. When the principal receives Mr. Choi's report, he asks for the source of the information. Mr. Choi indicates to the principal that unless absolute necessary, he will not disclose the pupil's identity.

Analysis and recommendations

Mr. Choi's handling of the case is appropriate. According to the ASCA's code of ethics, school counsellors have the responsibility to '[i]nform appropriate officials, in accordance with school policy, of conditions that may be potentially disruptive or damaging to the school's mission, personnel and property while honoring the confidentiality between the student and the school counselor.' The ACA, on the other hand, has no mention of a school-based context. Under the circumstances, Mr. Choi has appropriately reserved his right to reveal the identity of the source of information at a later stage if there is such a need. In the meantime, he has to try to respond to the query without disclosing Yu-ping's identity.

The above three scenarios reveal the ethical responsibilities involved in counselling work in the school system. On the one hand, the teacher has to abide by the confidentiality agreement made with the pupil-counsellee, and, on the other, he/she has to balance it out with his/her responsibility towards the parents/guardians, relevant teachers and the school authority. Under certain circumstances, apart from ethical considerations, the counsellor has to disclose information due to legal responsibility. The codes of ethics of many professional counselling bodies have clear guidelines concerning these circumstances. The following are citations from relevant content from the ASCA:

1. When there is a clear and present danger to the pupil-counsellee or a third party;
2. When the law requires the information to be disclosed;
3. When there are doubts about the validity of the information disclosed, and there is a need to consult suitable professionals.

Undoubtedly, the safeguarding of personal safety is the most important principle in the handling of all problems, and the teacher needs to recognize that he/she has a warning responsibility. Warning responsibility means when the client's behaviour is posing a serious danger to himself/herself or a third party, the teacher has the responsibility to warn his/her legal guardian or the third party. If the teacher is aware of a real danger but does not take reasonable preventive action, resulting in personal damage, it will amount to negligence in law. The following are two school counselling cases that involve legal and ethical issues. If you were the teacher in the cases, to whom should you issue a warning? How can you safeguard the optimal interest of the pupil counselled? What are the areas in the process that need special attention?

The confidentiality agreement is a very important code in the counselling profession. Teachers have to protect pupils' privacy by all means. If a teacher has doubts about the necessity of disclosing the information, he should seek professional advice. In the school context, the teacher can consult suitable professionals such as school social workers, guidance masters, and educational psychologists. During the consultation sessions, the teacher does not have to disclose the counsellee's

☐ **Activity 1**

Case Discussion 1

You are the English teacher and the class teacher of an S. 1 pupil, Ka-ho. One month into the new academic year, you have begun to follow up on Ka-ho's counselling because apart from his below-average academic performance, you have found on more than one occasion bruises on his body, which he put down to falls he has sustained. Not long after the beginning of the counselling sessions, Ka-ho shows you the flog marks on his legs. He also tells you his father is an alcoholic, and is afraid that his father might kill him one day. Even so, he stresses that you should keep it a secret.

How would you handle Ka-ho's predicament and his request for confidentiality?

Case Discussion 2

Chun-him has received a demerit from the school for fighting with classmates. As his teacher, you are responsible for following up on his case. Graduating in two months, this would-be school leaver tells you candidly he has taken ketamine on campus, and he is not alone. The fighting incident was related to drug trafficking in school.

Drug taking and trafficking are both illegal. How would you handle this case?

identity; he/she only needs to describe the case with the purpose of obtaining professional analysis and advice on ways to handle a particular situation. When the circumstances require the breaching of the confidentiality agreement, it would be advisable to first inform the counsellee. Scholars have emphasized the desirability of engaging the counsellee himself/herself in the process of making a decision; the more he/she takes part, the better (Mappes, Robb, and Angel 1985; Hill, Glaser, and Harden 1995; Corey, Corey, and Callanan 2003). This can reduce the damages done to the counselling relationship. In fact, it would be ideal, and something that should be practised by teachers, if before the actual counselling begins, the pupil-counsellee is made to understand the limits to the confidentiality, and sign the informed consent policy before entering into the counselling relationship. The following is an exposition on this important topic.

Informed consent policy

Both local and Western professional counselling bodies have guidelines that point to the importance of signing the informed consent document by the counsellee before a counselling relationship begins. This is not so much to protect the counsellor from ethical and legal liabilities as to protect the counsellee's rights. From an ethical point of view, informed consent is built mainly on the principles of autonomy and fidelity (Glosoff and Pate 2002). Glosoff and Pate (2002) point out that the exercise of informed consent is to give the counsellee the choice of whether to receive counselling, and to take the initiative to engage himself in the counselling process (autonomy). This measure also guarantees confidentiality (fidelity) to the counsellee.

From a legal point of view, three elements are fundamental to informed consent, namely, capacity, clarity of information and voluntariness (Anderson 1996). Corey, Corey, and Callanan (2003) have made clear explanations of these three elements. 'Capacity' means that the client has the ability to make rational decisions; when this capacity is lacking, the parents/guardians are typically responsible for giving the consent. 'Clarity of information' means the counsellor must provide the client with clear and sufficient information, including the benefits and risks in counselling procedures, possible adverse effects from treatments, and available alternatives. He/she is also responsible for checking that the client understands the information thus provided. 'Voluntariness' means when the client is giving consent, the client is acting autonomously in the decision-making process, and is legally and psychologically able to give consent.

It is apparent from the above that the client's autonomy and self-determination are crucial in the process of giving informed consent. The difficulties for this to be practised in a school setting are evident. Apart from not being able to give consent legally, pupils who are minors may not have the capacity to understand the content of the informed consent document, including his/her consent to receiving counselling, the aim and procedures of the counselling, and the confidentiality agreement and the limits to it. This problem can be clarified and resolved on two fronts. Firstly, for a client who is legally unable to give consent, the APA suggests that consent can be given by a legal proxy. The ACA's guidelines spells out even more clearly that a minor's family member can be included in the counselling process. This recommendation has its merits, and is supported by Lawrence and Kurpius (2000) who suggest that at the initial stages of the counselling, the counsellor should meet with the minor and his parent/guardian so that they could have a clear idea and consensus as to what information can be shared, thus helping build mutual trust between the three parties. The counsellor could also take the opportunity to encourage direct communication between the client and the parent/guardian.

Secondly, the teacher has to explain the content of the informed consent document to the pupil in accordance with the pupil's capacity and ability. Whether in verbal or written form, the teacher should define and explain with a vocabulary which is comprehensible to the pupil. Before he/she meets with the pupil, the teacher should prepare in advance for the content of the informed consent document, including what is to be told to the student, how detailed the information should be, and the way it is put. For example, for a Primary 3 pupil, the teacher can explain the meaning of, and limits to, confidentiality thus: 'Only you and I will know about what you are going to tell me, unless something makes me worry about your health or safety, in which case I will discuss with your parents. Do you have any questions?' However, for an S. 3 pupil, the teacher would need to explain more on the limits of confidentiality and give examples, to make him understand under what circumstances will there be a need to disclose the content of the counselling to his parents or the school staff (Glosoff and Pate 2002). Scholars have reminded counsellors not to mistake informed consent for merely the signing of a consent form by the client; they should treat it as an ongoing process (Glosoff and Pate 2002; Corey, Corey, and Callanan 2003). The teacher is probably not able to clarify all the content on the first meeting; nor should he/she assume that the pupil is able to remember all the explanations given at the time. In conveying important messages, the teacher should take care not to overload the student with information lest the counselling ambience would be rendered sombre and heavy. It should be borne in mind that informed consent is not confined to the early stages of counselling, but is an ongoing process (Corey, Corey, and Callanan 2003).

In primary and secondary schools in Hong Kong, the exercise of informed consent is understandably rare, probably due to the local school culture and teachers' sense of ethics. The reality is that schools often do not have the informed consent forms suitable for counselling; and it is also not uncommon for busy Hong Kong parents to find themselves unable to participate in the counselling process and to give informed consent. In such a case, the teacher should nonetheless obtain the pupil's verbal informed consent, so that the pupil would understand his autonomy right and the nature of confidentiality. The pupil should also know the various limits to the confidentiality. This can reduce the likelihood of the counselling relationship being damaged due to a need to disclose information at a later stage. Of course, pupils may not be able to grasp fully the content of the informed consent, but as pointed out by Margolin (1982), when providing counselling, it is always more desirable to attempt at some understanding regarding its purpose and process than not giving any explanations at all. Besides, letting the pupil ask questions is conducive to a clarification of the content for both parties.

❏ **Activity 2**

Play the role of a teacher who has to obtain informed consent from a junior primary/senior primary/junior secondary/senior secondary pupil on the first meeting. Try to rehearse the content you are to convey to the pupil.

Dual or multiple relationships

Dual or multiple relationships in psychotherapy refer to the presence of relationships between the client and the therapist which are other than the client-therapist relationship. This is one of the most pertinent factors for ethical quandaries faced by psychologists and other mental health professionals (Slack and Wassenaar 1999). The term 'dual relationships' first appeared in the APA's code of ethics (1958), which states clearly that psychologists are forbidden to enter into a counselling relationship with family members, friends, partners, students or others whose welfare may be jeopardized due to certain relationships (Mok 2003). Further developments saw the term 'multiple relationships' adopted in the APA's code of ethics (2002), which forbids categorically any other extant relationships that may jeopardize professional judgement or increase risks of exploitation. These include clinical relationships with one's employees, subordinates, friends or relatives. At the same time, the code of ethics also points out that multiple relationships are not deemed unethical if there is a reason to believe they will not lead to infringement, risks of exploitation or harm.

In the Hong Kong system of primary and secondary schools, teachers by nature assume the dual identities of 'teacher' and 'counsellor'. It follows that teacher and pupil will have unavoidable dual relationships. If the teacher is the pupil's class teacher or subject teacher, multiple relationships will be found. This is quite common as very often a teacher starts a counselling relationship because he/she has noticed the unusual behaviour, falling work standards and poor academic performance of the pupil in class.

Sometimes the pupil being counselled has already established trust in the counselling teacher who is his past or current teacher. Some of them even share their personal thoughts and stories with their teachers on their own initiative. In these cases, dual or multiple relationships have a positive effect on the counselling work. Compared to facing a social worker or a counsellor who is a stranger, the pupil would feel more secure and find it easier to express himself/herself. This would enhance the effectiveness of the counselling. Moreover, the empathy that stems from the teacher's knowledge on the pupil could also help the teacher support the pupil in and outside class more effectively.

Nevertheless, teachers must pay attention to the negative effects of dual or multiple relationships. First, a good teacher-student relationship may hamper the pupil's self-revelation in the counselling procedure. The following are possible scenarios:

1. Some pupils do not want to show their dark sides before their much-loved teachers, lest it would damage their image in the teachers' eyes;

2. Some pupils have heard their teachers criticize certain behaviours, and hence would not reveal they have those very behaviours;

3. The pupil understands that if the teacher knows about his/her offences, it would create a dilemma for the teacher. He/she does not want to be punished and does not want to make things difficult for the teacher. Hence he/she chooses to keep quiet;

4. Moreover, as the problems in interpersonal relationships recounted involve mostly classmates, the pupil may not want to disclose their private information to the teacher. Or he/she may think the teacher would take the side of the other classmates, and hence may choose not to tell.

The pupil-counsellee may feel constrained by the teacher's dual or multiple identities. In the same way, the teacher's counselling work may also be adversely affected by the dual or multiple relationships. The teacher's knowledge of the pupil outside the counselling room may very well affect his/her active listening, and create a lot of 'psychological noise' in the listening process. For example, when the pupil-counsellee says he/she has been making efforts in his academic performance, the teacher may be inadvertently reminded of the several pieces of missed homework he/she is supposed to have handed in. This kind of 'psychological noise' would undoubtedly be detrimental to the teacher's judgement.

When the relationship between the counsellor and counsellee is one which is not exclusively counselling-related, the professionalism of counselling may naturally be compromised by the vague boundary, since both the pupil and the teacher are inevitably prevented from completely immersing in the counselling relationship because of their other roles. Dual or multiple relationships are generally regarded as unavoidable in the Hong Kong school setting (Leung, Leung, and Chan 2003). In a study conducted by Leung, Leung, and Chan (2003), out of 114 Hong Kong secondary school counselling teachers, the majority (55.3 per cent) believe that there is no need for the teacher to avoid a multiple relationship. Moreover, about 73 per cent of the respondents indicate that they have not or have rarely experienced conflicts or contradictions arising out of their dual roles of teacher and counsellor. Are these results indicative of a lesser problem than is recognized by professional bodies regarding conflicts arising out of dual or multiple relationships? Or are the teachers in the study not fully aware of the existence of such conflicts and contradictions? These are questions that warrant attention. If ethical issues have not been discerned, it would have been difficult for counselling work to be conducted along ethical lines. A teacher has to be sensitive to the negative effects that dual or multiple relationships may have on the pupil being counselled. On this basis, the teacher has to make psychological or even environmental adjustments as required by each individual case. When serious conflicts arise from the different roles, actions such as case referral will have to be taken.

❏ **Activity 3**

Case Discussion

You are a P. 4 pupil Chiu-tak's maths as well as counselling teacher. Chiu-tak often forgets to bring his books, homework and exercises books. His academic performance is middling to low. Many pupils in the class do not like to get near him because they say his uniform is dirty. Chiu-Tak sometimes responds to it with foul language. Some classmates say he does not return borrowed stationery, and sometimes he forces them to buy him snacks. You have begun to see him for these symptoms. During the counselling process, you get to know that his family is poor; at a tender age he has to take care of a younger brother and sister. His father allegedly left home one day and never came back, and his mother, being a non-resident of Hong Kong, needs a two-way permit to travel between Hong Kong and the Mainland.

What kind of positive and negative effects would your dual relationships with Chiu-tak have on your counselling work? Discuss.

The influence of personal values

Every one of us lives by our own values, which are reflected in what we say and how we behave. As regards the ethical topic of 'personal values influence', teachers must not take it to mean maintaining a totally neutral position in terms of values during the counselling procedure. It is impossible and untenable. The ACA has a guideline regarding this issue: the counsellor must be aware of his/her own values, attitudes, beliefs and behaviour, and avoid imposing his/her own values upon the client. It is clear that the counselling practitioner must avoid unconsciously inculcating his/her own beliefs and values in the client's mind, and more importantly avoid a critical attitude towards the client due to a difference in personal values.

To avoid the above unethical practices, the teacher should first understand his/her own values: Which values are deemed most despicable by you? Which ideas are unacceptable to you? The following are the opinions and behaviour of ten pupils receiving counselling. Check what kind of opinion you will have of them.

Not only has a teacher to be clear about his/her own values, he/she should also be aware of how these values affect his/her counselling work. Regarding the above pupils' thoughts and behaviour, we are bound to make certain moral judgements. We would very likely have different points of view and feelings. The intensity of our reactions would also be different. In any case, the teacher's level of acceptance will have been revealed through words, facial expressions and other body language to the pupil (Corey, Corey, and Callanan 2003). Upon receipt of these signals, the pupil

❐ **Activity 4**

Put A, B, or C against each of the following to show your level of acceptance of the pupil.

  A: I can accept this pupil
  B: I find it rather difficult to accept this pupil
  C: I cannot accept this pupil

1. ( ) A senior secondary pupil intends to explore his homosexual tendency
2. ( ) An S. 5 female pupil leaves home to live with her boyfriend
3. ( ) A senior primary pupil feels that his father is quite useless
4. ( ) An S. 2 pupil fails to turn up for an exam because her dog has died
5. ( ) An S. 3 male pupil dates two girls at the same time
6. ( ) An S. 6 pupil thinks the swimming gala is a waste of time and hence was absent on that day
7. ( ) A P. 3 pupil discriminates against a classmate with speech impairment
8. ( ) A S. 1 pupil goes without lunch in order to buy a $1,000 idol item
9. ( ) A secondary female pupil weighing only some ninety pounds has fallen ill because she wants to lose weight
10. ( ) A S. 4 female pupil thinks that there is nothing wrong in having sex with someone

will interact with his interlocutor. For example, if you think that it is understandable for someone to skip an exam due to the death of a pet dog, and being absent at an exam is no big deal, then the pupil will have received a signal of understanding and empathy. To cite another example: you do not agree with the opinion of the pupil who thinks his father is useless, because 'all parents are infallible'. You explain to the pupil he should appreciate his father's difficulties, and tell him that parents always love their children. These examples show that the teacher's values influence the interactive process of the counselling work. In fact, some researchers have found that the client has a tendency to change in the direction towards the counsellor's values. It is quite often the client will accept the counsellor's values (Zinnbauer and Parament 2000).

Not only do teacher's values affect the interactive process in counselling, they also permeate other aspects such as the setting of counselling goals, the choice of theoretical framework and the application of counselling techniques. Hence, teachers should keep reflecting and asking this question: Am I doing it for myself or for the pupil? They should also put a higher premium on their own personal growth, reflect more on their opinions of people and issues, and nurture open-mindedness.

It is commonplace for teachers and their counsellees to hold conflicting values. In the case of the S. 4 female pupil who thinks there is nothing wrong to have sex, disagreeing teachers can make their values known. Just remember to make it clear that this is only your personal opinion. A non-judgmental attitude always fosters an open discussion. It is most important to create a climate of openness. On the one hand, it allows the teacher to listen more carefully to what this pupil means by 'there is nothing wrong'. What kind of experience or the lack of what kind of knowledge has led to her such belief? On the other hand, it would also allow the pupil to appreciate the concern and loving care behind the teacher's outward disagreeing stance. When all parties have had the chance to put their case clearly, and the issue has been teased out in a concrete way and their views clarified and explained, the counselling will have already been made effective as this process has enhanced the trust between the parties. The pupil may not exhibit a U-turn in her behaviour, but the myriad of worries and concerns raised by the teacher will probably leave something in her mind. More importantly, as the teacher has not shut the pupil out of communication due to a conflict in values, the teacher can continue to offer support in the pupil's growth and development.

Conclusion

This chapter discusses four ethical issues in school counselling: confidentiality agreement and warning responsibility, informed consent, dual or multiple relationships, and the influence of personal values. In the course of discussions it further brings out the important concepts of case conferences, professional consultation and case referral, the purpose of which is to help teachers carry out school counselling work along the ethical lines. The practice of ethics in counselling can be summarized in three aspects. First, teachers should have a good knowledge of the ethical guidelines of school-based counselling and the related resources. Teachers have to take the initiative to understand the storage system and the method of access to case data in their school, the availability of informed consent forms, and the information on professional counselling referral inside and outside school. Second, they have to adopt the right measures and make the right decisions along the ethical lines in the counselling procedure. Informed consent is an ongoing process which aims to safeguard the pupils' right to autonomy and fidelity. Inasmuch as the confidentiality agreement forms the basis of trust between the teacher and the pupil, there are limits to this agreement. When the need to breach the confidentiality agreement arises, the more the pupil has participated in the process, the better. Moreover, teachers should be more sensitive on the unavoidable issues of the dual or multiple relationships and the differences in personal values. Third, teachers should enrich their professional knowledge in counselling ethics. To be able to put it into practice, knowledge acquisition is the prerequisite. Whether it involves studying the codes of ethics or enrolling in professional courses, the teachers' very action of equipping themselves is already a concrete expression that they are taking and practising counselling ethics seriously. It is the hope of the author that as teachers place more emphasis on counselling ethics, school-based guidelines and related resources will thus be improved.

Questions for Discussion

1. Language teachers and class teachers may ask their pupils to write essays that touch upon their personal experience and feelings, such as 'jottings on everyday life' or 'bi-weekly journals'. Do you think it is necessary to have a confidentiality agreement with the pupils? Why?
2. It has been suggested that class teachers should obtain informed consent documents signed by parents at the beginning of the school term, so as to facilitate future student counselling work. Do you think this is feasible? Why?
3. Teachers who perform counselling duties may have their classroom teaching affected due to the dual or multiple relationships. Discuss the potential positive and negative influence.
4. How are personal values formed? What are the core values of the Hong Kong people? Which 'significant other(s)' (such as parents, teachers or friends) affect your views and behaviour the most?

Related Websites

1. American Counselling Association (ACA)
   http://www.counseling.org
2. American Psychological Association (APA)
   http://www.apa.org
3. American School Counsellor Association (ASCA)
   http://www.schoolcounselor.org/
4. National Association of Social Workers (NASW)
   http://www.socialworkers.org/pubs/code/code.asp
5. Hong Kong Professional Counselling Association (HKPCA)
   http://www.hkpca.org.hk/
6. Hong Kong Psychological Society (HKPS)
   http://www.hkps.org.hk/en/code.htm
7. Hong Kong Social Workers Association (HKSWA)
   http://www.hkswa.org.hk/en/node/60

Extended Readings

Cottone, R. R. (2007). *Counseling Ethics and Decision Making* (3rd ed.). Upper Saddle River, NJ: Pearson/Merrill Prentice Hall.

Remley, T. P., and Huey, W. C. (2002). An Ethics Quiz for School Counsellors. *Professional School Counseling*, 6(1): 3–11.

Mitchell, C. W., Disque, J. G., and Robertson, P. (2002). When Parents Want to Know: Responding to Parental Demands for Confidential Information. *Professional School Counseling*, 6(2): 156–61.

References

American Counseling Association. Code of Ethics. Accessed 1 January 2010. http://www.counseling.org.

American Psychological Association. Ethical Principles of Psychologists and Code of Conduct. Accessed 1 January 2010. http://www.apa.org.

American School Counseling Association. Ethical Standards for School Counsellors. Accessed 1 January 2010. http://www.schoolcounselor.org/.

Anderson, B. S. (1996). *The Counsellor and the Law* (4th ed.). Alexandria, VA: American Counseling Association.

Collins, N., and Knowles, A. D. (1995). Adolescents' Attitudes towards Confidentiality between the School Counsellor and the Adolescent Client. *Australian Psychologist*, 30(3): 179–82.

Corey, G., Corey, M. S., and Callahan, P. (2003). *Issues and Ethics in the Helping Professions* (6th ed.). Pacific Grove, CA: Brooks/Cole.

Glosoff, H. L., and Pate, R. H. (2002). Privacy and Confidentiality in School Counselling. *Professional School Counseling*, 6(1): 20–27.

Herlihy, B., and Corey, G. (1996). *ACA Ethical Standards Casebook* (5th ed.). Alexandria, VA: American Counseling Association.

Hill, M., Glaser, K., and Harden, J. (1995). A Feminist Model for Ethical Decision Making. In E. J. Rave and C. C. Larsen (eds.), *Ethical Decision Making in Therapy: Feminist Perspectives* (pp. 18–37). New York: Guilford Press.

Hong Kong Professional Counselling Association. Code of Conduct. Accessed 1 January 2010. http://www.hkpca.org.hk/.

Hong Kong Psychological Society. Professional Code of Practice. Accessed 1 January 2010. http://www.hkps.org.hk/en/code.htm.

Lawrence, G., and Kurpius, S. E. R. (2000). Legal and Ethical Issues Involved When Counselling Minors in Nonschool Settings. *Journal of Counseling and Development*, 78(2): 130–36.

Leung, S. A., Leung, T. K. M., and Chan, E. P. O. (2003). Ethical Counselling Practice: A Survey of Counselling Teachers in Hong Kong Secondary Schools. *Asian Journal of Counselling*, 10(1): 71–94.

Mappes, D. C., Robb, G. P., and Engels, D. W. (1985). Conflicts between Ethics and Law in Counselling and Psychotherapy. *Journal of Counseling and Development*, 64(4): 246–52.

Margolin, G. (1982). Ethical and Legal Considerations in Marital and Family Therapy. *American Psychologist*, 37(7): 788–801.

Mok, D. S. (2003). Multiple/Dual Relationships in counseling: implications for the asian context. *Asian Journal of Counselling*, 10(1): 95–125.

National Association of Social Workers (2008). Code of Ethics of the National Association of Social Workers. Accessed 1 January 2010. http://www.socialworkers.org/pubs/code/code.asp.

Slack, C. M., and Wassenaar, D. R. (1999). Ethical Dilemmas of South African Clinical Psychologists: International Comparisons. *European Psychologist*, 4(3): 179–86.

Welfel, E. R. (2002). *Ethics in Counselling and Psychotherapy: Standards, Research, and Emerging Issues* (2nd ed.). Pacific Grove, CA: Brooks/Cole.

Zinnbauer, B. J., and Pargament, K. I. (2000). Working with the Sacred: Four Approaches to Religious and Spiritual Issues in Counselling. *Journal of Counseling and Development*, 78(2): 162–71.

陳秉華（2003）：〈重建台灣／華人諮商倫理的文化思考〉。《亞洲輔導學報》，第 10 卷第 1 期，頁 11–32。

教育統籌局（2004）：《中學輔導》，瀏覽日期：2010 年 5 月 8 日，http://www.edb.gov.hk/FileManager/TC/Content_2264/role4_c.pdf.

林孟平（2008）：《輔導與心理治療》。香港：商務印書館。

Index